THE HUNGER MARCHERS IN BRITAIN
1920–1939

The Hunger Marchers
in Britain
1920–1939

by

PETER KINGSFORD

with a Foreword by Bill Paynter

LAWRENCE AND WISHART
London

Lawrence and Wishart Ltd
39 Museum Street
London WC1A 1LQ

First published 1982
Copyright © Peter Kingsford, 1982

Printed and bound in Great Britain at
The Camelot Press Ltd, Southampton

Contents

	Preface	7
	Abbreviations used in Reference Notes	8
	Foreword *by Bill Paynter*	9
1	Reserve Army of Labour	13
2	The First National March, 1922–3	33
3	Only the Miners Marching, 1923–8	73
4	'Not Genuinely Seeking Work', 1928–9	88
5	Marching Against a Labour Government, 1930	109
6	Climax of Conflict, 1932	129
7	Friends and Comrades, 1934	167
8	The Last March on London, 1936	200
9	Instead of Marching, 1937–40	223
10	Acceptance or Protest	232
	Index	239

Illustrations

Between pp. 128 and 129

Head of the Liverpool and Merseyside Hunger March, 1929

Women's reception committee for Hunger Marchers, Deptford, mid-1930s

Lancashire contingent of Hunger Marchers, joined by undergraduates, Oxford, 1932

Wal Hannington outside Pentonville Prison, 1932

Wal Hannington with NUWM leaders

Women' contingent marching against the means test

Head of Scottish women's contingent of Hunger Marchers, February 1934

A penny pamphlet issued by the NUWM in 1935

Harry Pollitt speaking in Trafalgar Square, March 1934

Welsh Hunger Marchers, October 1936

Unemployed demonstrators at the Ritz Hotel, Christmas 1938

Two unemployed demonstrators, Highbury FC, January 1939

Preface

The purpose of this book is to restore to the hunger marchers the place which they occupied during the inter-war years and their proper place in the history of those times. The myth that Jarrow alone can represent the protest against unemployment needs to be dispelled. Whereas two hundred men marched from Jarrow on one occasion, the hunger marchers trudged to London from every corner of the land: from Devon as well as from Scotland, from Kent as well as from Wales, from Norfolk as well as from Lancashire, six times, and in their thousands. Behind those thousands were more thousands willing to march and many more thousands who aided the marchers' departure from their homes and their progress along the roads of Britain. The persistent protest, against all odds, of these ill-fed, ill-clad, ill-housed heroes – and heroines – of depression offers a sharp contrast with those shabby decades.

My main debt is to those marchers and their relatives who wrote to me about their experiences: R. Davies of West-houghton, Bolton; I. Fisher of Highbridge; Mrs L. E. Jenkins of Taffs Well; Herb Morgan of Abertillery; Mrs A. Robinson of Pontypridd; D. O. Williams of Nantymoel. My grateful thanks are also due to Noreen Branson for reading the typescript and suggesting improvements, which have been embodied in the text, Marx Memorial Library where I spent many hours on the Hannington collection, and to the county archivists who have helped me but are too numerous to mention by name.

Abbreviations used in Reference Notes

CAB	Cabinet
CRO	County Record Office, e.g. HCRO – Hertfordshire County Record Office
GLC	Greater London Council
HO	Home Office
MEPOL	Metropolitan Police
MH	Ministry of Health
NAC	National Administrative Council
PL	Poor Law
PRO	Public Record Office

Foreword *by Bill Paynter*

Wal Hannington's *Unemployed Struggles, 1919–1936* – the classic account of the national hunger marches written by their organiser and the acknowledged leader of the unemployed – was first published in September 1936. Subtitled 'My Life and Struggle Amongst the Unemployed', Hannington's account was and still is an outstanding testimony of the struggles of the unemployed by one who was continuously in the thick of them.

This new study by Peter Kingsford provides the ideal complement to Hannington's to some extent autobiographical account. The product of thorough and original research in police and Home Office archives, it is presented with a clear understanding of the historical background to unemployment and in clear solidarity with those who struggled against it. It covers all the national hunger marches, including that of 1936, and describes in great detail the obstacles, harassment and persecution imposed upon the rank-and-file marchers by the authorities. Except for 1936, each march and each contingent met hostility and sometimes brutality at the hands of the police. I had personal experience of this both in 1931 and in 1932. Sleeping accommodation often had to be sought in workhouses where workhouse masters and inspectors were instructed to treat marchers as vagrants, which often meant the confiscation of all possessions and the imposition of tasks, though in most cases the marchers were able to resist such impositions. The whole period was one in which the police assumed power to decide the civil liberties of the people: the local Courts were truly 'police Courts'.

Mass unemployment again stalks the land as it did in the two decades between the world wars. It is appropriate that a book recalling the earlier struggles is published at this time. There are many similarities in the circumstances of then and now. Following the short-lived post-war boom, there was recession from 1920 onwards. As now, it was characterised by attacks on living standards of the employed and the unemployed. There were successive direct wage cuts for those employed, the harassment of the 'not genuinely seeking work regulations', and later, the family 'means and needs test' for the unemployed.

Anti-trade union legislation followed on the defeat of the 1926 General Strike, with the trade union leadership finding common cause with the employers. The crisis did not abate but intensified and created policy divisions in the labour movement leading to a split on the issue of harsh economy cuts, and the collapse of the second Labour Government. The position did not improve until the nation was on the eve of the Second World War – a solution to be avoided at all costs now.

This was the setting in which the Hunger Marches developed. Of course there have been many changes since, in technology, medical science, welfare and living standards, but the nature of the crisis is unchanged. The history of capitalism is one of booms and slumps. Since the end of the First World War, the booms and slumps have been relatively small periodic fluctuations in a condition of general crisis, for which there can be no permanent solution in an economic and social system of gross inequality of wealth distribution, and where social production is not accompanied by the social ownership of the means of production, distribution and exchange.

The principal difference in the two periods lies in the role of the trade union and labour movement. I was unemployed for most of the 1930s and took part in three marches, first in 1931 to the Trade Union Congress meeting in Bristol, and subsequently in 1932 and 1936, on the national marches to London.

The unemployed were in the main unorganised and isolated from organised labour. The only national organisation was the National Unemployed Workers' Movement, built up and led by Hannington, a national leader of the Communist Party. In fact, in most regions of the country the leaders of the unemployed were Communists themselves, unemployed and suffering the same hardship as their fellows.

Until the 1936 Hunger March the leadership of both the Trade Union Congress and the Labour Party was hostile to the unemployed struggles, and encouraged local organisations to adopt a similar attitude. It must be acknowledged, too, that the sectarianism of the Communist Party for a time intensified this attitude, although this changed with the development of united front councils of action in the middle of the decade.

The trade unions and the Labour Party are now in the vanguard of the campaign against unemployment and for full employment. The left in both organisations join with Communists and others in developing action in support of the campaign. However, the policy of setting up unemployed centres where the unemployed can meet and discuss common problems does not of itself create unified organisation and leadership, and trade unions tend to be preoccupied with the problems of the employed. There is therefore need for an organisation giving priority to organising the unemployed in action around the demand for jobs or full maintenance.

There is a lesson for the trade union and labour movement in the experiences of those who fought the same battles years ago. This is that there is no prospect of success for the unemployed if organisations try 'going it alone'. The most successful of the Hunger Marches was in 1936. This was made possible by united front and popular front movements throughout the country. There was a minimum of police and other harassment. There were broad reception committees and sleeping accommodation at each stage of the march for all contingents. In London, although there was no meeting with the Prime Minister, there was broad parliamentary support. Such unity in action by progressive organisations on an agreed programme of demands is essential to successful campaigning.

1936 was of course also the year of the Jarrow march, which arrived in London some weeks before the National Hunger March of that year and had the blessing of the Establishment. It is one of the virtues of Peter Kingsford's book that – without denigrating it – he puts the Jarrow march in perspective, and shows how, contrary to popular belief, it did not encounter the degree of hardship and persecution experienced by the other marches.

Bill Paynter
March 1982

1

Reserve Army of Labour

In the early afternoon of 18 October 1920 thousands of unemployed men were struggling with the police along the whole length of Whitehall and in the roads leading to it, while many more thousands stood waiting in orderly columns of four on the Victoria Embankment and Bridge Street or pressed forward in a solid mass to support their deputation to the Prime Minister.

That day had been preceded by weeks of preparation for a demonstration to the Government on behalf of the unemployed of London. Fifteen mayors of the borough, including those of Stepney, Fulham and Shoreditch, had been granted an interview with Lloyd George. They were to be accompanied as far as the Embankment by a massive demonstration of unemployed, each mayor marching with the contingent from his borough. The town clerk of Deptford, writing as secretary of the organising committee, informed the Commissioner of the Metropolitan Police of the assembly point and time for each contingent, and the final arrangements were agreed between the mayors of Fulham and Shoreditch, the London County Council and the Commissioner. The unemployed columns were to wait on Victoria Embankment until the mayors returned from their interview at 10 Downing Street to inform them of the result. This arrangement seemed to suit all parties admirably since it was calculated to preserve order and to ensure the mayors an audience. The mayors, as justices of the peace, pledged their contingents to be orderly and appealed to the unemployed to keep the pledge, 'placing them upon their honour' to do so. The police made their preparations. This was likely to be the biggest demonstration of unemployed so far. The miners were due to start a national strike on the same day, army leave had been stopped, and the Coldstream Guards had been ordered from Aldershot to London. Thirteen hundred foot police and one hundred mounted were ordered out for 18 October, some to accompany the contingents from their starting points, some to preserve order in the area surrounding Whitehall, others – amounting to some six hundred – in reserve in the Foreign Office yard, the guard room of Buckingham Palace, and the National Gallery, to deal with general disorder. Their orders confirmed that the mayors would return from Lloyd George to the assembled unemployed on the Embankment. These were then to be escorted back safely to their own gathering-points north and south of the Thames, in Hackney, Hammersmith, Battersea or St Pancras. Officially about ten thousand were expected, but double that number came.

While the mayors, led by Major Attlee, were ushered into 10 Downing Street, the columns waited patiently on the Embankment. Mrs Despard, now an old woman, was amongst them. A dozen fire-engines driven through the ranks, whether by accident or design, caused some resentment. Two councillors from Battersea tried to address the multitude and, when forbidden by the police, climbed a tree at the end of Horse Guards Avenue and continued to speak amid wild enthusiasm. The police dispersed a hostile crowd outside New Scotland Yard and, contrary to the agreed arrangement, moved the columns of unemployed off the Embankment towards Whitehall. The skirmishing with the crowd which had gathered at Downing Street intensified. A mounted constable was pulled off his horse. The stone balustrade outside the Privy Council office gave way under the pressure. The police seized and destroyed all red banners in sight.

When the deputation of mayors emerged from 10 Downing Street, the excitement grew amongst the unorganised crowd and the heads of the columns mixed together. Men retaliated against the police with stone throwing. The mounted police drew their batons and charged straight at the dense mass of demonstrators, orderly marchers and disorderly crowd together. Battle raged and casualties were heavy until Whitehall was cleared. Many ex-servicemen fought back. Albert Fletcher, a labourer, attacked a policeman who was trying to arrest a woman; she escaped. William MacGillivray, painter and member of Willesden Council of Action, engaged a mounted officer with his umbrella. Many fled into Richmond Terrace where they closed the gates, barricaded them with railings torn up from the gardens and let fly with volleys of stones until they were taken by storm. Other groups, harried and beaten up near Whitehall, clutching their torn banners, tried to hold a meeting in Trafalgar Square only to be chased out along Northumberland Avenue.[1] *

When the London County Council met on the morning after, the unemployed were in the gallery in full force. They had heard of Lloyd George's response to the London mayors. He had admitted that the Government had made promises to ex-soldiers which had to be kept and now he would request the London County Council to start work on the scheme for arterial roads with a 50 per cent Government grant. 'Lloyd George told us to come here to get a hearing' was the cry from the gallery, and the repeated chant, 'We want grub, grub, grub' stopped only when the Shoreditch councillor shouted from the floor, 'We are going to have food for the unemployed.' When Harry Gosling, leader of the transport workers, declared, 'It is clear that the proceedings in Whitehall have lent the Government wings. It is an awful feeling to know you are going home without any food for the kiddies. You can't argue like well-fed people. The unemployed are not going to stand still this winter and starve', there was a shout from the gallery, 'No, by God we are not.'[2]

The violent conflict on 18 October made men think about getting organised, and the resentment it produced gave rise to the first steps towards a national organisation of the unemployed.

The 'Battle of Downing Street' had its origins in the war of 1914–18 and before. When the post-war boom collapsed in 1920 the rate of unemployment rose to 6 per cent by the end of that year. As the unemployed ex-servicemen found that 'the land fit for heroes' was not to materialise, local committees sprang up spontaneously. The danger of unemployment arising from demobilisation had been recognised by the Government in making the 'donation', and *ex gratia* weekly allowance to ex-soldiers and civilian war workers. For the latter the donation had been stopped in November 1919; at the same time unemployment benefit was raised from seven to eleven shillings

---

* See end of each chapter for references.

per week. In these conditions the activity of the local committees of unemployed was limited to collecting money to relieve distress; in effect they could do little more than beg. Even the more independent National Union of Ex-Servicemen could not take the further step of challenging the Government with demands for a better deal. To transform the unemployed from a passive lump – a reserve army of labour presenting a constant threat to the employed – into a force to confront the authorities, a different group of men was required. These men were the shop stewards of the wartime engineering industry.

The war of 1914–18 had used up such resources of men and materials that the ability to continue it, let alone win victory, had depended completely on the willingness of the workers to make sacrifices. The trade unions had therefore agreed with the Government to give up any of their rules and practices which might interfere with maximum production and to abandon for the duration the right to strike.

The Treasury Agreement of 19 March 1915 became law under the Munitions of War Act of June that year. The most important of those rules and practices had been to ensure that skilled work was done by skilled men. They were to be suspended so that greater use could be made of unskilled and semi-skilled labour, the process of 'dilution of labour'. But, as Pribicevic says: 'It was one thing to get the trade union officials to sign the Treasury Agreement and quite another to persuade craftsmen in the workshops to accept dilution.'[3] It took over a year to do so. The very large number of problems which arose could be dealt with only at the workshop level and by the leaders to be elected in the workshops, the shop stewards. The craft unions themsleves could not do this because their local branches were based on residence not on workplace and, moreover, each union catered for its own section of skilled men. Accordingly there arose the alternative leadership of the shop stewards which could negotiate with management about grievances of dilution and government control of labour. In some places shop stewards already existed but usually with the sole function of collecting subscriptions. Now, as representatives of the workers, the stewards became a power in the land which trade unions, employers and the Government had to recognise. They were officially recognised in national agreements made in 1917 and in 1919.

The next development came when the shop stewards in a particular industrial town or area formed a local workers' committee. The first and foremost was the Clyde Workers' Committee in the summer of 1915, composed of shop stewards who were delegates elected from the workshops affiliated to it. Always in the forefront of struggles with the Government and employers, it gained such a name that other shop stewards followed its example in 1916 in, for instance, London, Manchester and Barrow-in-Furness, and in 1917 in Sheffield. This development continued so that nearly every engineering centre had a Workers' Committee by the end of the war. The Workers' Committees were at the head of the main strikes in the engineering industry during the war. They were democratic bodies, not attempting to impose leadership, responding to the grievances and demands of the workers, and inclined rather to leave control of policy and action in the hands of the rank and file.

They were also more explicitly anti-capitalist and revolutionary in outlook than were the workshop committees, to some extent because many of their leading members belonged to one or other of the pre-war socialist parties, the Socialist Labour Party, the Independent Labour Party or the British Socialist Party.

As the Workers' Committees grew in number so the need arose for coordination between them to deal with national issues and to gain strength *vis-à-vis* both trade union officials and employers. In 1917 they established a national organisation, the National Shop Stewards' and Workers' Committee Movement (NSS & WCM), with its annual conferences and national administrative council, which included in its aims 'the organisation of the workers upon a class basis to prosecute the interests of the working class until the triumph of the workers is established'. At the end of the war the power of the NSS & WCM was weakened and the national movement came to an end in 1922 for several reasons. The shop stewards had been brought into the official trade union structure by the Shop Stewards' Agreement in 1919. The run-down of the munitions industry reduced the movement's base in industry, and the slump in 1920 gave employers the opportunity to discharge the key men amongst the shop stewards. Amongst those weeded out were two men who became leaders of the organised unemployed, Wal Hannington of London and Tom Dingley of Coventry. When the Amalgamated Engineering Union faced a national lockout in 1922, the newly formed National Unemployed Workers' Committee Movement gave it valuable help. In the same year the NSS & WCM was merged into the British Bureau of the Red International of Labour Unions to which it had already affiliated in 1920.

While the industrial influence of the NSS & WCM shrank, its political commitment increased. The link between it and the new national organisation of the unemployed of 1921 was paralleled by a link, though of a different kind, with the formation of the Communist Party of Great Britain in 1920. This second link developed under two major influences. Wartime experience in the Workers' Committees had led the shop stewards' leaders to believe that because those bodies were essentially rank-and-file ones, independent and powerful, they had a revolutionary potential far greater than the pre-war ideas of syndicalism and industrial unionism. The example of the Russian Revolution also persuaded them to see the Workers' Committees as 'soviets' which could have the same function in the overthrowing of capitalism as in Russia.

These shop stewards were convinced that, since it was the Communist Party in Russia which had guided the soviets to power, a communist party was required in Britain. The movement in that direction started when the resolution of the British Socialist Party in 1918, 'That the time has arrived for the cooperation of all Socialist forces', overcame internal differences in the parties, and culminated in the Unity Conference of 1920. The conference, which led to the formation of the CPGB, and its acceptance as the British section of the Communist International, was supported by the NSS & WCM. 'Of the eight members of the National Administrative Council (of the NSS & WCM) elected in 1917, six joined the Communist Party by January 1921.'[4]

Arising from the London shop stewards' call for action, the Hands Off Russia Committee was set up in London four months after the October Revolution. As this quickly grew into a national committee, shop stewards were joined by trade union leaders. After Britain stopped direct intervention in Russia, she continued to help Russia's enemy, Poland, until London dockers refused to load munitions for use against Russia. When Britain threatened action against the advance of the Red Army, the likelihood of a new war was reduced by the National Council of Action, formed in haste by the trade union leaders and the Labour Party and supported by over three hundred local Councils of Action. In all these events the shop stewards were prominent. Some of them, including Tom Dingley and Wal Hannington, linked with local groups of unemployed in order to give them a new direction. Hannington, British Socialist Party member, joined the group in St Pancras and began to urge union with other London groups, but met with resistance from ex-servicemen without industrial experience who could not see the purpose or the benefits to be derived. Groups such as this formed the demonstration on 18 October. Hannington marched with the section from North London. After the eruption of violence on that day the opposition to organisation faded away.

The newly formed Communist Party also mobilised its members. Three days after the 'Battle of Downing Street' the Party circularised all branches calling on them to give maximum support to the unemployed. 'Our branches are called upon to play their part in the forthcoming struggles and must, where possible, take the lead.' By the end of the month the St Pancras committee, on Hannington's initiative, called a conference of all other unemployed groups in London at which a dozen were represented; as a result the London District Council of the Unemployed was formed with, very soon, delegates from thirty-one London boroughs. Its chairman, secretary and organiser, Jack Holt, Percy Haye and Wal Hannington, had all been shop stewards in the engineering industry and were all members of the Communist Party.

As unemployment continued to rise to a peak of 18 per cent in June 1921, the struggle of the unemployed for a square deal became more vigorous under the new leadership, particularly in London. It took the direction of an attack on the Poor Law Regulations which governed the lives of many unemployed. Under these regulations the guardians of the poor might not grant outdoor relief except on special conditions, the most onerous of which were that the applicant must be put to task-work and receive half the relief in kind. Adopting the slogan 'Go to the Guardians', the unemployed marched to the poor law offices all over London to demand unconditional relief, and occupied the guardians' board rooms until it was granted or until they were expelled by the police. Similar methods of direct action also came into use when the Unemployed Council raised a demand for premises where the committees could hold meetings.

Many boroughs met the demand, but when they did not, the local committee took possession of whatever premises were available – empty houses, libraries, public baths – and held them until evicted. The public library in Islington, where there were ten thousand unemployed, was seized and held for three weeks. When the police recaptured it the Unemployed Council laid a plan to occupy the town hall instead. A raiding-party was to seize the building while several thousand men were to march on Islington from the St Pancras, Lambeth, Stepney, Edmonton, Willesden, Tottenham, Poplar and Hoxton committees. Instructions for the raiders went out from Dennis Jennett, shoemaker and chairman of the Islington Committee, to Sullivan, chairman of the Poplar committee: 'I am working this so that within three minutes four car-loads of men will be landed within twenty-five or fifty yards of the town hall, I am trying to keep the police busy elsewhere.' The supporting march set off headed by the St Pancras banner – '1914 Wanted. 1920 Forgotten. We Demand Work or Maintenance' – but the police having been tipped off, were ready in force in the town hall and set about the raiding-party and the marchers. Hannington was one of many struck down. In the affray, a smaller scale 'Battle of Downing Street', nineteen unemployed were arrested and thirteen police injured. Jennett, charged with disturbing the peace, was ordered to prison for three months or to give two sureties of £25 each; the magistrate refused sureties from the chairman of the board of guardians and a fellow guardian. In nearby Edmonton the committee denied the police story that they had armed their contingent with lengths of piping. They were only too happy to be in possession of their own town hall. 'It is our home now,' they said, 'and we treat it as such.'[5]

The new burst of organised action was not confined to London. In Norwich the unemployed committee successfully protested against the guardians' intention to reduce outdoor relief. They marched to Sunday service in the cathedral headed by their ex-servicemen's band, to be welcomed in by the bishop. The chairman of the trades council at Lowestoft urged a mass demonstration to set up its local committee and to 'Go to the Guardians'. In November 1920 the movement claimed success for its agitation and organisation, when the Government raised the rate of unemployment benefit to fifteen shillings for men and twelve shillings for women. As yet there were no allowances for wife or child.

Several factors now combined to lead to the formation of a national body for the unemployed. One was the reluctance of most of the labour leaders to be involved in 'direct action'. There was, indeed, a great division of opinion in the labour movement over this issue. One form of 'direct action' – the political use of the strike weapon – had already been debated by the TUC and the Labour Party in relation to the nationalisation of the mines, on the occasion of the British intervention in the Russo-Polish war, and in connection with the Government's policy in Ireland. Certain trade union leaders – Robert Williams, Robert Smillie and Fred Bramley – had spoken in favour of direct action. On the nationalisation of the mines, the TUC backed down from strike action; in regard to Ireland a special trade union conference called for a ballot on strike action for a peace settlement, but the matter went no further. But on the Russo-Polish issue the labour movement formed Councils of Action strong enough to be instrumental in averting war with Soviet Russia. The inconsistency is explained by Ralph Miliband in terms of class. When the labour leaders saw direct action as serving a national interest, as with Russia and Ireland, they were prepared to support it; not so when there was a class issue as in the case of the mines.[6] Unemployment, against which the movement had already distinguished itself by direct action, certainly seemed a class issue. On this ground alone the unwillingness of the Labour leadership to associate themselves with an unemployed movement might be accounted for. There was also the fact that the newly-formed Communist Party, the party of direct action, had applied for affiliation to the Labour Party. The application was rejected, as were also the Communist leaders of the unemployed. The upsurge of activity in London and the spread of direct action to the provinces prompted the London Unemployed Council to call a national conference in April 1921. There was also the important fact that although the Government had again in March increased unemployment benefits to twenty shillings for men and sixteen shillings for women, it had at the same time abolished the wartime 'donation' for ex-servicemen.

The national conference, representing seventy to eighty committees, established the National Unemployed Workers' Committee Movement henceforth referred to as the Movement, with a national administrative council from five areas and the same three men – Holt, Haye and Hannington – as chairman, secretary and organiser as for the London Council. 'Work or Full Maintenance at Trade Union Rates of Wages' was its simple but radical demand. Full maintenance meant in detail thirty-six shillings per week for man and wife; five shillings for each child up to sixteen years of age; rent up to fifteen shillings a week, plus one hundredweight of coal or its equivalent in gas; thirty shillings for single persons eighteen years and over; fifteen shillings for single persons between sixteen and eighteen. But as well as these basic demands the Movement had socialism as its purpose. Its members took an oath 'never to cease from active strife until capitalism is abolished'. Six months later such progress had been made that a hundred and forty committees were affiliated and the sale of the Movement's fortnightly paper, *Out of Work*, reached fifty thousand.

Three months after the unemployment benefit had been raised, the Government reduced it back to the 1920 level, thereby adding fuel to the fire of the Movement. A demonstration of tens of thousands, with a deputation to the Minister of Labour, received little satisfaction beyond the statement that the insurance fund was insolvent. A national campaign to restore the cuts continued throughout the summer and autumn of 1921. In Sheffield thousands marched to the town hall to demand that when applicants for relief were put on task-work this should not last more than two days, and in Bristol demonstrations persuaded the guardians to offer improved scales of relief which were not less than the unemployment benefit.

Many boards of guardians became overwhelmed by the demands for relief, but when they tried to reduce the number of applicants the Movement had an answer. As soon as the Wandsworth guardians had announced that tickets for admission to the workhouse would be given instead of outdoor relief, the Battersea and Wandsworth Unemployed Committee arranged for everyone to take the tickets offered, and two hundred men with their families – seven hundred people in all – marched, with band playing, to the workhouse which, with a capacity of nine hundred, already had seven hundred inmates. Necessarily admitted, they virtually took over the institution, exacted better food, sang 'The Red Flag', flew it from the roof, and refused to leave until the guardians agreed to grant outdoor relief.

An acute problem of massive expenditure remained with the guardians wherever there was heavy unemployment, sandwiched as they were between harassed ratepayers and tight control by the Government. At a London conference they called on the Government to finance unemployment relief. A Woolwich guardian told it: 'A hungry man is an angry man and there are people who cried out for a bloody revolution leading the unemployed. What stood between the country and revolution was food.' This situation gave rise to 'Poplarism', a protest by George Lansbury's borough against bearing an unfair burden of relief payments. The Poplar Council refused to pay the precept due to the London County Council and went to prison for contempt of court until hurried legislation did something to even the expenditure between rich and poor boroughs. The unemployed committee demonstrated daily outside Brixton and Holloway prisons in support of the councillors. In nearby Shoreditch the committee used different tactics, in the form of a rent strike. 'No work, No Rent' was the slogan. 'What will come out of it all?' asked *The Communist*. 'The Revolution? We must not dismiss the possibility too lightly. All the same we do not anticipate it this winter. Most of this winter's battle will be a one-sided affair. The unemployed are not yet armed. This winter the unemployed will be beaten because they will not be able to fight, though they may in certain districts fight enough to gain some crumbs.'[7]

During the second half of 1921 the increased influence derived from organisation on a national scale made itself felt. As the Movement's agitation for its twin aims of restoration of the cuts in unemployment benefit and of a standard rate of poor relief grew throughout the country, the Special Branch at Scotland Yard received reports of hundreds of meetings of unemployed from Glasgow to Eastbourne and from Sheerness to St Helens. In some places the demands for a living scale of relief were partly successful, in others not. In Liverpool, where demonstrations took place almost daily, the committee published *Justice for All*, edited by a clergyman and a local journalist, and maintained the right of the hungry to steal food. An attempt to protest inside the Art Gallery, giving rise to criticism of alleged excessive police batoning, was followed by the guardians conceding increased relief and promising to take action if relieving officers refused it. At Leicester there was no progress in spite of the efforts of Dennis Jennett, the Islington shoemaker, who had come with others from London to give help. Groups of unemployed who demanded free food in restaurants and coffee houses were arrested. An attempt to take possession of the trades hall was prevented by the police, and a march of fifteen hundred on the poor law offices was met with a baton charge, arrests and a month in prison for Jennett. In Cardiff the guardians responded with increased relief but well below the scale demanded.

New local committees sprang up every week under the guidance of the Movement's national administrative council. Local secretaries received advice on how to act:

> Concerning the powers of the Board of Guardians, I don't think that you can do better than obtain the book entitled *Poor Law Administration* which should be obtained from the local library. On the question as to how far they are allowed to go, if you will take into consideration that the Ministry of Health sent out notices to all the Guardians to the effect that they *must* reduce the allowances given in relief as much as possible and also endeavour to establish as a principle – that all relief is granted as a loan, you will understand how far they are allowed to go. It is just this far: as far as you can *make* them.[8]

New committees appeared in Nottingham and the outlying districts of Beeston, Carlton, Colwick and Netherfield. In Birmingham, where the division organiser was busy, there were seventeen new committees which held sixty-three meetings each attended by about four hundred men. As a result of progress there, the Wolverhampton unemployed informed the Chief Constable that if the guardians would give the same scale of relief as in Birmingham they would not cause any trouble. Organisation in Scotland was not so well developed until the local groups were linked up, but in Glasgow, in spite of the imprisonment of John MacLean, what Scotland Yard called his hooligan followers were demonstrating daily under the leadership of McShane, Duffy and Dundas. The authorities sometimes reacted to these activities by labelling the local committees as not genuine and by trying to establish rival 'genuine' committees. In Sunderland the lord mayor, supported by councillors and a police superintendent, presided over a meeting called for that purpose, but when he refused to accept a motion of no confidence moved by the local branch of the Movement, the whole meeting broke up.

On the issue of restoration of the cuts in benefit, the London District Council decided on a massive demonstration. The *Daily Herald* gave it the fullest encouragement. On 4 October some twenty thousand unemployed marched in good formation from all parts and assembled outside the London County Council offices on the Embankment, stretching in an unbroken line four to twelve deep from Temple station to Blackfriars Bridge. Stewards wore red armbands, banners proclaimed: '1914 Popularity and Fags – 1921 Charity and Rags'; '1914 Mobilisation and War – 1921 Starvation and Jaw'; '1918 End of the War – 1921 Volunteer for More'. *Daily Herald* posters urged the release of the Poplar councillors. Posters for *Out of Work*, which was selling freely, announced 'Getting Them on the Run'. The Movement was determined to demonstrate in Trafalgar Square although, or because, that had been forbidden by the Commissioner of Police. In Hyde Park Hannington's invitation to march to the Square met with a shout: 'Let's go to the Square.' The columns disbanded, banners were furled and men infiltrated into the Square. The police thought that this was so that the banner poles could be used as weapons. They also believed that the redoubtable Mrs Thring, editor of *Out of Work*, had advised that mounted police could be easily unhorsed by twisting the toes of their left feet downwards. Many men forced their way through to raise the red flag on Nelson's plinth, but repeated baton charges by mounted and foot police ensured their defeat after a general conflict of a quarter of an hour. Among those arrested was Mrs Thring who was bound over to keep the peace in the sum of £5.[9]

Two days later the Movement asked Lloyd George to receive a deputation. When it was refused on the grounds that the Cabinet was giving the problem its constant and unremitting attention, and moreover that the Prime Minister was in touch with the representatives of organised labour and intended to make a statement in Parliament, the deputation had to make do with the Ministers of Health and Labour. Its demands were comprehensive; work schemes at trade union rates, the abolition of relief given as a loan, free milk for children and expectant mothers, as well as restoration of the insurance benefits and a national scale of poor relief. They received in reply Sir Alfred Mond's assurance that everything possible would be done and that every avenue was being explored. A week later the Movement could celebrate a major advance. When Parliament reassembled on 18 October the unemployed learned that for the first time insurance benefits were to include allowances for dependants, five shillings for a wife, one shilling for each child. Three months later a further success could be recorded. Sir Alfred Mond announced a new scale of poor relief for London which, while it still fell short of the amounts which had been obtained from some boards of guardians, was a big advance on any previous scales issued by his Department. At the same time the Minister emphasised that the principle of less eligibility should always be applied to anyone receiving relief under the Poor Law, as enunciated in the Poor Law Report of 1834 'that his situation on the whole shall not be made really or apparently so eligible as the situation of the independent labourer of the lowest class'.

In November 1921 the Movement, holding its second national conference, had been greatly encouraged by the number present – a hundred and forty delegates from ninety committees who found the money to make the journey. The organisational structure was established – a pyramid from the base of the branches to the district councils and the national administrative council, with a head office in London staffed by national officers, financed by members' contributions of one penny per week. As well as confirming the aims over which the struggle had already developed, the conference added others: three meals a day for the children of the unemployed, no distraint for rent or rates on the goods of an unemployed person, poor relief to be a charge on the national exchequer instead of on the local rates and to be administered through the trade unions, the Movement to be represented on all official Labour Exchange committees, the abolition of overtime in industry so as to share out the work available. All these implied a number of targets for agitation – government departments, local government councils, boards of guardians and industrial employers. At the same time they underlined the desire to be closely connected with the trade union and labour movement in spite of the rebuffs from its leadership.

For the rest of 1921 and during the greater part of 1922 the Movement worked out its tactics for raids on factories and support to workers on strike, raids on guardians' offices, resistance to low wages for relief work, and refusal to allow eviction for rent arrears. The raids on London factories were carried out in Kilburn, Tottenham, Islington, St Pancras, Edmonton and Walthamstow. Their object was usually to prevent the working of overtime and sometimes the payment of wages below the normal trade-union rates. Led and carefully planned by former shop stewards the raids were often successful. A strong force of unemployed rushed the gates, occupied the machine shops, turned off the power, seized telephones and exits and called a meeting of the workers, while its leaders negotiated with the management. During one foray on the Auto-Triumph Works in York Road, Islington, the manager was told that if overtime continued thousands more would raid the works and stop it. The police could do little inside the workshops. The attitude of the managers was, more often than not, flexible enough to arrive at a satisfactory agreement to ban or restrict overtime or to pay the normal wages. There were considerable repercussions in the engineering industry. The campaign was intended, as much as anything, to prevent a split between employed and unemployed, who were sometimes regarded by trade unionists as parasitic nuisances and looked on as paupers when they attended branch meetings.[10] Now, because of the post-war slump, over fifty thousand engineering workers had lost their jobs. The Amalgamated Engineering Union had refused to make an agreement with the employers which would have left the working of overtime solely at their discretion. 'Must I work overtime whilst my mate and his family starve for want of work?' was the question asked on a union broadsheet. The national lockout, which followed in April 1922 and lasted three months, gave the Movement the opportunity to demonstrate its solidarity. Local committees helped with picketing, raided factories which were employing non-union labour, and by mass demonstrations put pressure on the poor law guardians to pay outdoor relief to locked-out workers at the same rate as to the unemployed. It was an increasingly difficult situation for the trade unions as a whole which, weakened by heavy unemployment, were engaged in a rearguard action against a general reduction in wages.

On the local government front, the Movement pressed forward with increased vigour and effectiveness. At the time of the meetings with Government ministers in October 1921, instructions sent from the National council to the local committees had set the pace:

> No Committees must allow their efforts to relax after Thursday, but rather, if possible, they should increase the agitation, not being content with mere assurances or meet half-way proposals by the Local Authorities, but cut for the main essential and definite object WORK OR FULL MAINTENANCE.
>
> Don't attempt to stand on ceremony with these people. If they are antagonistic, refuse to see you, or may be on holidays, just give them to understand that you mean business. The time and day for constitutional action has long past. It is now three years after the Armistice and our numbers are still increasing. IT IS NOT THE TIME FOR PARLOUR TALK. IT IS THE TIME FOR ACTION. UP THE UNEMPLOYED.[11]

The pressure was raised against all those guardians who had refused, or failed, to raise their scales of relief nearer to the national scale demanded by the Movement. During one month, February 1922, hundreds of demonstrations to the guardians' offices were made throughout the country, from Kent to Cumberland and from Devonport to Southend. Often the demonstration was also a raid; the unemployed penetrated to the boardroom while the guardians were in session, occupied it, sealed off the meeting, and surrounded the guardians in their chairs until they made a concession in cash or kind, or until the police ejected them.

There was also direct action against low wages paid by local councils for work on relief schemes. The Ministry of Health had authorised councils to start schemes of work for the unemployed, but stipulated that the wage was to be not more than seventy-five per cent of the trade-union rate. The Movement set out to defeat this and at Basingstoke, after a meeting in the cinema, three hundred men, led by Wal Hannington, marched out to the site, persuaded some of the workers to stop, confiscated the tools of those who would not, marched back and deposited two hundred muddy picks and shovels in the district surveyor's office. Action on relief-work schemes took place throughout the country. At Rochdale the wages for work on a relief scheme at the cemetery and the recreation ground had been reduced to seventy-five per cent of the rate set by the Civil Engineering and Construction Conciliation Board. Sixty men marched to the site and seized tools and wheel-barrows. One of them, Robert Dawson, defending himself in court with the help of the Movement's divisional organiser, urged the unemployed to 'take up something stronger than batons', and was bound over, for his pains, in the sum of £10. The local *Observer* offered the advice that 'three-quarters of a loaf was better than no bread',[12] and opined that the unemployed were really eager for work at any wage if they were left to themselves; in any case there was always the mayor's unemployment committee which would continue to provide them with meals, clothing and boots.

In the same month of January, when the West Bromwich Council started a relief scheme at the sewerage works, the unemployed taken on there went on strike for the trade-union rate of 1s 5d per hour. Their view was that if Poplar could give the full rate so could West Bromwich. After twenty-two men had gone back to work three hundred marched to the site and persuaded them to stop. Walter Rigby, James Baggott, John Swain and William Carpenter, were arrested and charged under the Conspiracy and Protection of Property Act of 1875.

In court Rigby explained: 'I want you to realise that I am out to get the necessities of life for myself and my wife and because I am striving against the system of society we are in. This is the position I find myself in and I want you to look at it from a logical point of view.' Such logic did not appeal to the magistrate whose view was simply that twenty-two men had been prevented from working. Swain denied that the men had been prevented. They had decided to come out but the police had ordered them back. When bail was refused he burst out: 'I don't see that you can send us to prison without bail. The point is you want to get rid of us. But I want justice and justice I demand', an expression which the magistrate did not like either, and threatened to commit him for contempt of court. Prosecuting counsel concentrated on establishing that the defendants were communists, the police inspector giving the evidence asserted that Swain was a 'red-hot Communist', followed no employment, and was nothing but an agitator. Counsel for the defence deplored the Communist bogy. It was a fact that the police wanted to stop unemployed meetings. Swain received one month's hard labour, Rigby and Baggott twenty-one days each.[13]

In April 1922 the policy of the gap in benefit appeared. During the previous year the Government had increased from fifteen to twenty-six the number of weeks in which a man could draw statutory benefit in any one year, and he could draw uncovenanted benefit if he was out of work for more than twenty-six weeks. The intention was that men would not have recourse to poor relief in undue numbers. This policy was found to be too generous and it was therefore enacted that there was to be a gap of five weeks in the payments. This meant that any man who had exhausted his statutory benefit had to wait five weeks for his uncovenanted benefit if he was still unemployed. When he had received that for five weeks, he had to wait another five weeks, and so on. As about half the unemployed who queued at the labour exchanges were drawing uncovenanted benefit, the result of this latest device was that hundreds of thousands had to apply for poor relief, to the dismay of the boards of guardians. The Movement, harnessing the fierce resentment felt, mobilised its forces against the gap.

One effect of the gap was that some boards of guardians tried to reduce the demands on them by refusing any relief to men who were already receiving benefit from the labour exchanges, if, for instance, it was needed to pay the rent. In Birmingham, in May 1922, two massive demonstrations in the Bull Ring marched and fought with the police all day against this policy. The guardians had been told that the maximum relief was to be ten shillings less than a labourer's wage and that they should therefore reduce what they were paying.[14] In June a week's continuous nation-wide campaign culminated in rallies in hundreds of towns. In July the Government reduced the gap from five weeks to one. The Movement claimed victory.

Simultaneously it was engaged in another struggle. The operation of the gap had had the effect of increasing the evictions of unemployed from their homes for inability to pay rent and rates. Wherever such evictions became frequent, as in Glasgow, the Movement organised tenants' groups. When the tenants' scouts raised the alarm, supporters gathered and prevented the bailiffs removing furniture or moved it back in again after eviction. In one struggle in that city, a group led by Harry McShane, defending a tenement in the Gorbals, resisted siege by bailiffs and police for two days before being overcome and taken to prison. In Sheffield attempts to restore families to their homes developed into a battle with the police, and in Smethwick the leaders of a group which reinstalled furniture were arrested. Resistance in London took the shape of organised squatting in empty houses. In the campaign against the gap the Movement had also taken the issue to Whitehall. From this came the origin of the big marches on London. In June 1921 there had been a march of two hundred unemployed from London to the Labour Party conference at Brighton. In July 1922 thirty men made a longer march of nine days from Birmingham to London. An interview with the Minister of Labour brought little satisfaction beyond expressions of sympathy, explanations of the difficulties under which he laboured, and a cup of tea in his office. The marchers were fed and housed by the Poplar Council for ten days. At a civic reception in their honour the mayor, Charles Sumner, urged them to do more. 'It is a sign of the times and a tribute to your organisation,' he said. 'I hope that this will be but the forerunner of many other such marches. Let them all march to London and perhaps the Government would then wake up to its responsibilities.'

Another pointer appeared in a leading article in the *Daily Herald*, at that period a staunch supporter of the Movement: 'Nor would it be amiss if half a dozen of the unemployed from every town set out to meet the Premier on a given day.'[15]

Developed and hardened by two years' of struggle, encouraged by successes and aided by the thriving circulation of *Out of Work* and of the *Communist*, the Movement now felt strong enough to put the idea of a march on London into practice. In September 1922, having received strong expressions of support from branches throughout the country, it started to organise the first national march.

REFERENCES

1. PRO Mepol 2/1958; *Morning Post*, 19 & 20.10.20; *Daily Herald*, 18–21.10.20; Hannington, W., *Never On Our Knees*, 1967, pp. 80–2.
2. *Daily Herald*, 20.10.20.
3. Pribicevic, P., *Shop Stewards' Movement and Workers Control*, 1959, p. 34.
4. Kendall, W., *Revolutionary Movement in Britain 1920–21*, 1969.
5. Hannington, op. cit., pp. 83, 94–7; *Daily Herald*, 4 & 25.1.21.
6. Miliband, R., *Parliamentary Socialism*, 1973, p. 82.
7. *Sheffield Daily Telegraph*, 12.8.21; *Communist*, 5.8.20. For 'poplarism' see Noreen Branson's *Poplarism, 1919–1925*, 1979.
8. PRO CAB 24/128; Mepol 2/1958.
9. *Out of Work*, November 1921; *Communist*, 17.12.21.
10. Hannington, W., *Unemployed Struggles*, 1936; reprinted 1977, pp. 45–50.
11. PRO CAB 24/128.
12. *Rochdale Observer*, 4.1.22.
13. *West Bromwich Midland Chronicle*, 6.1.22–3.2.22.
14. Hannington, W., op. cit. p. 75.
15. *Daily Herald*, 21.8.22.

2

The First National March, 1922–3

On 16 September 1922 a call went out to all branches of the National Unemployed Workers' Committee Movement signed by Jack Holt and Percy Haye:[1]

Each Committee must consider VERY SERIOUSLY the implications of the March.

Every participant must have on his or her heart the CAUSE for which we fight: THE EMANCIPATION OF OUR CLASS.

The bigger the contingent the better but DON'T BRING OR SEND OTHERS THAN THOSE THAT CAN BE RELIED UPON.

A month later the unemployed were on the march. First off the mark were iron-and-steel workers from Scotland, then shipyard workers of the Tyne, shipwrights of Barrow-in-Furness, dockers and seamen of Liverpool, iron-ore miners of Cumberland, cotton operatives of Lancashire, coal-miners of the South Wales valleys, engineers and mechanics from the Midlands, labourers from all parts of Britain. By 27 October the men from Newcastle and South Shields had reached Northallerton, fifty miles to the south, where they spent the night in the workhouse. This band of seventeen was made up of two boilermakers, two fitters, two blacksmiths, one turner, one domestic engineer, one holder-up, and eight labourers. Their ages averaged thirty, ranging between twenty and forty-eight. Many of them were ex-servicemen. One, a fitter, was alleged to be going to Moscow. Such a mixture of skills, ages, experience and political commitment was typical of the contingents converging on London.

At Westminster Lloyd George had just come to the end of his reign. The Conservatives had revolted against the coalition and decided on 19 October at the Carlton Club to govern the country by themselves under the leadership of Bonar Law. Throughout the whole fortnight of electioneering which followed, the hunger marchers carried their banners through the towns and villages, and reached London two days after polling day on 15 November. Bonar Law promised an era of tranquillity, the marchers were out to distrub it. 'The nation's first need,' Bonar Law declared, 'is, in every walk of life, to get on with its own work, with the minimum of interference at home and of disturbance abroad.' There were still one and a half million men who were not able to get on with any work at all and whose hope lay in intervention by the Government on a massive scale.

The marchers' demands were clear and definite. Each man knew that what he was marching for was – work or full maintenance at trade union rates. He knew what the demand for full maintenance meant: for a man and wife thirty-six shillings a week, plus five shillings for each child up to sixteen years old, rent up to fifteen shillings and one hundredweight of coal or its equivalent in gas; for single persons eighteen years and over, thirty shillings and a hundredweight of coal or gas; and for single persons under eighteen, fifteen shillings per week. On such money, compared with the unemployment benefit of twenty shillings for man and wife plus one shilling for each child, he would have been able to live decently. He realised that the demand was for something near a living wage and he believed that it was worth fighting for because he had a right to it. The men, of whom there were many in the ranks who, having exhausted their insurance benefit, had been obliged to go to the boards of guardians for poor relief, had most to gain and nothing to lose. These men were well aware that the guardians in some towns gave less relief than those in others. So the demand was that payments for maintenance should be on a national scale, not subject to local variation, and also that the cost should be borne wholly by the Government not by the local ratepayers. This, they calculated, would win them the support of all ratepaying citizens.

Each man had his copy of *The Programme of the Great National Hunger March on London*, published by the National Administrative Council of Unemployed at 3 Queen Square, London, WC1 for one penny, which enrolled him behind 'the general uplifting of the working class as a whole until emancipation from the clutches of a decaying system of society based upon Rent, Interest and Profit is achieved'. Already, as a local activist, he had pledged himself:

Realising that only by the abolition of this hideous capitalist system can the horror of unemployment be removed from our midst, I here and now take upon myself a binding oath, to never cease from active strife against this system until capitalism is abolished and our country and all its resources truly belong to the people.

Picked out from the ranks of volunteers, he had accepted the Rules of the March printed in the Programme, the necessity of strict discipline on the road and obedience to the marshals' instructions. The Rules stipulated that each contingent must have its own banner showing the name of its town. It must have its finance sub-committee of three and a treasurer to ensure that money, particularly the collections on the road, was properly handled, and its arrangements committee to obtain accommodation and food. It should have cyclists as messengers and scouts to explore the road ahead. It would march an average of twelve miles a day.

Each man's deep sense of grievance, combined with a hope of improvement, was the spur to face the hardships on the road and the uncertainties in his mind. There were plenty of these, money for one; would he get unemployment benefit on the march? He might, but only if he had got a travelling-card from his local exchange and could persuade the exchanges on the way to London that he was marching in search of work. But no one could tell if this would happen. How would his family be able to manage? That would depend on the guardians of the poor. If they were hostile to the march or likely to refuse outdoor relief in any case, and if there was no unemployment benefit, then local comrades would have to help and his own branch of the Movement would have to raise funds for the wives and children. On the road the money for food would have to come from the collecting boxes which he and his comrades would be shaking all along the way. He had no guidance what to take with him, what clothing, bedding, pots and pans and means of cooking. Meal and a bed would have to be taken where they could be found.

By the end of October, information had reached Government ministers in London. Having been in office only a few days, they were pre-occupied with the general election pending. 'What are we doing about the marches to London of the unemployed? I presume we are prepared for it,' inquired the

Home Secretary, W. C. Bridgeman. He was reassured by General Horwood, Commissioner of the Metropolitan Police, who thought that the march would probably prove to be 'a frost'. Few of those who set out would reach London, in his view. Bridgeman was also told of the marchers' demand that the national exchequer instead of the local authorities should pay for their maintenance. The next day the Government announced that the cabinet had formed an unemployment committee.[2]

The Scots had started a fortnight before. Thomas Cooper, James Bean, James Clark and Thomas Waddell of Aberdeen had intended to walk to Glasgow, but instructions from London arrived too late, so when the local unemployed workers' committee had found the money for their fares they took the boat to Leith. They did not have to worry about dependants. Single men only were chosen because the parish council had refused to pay relief to the families of any men away on the march. They expected to be joined by comrades at Edinburgh and by others from Falkirk, Alloa, Motherwell and Hamilton, as they made their way by bus and on foot to Glasgow.

Only a dozen joined the group at Glasgow but together they elected a committee, appointed their chief marshal, Robert Wemyss, four deputy marshals, and set off on 17 October on the four hundred miles to London via Carlisle. In their native land they had mixed fortunes. Kilmarnock welcomed them with two recruits but at the next stop, Cumnock, their cycling advance party was refused the use of the hall from its custodian, miners' secretary, town councillor and member of the Independent Labour Party though he was. It was the minister who gave the use of the church, food, and boots for the marchers, and the townspeople who told them to 'knock Lloyd George's head off.' Further on at Sanquhar, where they slept in the town hall, there was a collection for them at the end of a concert. The next day, at Thornhill in Buccleuch territory, people stayed away from the marchers' meeting, but in Dumfries they marched in with banners flying – 'National Unemployed Workers Committee Movement – Aberdeen Deputation to Interview Lloyd George, Sir Alfred Mond and the Minister of Labour', and got a good hearing at meetings in Queensberry Square. Work of a kind was available there. On going to the labour exchange to get their cards signed they were offered work at the rate of 4s 6d a day. They refused what in their opinion were sweated wages, and were told that their local labour exchange would be informed accordingly for the appropriate action to be taken.[3]

At the other end of the kingdom ten days later twenty-seven men from the dockyards of Devon were getting ready to start from Plymouth. On 27 October they were entertained with their relations by Herman Darewski and his music at the Palace Theatre and benefited from collections there and at the boxing gymnasium. The following day, after a demonstration in the Guildhall Square, the marchers set out, led by the red flag and brass band of the Plymouth unemployed, and escorted by the police as far as Plympton. They too had mixed fortunes. The first night was spent well enough in the workhouse at Totnes but, after passing through Exeter, Honiton and Chard, the fifth night at Yeovil was severe hardship. The mayor refused them accommodation and there was nowhere else to go. They could not continue marching after seventeen miles on the road, so they spent the night in the open, sleeping as best they could on the steps of the new war memorial.[4]

In Lancashire it was difficult to choose who should go, so many wanted to march, whether they were shipyard workers from Barrow-in-Furness or cotton operatives from Bolton and Manchester. In Barrow every other man was out of work. Seventy of them, with their own brass band, got off to a good start on 27 October. The guardians of the poor, at their wits' end to make ends meet, were strongly in favour of the demand that maintenance should be paid for by the Government, and they gave the marchers clothing and boots and promised boards of guardians along the route that they would repay the cost of night's lodging in the workhouse.

The marchers fared well with free food and lodging at Milnthorpe and better still on arrival at Lancaster, where they were received by the Trades Council and that evening saw a revue at the Grand Theatre, at the close of which their brass band played on the stage and earned a handsome collection. The next morning they set off for Preston, Wigan and Warrington, bound for Wolverhampton, Birmingham and the south. The other Lancashire men, those from Bolton, went a different way. Seventy marchers gathered in Victoria Square on the misty morning of 31 October and, as they exchanged memories of the old army days, fell into line at the order 'Company, number-r-r!'. A large crowd listened to speeches and showered coppers into the ring of caps. The mayor had sent a message of good luck with a substantial donation, the tradespeople had given tins of food and clothing, and the local Right to Work Council had raised enough funds to hand each marcher an envelope containing some money. Spirits were high as they said goodbye to wives and children; to some shouldering their packs, it seemed like the more serious farewells of wartime. Now they were, for a time, their own men. 'We have nothing to do with the communists,' one said. 'They have tried to break us, and we are against them. We want to act constitutionally, and we do not recognise any particular party.' Next morning in Manchester, as some two hundred men from the city, Salford and Openshaw joined the Bolton men, a cold wind and rain soaked their underfed, ill-clothed bodies. These men were not so well provided; many were without outdoor coats. The ex-servicemen among them had a change of clothing in their packs but the others, not a few of whom were elderly, hugged brown-paper parcels which revealed saturated shirts and socks. Wives and mothers realised that their men would have to go to the boards of guardians en route for food and a bed or a heap of straw in the casual ward of the workhouse, and wept as they said goodbye. All knew that although a good deal had been organised in advance, at some places which had refused to take them in they would have to rely on the generosity of the townspeople.[5]

As they got into Staffordshire there were complaints about the unvaried diet of bread and cheese. It constituted dinner at Stockport, supper at Macclesfield and again dinner on the second day. Tom McKay, chief marshal and unsympathetic to grumblers, told them they would have to vary it with cheese and bread. At Leek, they had butter and jam with it, thanks to the initiative of the Labour parliamentary candidate who was in the thick of his election campaign, and the Trades and Labour Council which met the cost. There was no room at the workhouse for close on three hundred and the council members, and their wives and daughters saw to it that the marchers were more or less comfortably bedded down in the Butter Market and had a good breakfast. One banner bore a skull and crossbones and the words 'Death is better than starvation'. The situation at Ashbourne the next stop was grim, for there was a desperate search for enough food. Derby, strong for Labour with its railwaymen, engineering workers and its representation in Parliament by Jimmy Thomas, did them very well. The borough handed them the Orchard Street schools for the weekend, the Sherwood Foresters' regimental depot gave a hundred tins of bully-beef, and the board of guardians authorised the Co-operative Society to supply £30 worth of provisions, thereby incurring the grave displeasure of the Ministry of Health. When forty Scots also marched in, more food was willingly found for them. The Scots, as they came through Yorkshire, had seen men fighting for work at the labour exchange in Sheffield. Rumours that thousands of men would get work on constructing a new road had drawn hundreds to the exchange, only to learn that a mere fifty were wanted.

This junction of Lancashire men and Scots took place according to plan. Tom McKay, the Lancashire chief marshal took the Scots also under his command as laid down in the Programme – 'where contingents meet with each other on the road the Chief Marshal of the largest contingent will act as Chief Marshal of the whole Mass Contingent'. Sunday breakfast, supplied by the York and Clarendon hotels, was the best for a very long time. The company, now numbering three hundred and twenty, fell into line at the bugle call, marched to and fro between the central hall and the schools for dinner, a social afternoon, and tea, its men wearing red rosettes alongside their war ribbons and singing 'The Red Flag' behind the red banners.

They left, well rested and well fed, heartened by the knowledge of having given an orderly demonstration of their case to the electorate of Derby. Tom McKay, giving their thanks to the guardians, declared that Derby had treated them better than anywhere else. At Shardlow seven miles along the road, there would be tea to wash down the guardians' issue of bread and cheese, and after another ten miles, at Loughborough, there would be jam with the bread instead of the eternal cheese.[6] But they found Loughborough very different from Derby. Every man from chief marshal to drummer was soaking wet and the only shelter offered by the guardians was a disused drill hall, without beds, boards, blankets, or any means of washing or drying clothes. There was bread and jam and cocoa, the 'menu', as one of the guardians put it, having been altered at the marchers' request. When they demanded, 'Where are the blankets?' they were told that as there were only fifty it would not be fair to issue them. Some men shouted that they should go in to the town and knock at doors until they got enough blankets, but discipline prevailed, and all settled down to sleep in their wet clothes without any other covering. In the morning the guardians added two ounces of margarine per head to the menu of bread, corned beef, tea, milk and sugar. Twenty marchers were left behind in the workhouse infirmary, suffering from throat and chest ailments. The guardians were more concerned with the cost of their hospitality. 'Who is going to pay for this?' asked Sir Edward Packe, KBE, Lord Lieutenant of the county and lately private secretary to the First Lord of the Admiralty, 'Cannot we write to the Ministry of Health and ask them to get it from Manchester?' The clerk reassured them, 'They could thoroughly congratulate themselves that they had got rid of these men so cheaply.' After all, he said, they must remember that they had certain liabilities to make some provision, and in fact the cost of the food had been very little more than that of the standard diet for vagrants. The guardians sent to the Home Office their protest against 'large bodies of men being allowed to parade the country in this manner, and especially in view of the statement of the Prime Minister that no useful purpose can result from the hunger march'.[7]

Twenty other contingents were converging on London, amongst whom the South Wales miners had been on the move since 3 November. First to start were the Rhondda Valley men, marching sixteen miles before joining their comrades in Cardiff where the Trades and Labour Council looked after them. At the place in Cathays Park known as 'unemployed corner' they were addressed by the Labour parliamentary candidate and by their leader, W. Mainwaring, who said what they wanted to hear:

We have been told that our mission is useless since the late Government collapsed. Personally, I think that it has taken on new importance from that fact. At all events, we are going to get to London, and once there a couple of thousands of determined men, and we are that, can accomplish something. At all events, the trickle of these little streams from all parts of the country just now will awaken the public to the fact that we are not a newspaper paragraph, or a recorded statistic, but men who wear boots and clothes, who eat, drink, sleep, love, and laugh and cry like themselves. We are sick of being a newspaper paragraph.[8]

As they moved off in the morning, the local unemployed gathered and passed them little gifts of fruit, a few coppers, a handful of Woodbine cigarettes. At Newport, again the Trades Council sheltered them with the help of blankets from the guardians. Recruits from Monmouthshire, from Brynmawr, Blaina, Nantyglo and Abertillery, came in as they entered Bristol, increasing their number to over a hundred. After they had bedded down in the corporation rest house in Leek Lane they went out to help the Labour candidate, Brigadier-General C. B. Thomson, CBE, DSO, formerly military representative at the Supreme War Council in Versailles, whose personal knowledge of Lenin during his work in Russia commended him strongly to the communists amongst the marchers. They vigorously supported his demands for a national minimum standard of life and for a capital levy to reduce the national debt. Their own grievance gave an edge to the first of these, for they had found that the scales of poor relief paid in Bristol were well above those which their own poverty stricken boards of guardians at home could pay. However, that wealthy city had earned their appreciation as their leader, now Sid Elias, said in thanking the corporation for their kindly reception. On leaving, they split into two to relieve the problem of accommodation in the country towns through which they would now pass. The Glamorganshire men made for Swindon where they could count on support from the railwaymen while those from Monmouthshire penetrated the Tory countryside to the south, to rejoin forces at Reading. The first group were 'in the pink', as they reported, after being given hot baths and hospitality by the Trades Council, while the second found that in rural Wiltshire miners could always expect sympathy. There was kindness on all sides, in the market town of Devizes and in Marlborough where a concert presided over by the mayor was given for them. At Reading, in the last week of the election campaign, there was plenty of hospitality from both ends of the political spectrum. The British Legion housed them in St Saviour's Hall and combined with the Trade Union Club to pay for three days' meals for a hundred and thirty men. They stirred up the election campaign, notably the meeting of Hall Caine, the Labour candidate, and left the day before polling day, 15 November.[9]

The contingents from Scotland and Lancashire were also by now approaching the home counties. The Scots and the Manchester men slept in beds for the first time at Leicester. 'We not only had a good tea last night,' one of the street collectors told the press, 'but we had a good bed to lie on, a refreshing bath that has made us feel as different again, and a splendid breakfast that will enable us to march, march, march for miles.' The advance guard had persuaded the guardians and the Urban District Council at Kettering to add to the diet prescribed for casual wards, so that when the column arrived there were meat teas in the Corn Market Hall and cocoa in the workhouse, before bedding down, and each man had a pillow and blankets. For 'so kindly dealing with the unemployed marchers' the guardians earned the thanks of the Trades and Labour Council and the displeasure of the Ministry of Health. Further on at Rushden there was another government department to deal with. The clerk at the labour exchange refused to sign their travelling cards so that they could not claim unemployment benefit.[10]

The other Lancashire column, the men from Barrow, having passed through Wolverhampton and gathered in recruits from Smethwick and Walsall, assembled, a hundred strong, in the Bull Ring at Birmingham and marched for Coventry under their leader McMahon. There was grumbling in the ranks about the monotony of the food; there seemed to be no end to bully beef. At the end of a march of eighteen miles, Coventry could only offer bully beef and dry bread and, to sleep on, bare boards in the drill hall. The guardians, charged with shabby treatment, promised to ask other guardians on the route to provide hot meals, but without effect, for at Rugby it was again bully beef. They made a solemn public protest. In the cemetery George Garrett, 'Clerk in Holy Trousers', read the burial service – 'Ashes to ashes, dust to dust, Goodbye bully, our bellies you've bust', and as the drums rolled and the bugles sounded the 'Last Post', a tin of bully beef was consigned to its last resting-place.[11]

From Yorkshire, Tyneside, Plymouth, Lincoln and Kent other columns slowly advanced. The Yorkshire men from Rotherham joined up with comrades at Nottingham and, after their boots had been renewed, pressed on through the hunting counties to Kettering and Bedfordshire, undeterred by the news that the guardians at home had been refused permission by the Ministry to pay them emergency relief. On the east the Newcastle column was awaited with apprehension by the Doncaster guardians. 'What preparations were to be made for this "battalion of unemployed"?' they asked; presumably the marchers would be put in the casual ward and be detained for two days in accordance with the regulations. At any rate the workhouse master would no doubt do his best in the special circumstances. He knew well that there was no hope of enforcing the detention rule, but in fact it suited the marchers to stay two nights, for two men had had to give up. At Stilton they met the men from Lincolnshire who had had to rest there. The Lincoln men had started in good heart from St Benedict's Square, where the Labour parliamentary candidate had spoken a few words of encouragement and explained to a big crowd the objects of the march. 'We're tired out but in good spirits,' they reported. Though well looked after at Peterborough by the trades council, their feet had given up. Two other parties, one from Dover, the other from Ramsgate, had set off and joined up at Canterbury, where the Labour Party gave them a meal and lodgings for the night. They, too, slept in beds for the first time. As they left for Sittingbourne their banner broadcast the message, 'In the Trenches Yesterday, Unemployed Today'.[12]

The men of Devon had made such good progress that they were a day ahead of schedule at Salisbury and stayed two nights there in spite of a frosty reception from the guardians and from the police who, anxious not to have the calm of the cathedral town disturbed, forbade them to sell their programmes in the streets. Like all the contingents, they had stirred up activity and debate as they went. Soon after the men had passed through Newton Abbot, the unemployed of that town renewed activity. They sent a deputation to the board of guardians requesting full work or full maintenance by which they meant a definite scale of relief and a hundredweight of coal per week during the winter months. In response to the guardians' offer of sympathy they said – 'we appreciate your sympathy but we want practical help'. The relieving officer reported that out of the deputation of five, two were in work, the third was paid 7 shillings a week from the guardians and 25 shillings from the unemployment committee, the fourth had 9 shillings from the guardians and 23 shillings from the committee, and the fifth, a woman, had 10 shillings from the committee and 8 shillings eight pence in kind from the guardians. Encouraged by these facts a guardian spoke up – the deputation had given no concrete evidence of insufficient relief; it was simply trying to force the doctrine of communism on people who, whatever their personal views might be, were not in a position to give effect to such doctrines – and the board unanimously resolved that no action be taken. The deputation told it that they would see what happened next and struck up 'The Red Flag' as they left.

By then the Devon contingent had arrived at Bagshot, where it found the tradespeople generous with food and the police more helpful.[13]

On 15 November the converging columns arrived punctually on the outskirts of London at the prearranged assembly points; Barnet, Hounslow, Tooting, and Woolwich. The small town of Barnet received by far the biggest gathering. Five hundred and twenty-six men, from Scotland, Lancashire, Yorkshire, Tyneside, Lincolnshire, the Black Country and the Midlands marched in, escorted by a strong body of police. They found the board of guardians well prepared with an equal number of pints of hot tea. Half of the men went to the workhouse where the board room and the old infirmary were ready, the other half to the army huts at the barracks. They lined up for a straw bed and two blankets each and sat down to a hot meal, shepherd's pie, bread and margarine, with more tea. They spent the evening in various ways. The day's collection was shared out equally among each contingent. For one man it would be just enough for a shave and haircut and a packet of fags, for another a collar and some stamps, for another a pair of braces and some tobacco. Twenty pairs of boots were repaired free of charge. Most then took advantage of the concerts for them at the workhouse and at the Wesleyan Hall. They felt no call to demonstrate in the streets of such a hospitable town. A few sought the public houses for pints of local brew. The ex-servicemen talked to a borough councillor and welfare workers, 'Hi guvner, 'ast seen owt like this?' one asked, pulling up his shirt and exposing a long scar of a shell wound. A second who lacked fingers on one hand explained, 'Left 'em o'er t'other side o' Channel'. A third who walked so badly that the visitors asked how he could march, answered: 'I could march with the best of 'em afore I lost my toes ower yon.' Another marcher told the visitors: 'The last time I was in London was when my battalion crossed to Waterloo en route for France. Then luxuries of all kinds were pressed in my hands and pockets, and the flags were waving for us, and – well I was thinking of the different reception we shall get tomorrow.'

Fifty-seven men found sleeping space on the floor of the workhouse boardroom. After breakfast of bully-beef, bread, margarine and tea the long column moved off with bread and cheese for lunch and in good order for Edmonton. There was satisfaction on all sides. Tom McKay told the press that the hospitality had been more generous than anywhere. The guardians were also well pleased. Their reverend member criticised the expense which the ratepayers would have to bear but he was assured that the cost per head would not amount to much. There was great relief that the whole thing had passed off so peacefully. The local newspaper called for reduced taxes to stimulate the economy:

Few who saw the pathetic procession of unemployed could be unmoved by sympathy and pity. It was obvious that the great majority were genuine hard working men. Particularly sad were the cases of crippled ex-servicemen. It is not enough to be sorry for them. The Government must grapple with the problem. Doles are no solution. They are the cause of the rate burden which so hampers industry. Thus the cost of the dole, is actually depriving men of work. The remedy for unemployment which is becoming a serious menace to the tranquillity of this country is a revival of trade and therefore there must be a reduction in taxation.

The loud cry, repeated along the length of the departing column, 'We shall not leave London once we get there without seeing the Prime Minister!', was for the Government to deal with.[14]

The last stage of the March was to quarters in London. For the men from Devon and Wales these were in Wandsworth; for those from the South, Battersea; and for the men of Kent, Deptford. They were all reached on the appointed day, 16 November. The five hundred men from the north were covering the last few miles through Finchley, Holloway and up the Seven Sisters Road to Edmonton. The *Daily Herald* was out early to meet them. Girls carrying *Herald* placards stepped out along-side the column. A reporter marching in the ranks was mocked by a white-haired sixty year old from Sheffield, 'Aye, you eat too much. If you could only lose your job you'd eat less. Then you wouldn't sweat so easily with a walk. You'd get in good condition.' Another veteran, Edward Tuck from Coventry, declared, 'I am just seventy and I was never fitter in my life.' 'He's the youngest man amongst us,' they said. Quite a few men were still lame, 'But they are all with us for the final assault' claimed Tom Dingley, ambulance chief and Coventry marshal. The Scots boasted too that all were present after a month on the road, led all the way by Gordon Currie, their own marshal. 'Meet the marchers' padre,' they urged, 'he's one of us.' The Reverend Thomas Pickering was at the head of the column: 'Yes, I have shared the men's hardships since Sheffield and we have had some hard times. The worst experience was at Clowne in Derbyshire. Through police action we of the Sheffield and Rotherham contingent were out all night. At first it was freezing, then raining, then snowing. The villagers took compassion on us at eight o'clock in the morning and took us in, giving us rest and food. But I have gained much. I have found a spirit of comradeship nearer to real Christianity than I have found in the Christian churches. I could tell of many acts of unselfishness and self sacrifice. These men, ticketed as the worst rebels, I have found to be possessed of qualities above price.'[15]

Then came 17 November the day of assembly in Hyde Park, the day of union with comrades in other contingents and with the workers of London. The London branches of the unemployed movement had assembled in the Park with bands and banners at two o'clock, but at three o'clock a dense crowd of some 20,000 was still waiting. Cyclists were sent out for news of the marchers. The Welsh and the Devon men, headed by Abertillery, were seen swinging up Park Lane, singing:

> Lloyd George won the war
> So let him win the next
> And we'll all stop at home.

The five hundred from the north were marching along Oxford Street to Marble Arch with their song:

> Law and order's got the wind up!
> Law and order's got the wind up!
> Law and order's got the wind up!
> But they can't put the wind up us!

and as they reached the Park gates there was a special cheer for the Scottish banner which had come farthest of all. The men of Kent came up, 150 strong, and the Hampshire and Sussex men, each shouting as they came in, 'Are we down-hearted? No!.' Wal Hannington had a message to deliver. They had heard that the Prime Minister's secretary had written to say that Bonar Law could not receive any deputation but that the Ministers of Labour and Health would see them. 'It is the Premier these men have marched to London to see, and they are not going to leave London until they have seen him,' he cried. 'We do not want to see the nincompoops of the Government, we want to see Mr Bonar Law.' Caps were doffed as 'The Red Flag' was sung, and in good order, watched by a strong force of police, the marchers re-formed and departed to their shelter for the night.[16]

Some resented the accommodation, others accepted it as inevitable. The London branches responsible for providing accommodation and food had done their best, but the only marchers lucky enough to go to comrades' homes were thirty-five men from Ramsgate who marched out to Eltham. For the rest there were public and charitable institutions of one kind or another. The contingents were broken up into manageable sections; the Bolton men split into four, one group dropping off at the West Ham workhouse, the others at the Young Men's Christian Association hostel, and at the Seamen's Rest and Lees Hall in Barking Road. The workhouse in Edmonton took in a hundred and fifty Manchester men. Public baths were used; thirty from Maidstone were in Leytonstone Baths and in Battersea forty-four men from as far apart as Nottingham and Deal found themselves together in the Latchmere Road Baths. Others were taken to Salvation Army barracks; a hundred and fifty from Scotland, Newcastle, Coventry and Lincoln were in the care of the Army at Harlesden. Although the comradeship and discipline forged on the march were weakened, men from widely different parts of the country came together in companionship and knowledge of each others's homes. One party were all miners, but they came from Wigan as well as from Wales. This group was glad to go to Poplar, for every man had heard of George Lansbury and Poplarism. All eighty-four sat down to a meal as the guests of John Scurr, the mayor. Each man had a bed in the old army lodging-house in the high street and could look forward to a civic welcome by the mayor, aldermen and councillors next day.[17]

Saturday was a day for settling in, for getting to know new comrades, exploring the district, nursing sore feet and reading the papers. The workhouse masters did not venture to impose the rules, marchers went out after breakfast and returned for tea as they wished. The Manchester men at Edmonton workhouse had free tickets from the Tottenham Football Club. Lansbury's *Daily Herald* was the favoured reading matter, the only paper in which men could see reports of their arrival. It announced – 'Labour Triumph in the General Election'. With 142 seats Labour had become the official opposition, with a million and a half fewer votes than the Conservatives. George Lansbury and Shapurji Saklatvala were back in Parliament and more like them.[18]

On Sunday everyone was marching to Trafalgar Square. So great was the crowd that three sides of Nelson's column were used for speeches simultaneously. From the north side of the plinth Wal Hannington repeated the marchers' purpose to state their case to the Prime Minister personally, and at the same time to fight their claims for unemployment benefit with the courts of referees and the umpire who judged those claims:

> The Umpire is prepared to consider the cases on Wednesday afternoon, the very day that the deputation is due to see the Premier. We have sufficient talent amongst us to send a deputation to see the Umpire as well as the Premier. Get that right into your heads. These men are not leaving London until they have interviewed Bonar Law and they are going to see to it, going to use every power they have, to see to it that their dependants are not robbed of what they are entitled to because they have come on the march.

Tom McKay emphasised the message by calling for 'a bumper demonstration on Wednesday so as to compel Mr Bonar Law to eat his own words'. 'Sak' spoke, Shapurji Saklatvala, member of Parliament for Battersea: 'We have been telling you ever since the revolution in Russia in 1917 that mankind has discovered another cure for unemployment.' The padre, the Reverend Pickering, gave them more of a sermon than a speech. George Garrett, seaman from Liverpool, the mock clergyman at Rugby, appealed to the Londoners, 'We do not want to go back to our towns and tell the people that the comrades in London gave us a clap, that they treated us very fine. We want to say that our comrades in London are preparing, not for the tranquillity that suits Mr Bonar Law, but the tranquillity that will suit the working class.' Gordon Currie carried the argument further:

> It is not merely a fight for 36 shillings per week, for the national demands. In my estimation it is a fight for possession. It is a fight for the workshops and the factories, for the land, for the things that go to make life worth living. That is the fight, the greatest fight. No matter how many doles you get, so long as Capitalism remains in existence, so long as a small class owns and controls everything, you will always be slaves.

George Cook, who had come with them from Altrincham, also called on London for support:

> Do all the clapping and cheering when we have shifted away the parasites of society. We are here to be heard, to be seen, and if necessary to be felt. Seventy-five per cent of the men who came on

the march from Manchester are ex-servicemen and we came up in military formation, all the way from Manchester with our commanding officer, our battalion sergeant-major and our company sergeant-major, I happened to be the company sergeant-major, and were so military disciplined that we were nothing short but ammunition, and I believe we can get the ammunition when it is necessary, and I do not give a damn whether we use it this week or the week after. We, as the ex-industrial workers of the country, have produced the whole of the wealth of the country, and when we have produced it, we say to our masters, 'We have produced this wealth, we give it unto you that you may give unto us what you think we deserve.' He turns to us and says, 'Well done, thou good and faithful servant, I will give thee one third of the wealth thou hast produced keeping the two thirds for myself.' Now friends, you who are unemployed. I want you to realise that this is your fight as ours, and you can help us by your organisation, by your finance and we are out to demand from the Government work at trade union wages, and failing work, adequate maintenance.

On the east side of the plinth there were fiery words from Jack Riley, leader of the men of Kent:

We can tell Bonar Law that there is a greater power than any government, that is the power of the working-class movement. Too long have we suffered. We of the working classes who are on this platform, we use our intelligence, and we say to you, get into the working-class organisations, and unite in a strong solid body to rule your own destinies. We are not going to have a parasite class on our backs. They asked us in 1914 to go to war, and I was one of the damned mugs that went. They said we were going to fight for liberty. What liberty did we fight for? The only liberty we fought for was the liberty to starve. We will compel Bonar Law to listen to our demands. We don't care for the men in blue or the men in khaki. The time will come when the workers will organise their own army, and then God help them. We will be prepared to meet force with force, and we will fight on towards the goal that we are out for.

Tom Dingley reasoned with all workers:

Today we have reached another stage in the history of the working-class movement. But do you really understand the economic foundation of the capitalist system that brings these comrades to travel five and six hundred miles to lay their grievances before the human race? An old historian who analysed the starvation that existed in the time of Wat Tyler says that the masses are now more servile than they were hundreds of years ago. Why is it now necessary that we should demonstrate? Because we are fighting for our self-preservation in human society. Your vote will not get you what you require, votes are only the replica (*sic.*) whereby your position in society is altered. The point that we have got to look for is to get down to the industrial economic situation. I do not care one jot how you vote, but I do desire that you allow your mental capacity to realise what you have got to go through. You are victims of your own ignorance. But make no mistake, let no one misguide you for a moment. If they wanted tomorrow to employ you, they would employ you for profit and gain. But on the other side, just the same, there is the unemployed, and they cannot find you a situation even if you give them your labour free.

Never mind about raising your hats to the Red Flag, raise your mental capacity. I want you to bring yourself to your own common sense. I ask you to get into the van of the revolutionary movement, break down the barricade of the capitalist system and enter into the workers' republic.

On the west side, George Cook came round from the north side:

I am informed that Downing Street is barricaded. I don't care a damn as an individual for their barricades. In the war we used a tank to 'fight for small nations'. In this war we are going to use our voices first. If that brings no result there is only one course left to us, and God help the authorities.[19]

The opening of Parliament was to take place on 23 November. The marchers intended to send a deputation to 10 Downing Street on the previous day in spite of the Prime Minister's refusal to see it. In the meantime delegates from the marchers and from the London Unemployed met at the Brotherhood Church in Islington to work out their tactics. They elected the deputation, two men from each contingent, and sent a telegram to Bonar Law that if he still refused to see them they would not be responsible for the consequences.

They learned that the test cases at the court of referees had been decided against them. 'So much more fuel for Wednesday,' said Percy Haye. He told the *Daily Herald*, 'I want to see at least a hundred thousand on the streets on Wednesday. I hope we shall not hesitate, if we are refused by Bonar Law, to march down Whitehall and if necessary to Downing Street itself.' A sub-committee met in secret to plan action in the streets on the day.

The *Pall Mall Gazette* announced – 'Communist Plot in London, The Truth about Tomorrow's March of Unemployed, Organised Plan to Provoke a Riot at Dictation of Moscow'.

The *Pall Mall* considers that the time has now come to make a complete exposure, in detail, of the tone and revolutionary character of the march of the unemployed from all parts of the country which has brought to London a body of men numbering upwards of two thousand.

We state with a sure knowledge of the facts that this is not a genuine demonstration of the unemployed.

It is a revolutionary move, and the men are prepared to use whatever force is necessary to achieve their aims.

A collision with the police is inevitable, and the men are deliberately engineering it in order to gain sympathy of the public by an 'unwarrantable attack on defenceless unemployed'.

ORDERS FROM MOSCOW

The men are led by some of the most revolutionary Communists in the country, men who are in almost daily communication with Moscow.

The chief aim of the demonstration is not to get relief for the unemployed, but to justify an immediate demand for a large sum of money from Moscow, without which the Communist organisation in this country is in danger of starving.

Moscow has refused to pay out more money unless some big coup is brought off to justify it.

Hence this elaborately planned move.

Details followed: a fighting force in sections of eight under the command of ex non-commissioned officers would take their orders from Hannington. The force would be armed with sticks, some with revolvers and knives. Hannington's statement that every man must be prepared to fight was quoted, and the intention to march to Downing Street.

When it was all over the Communists would send a message to Moscow – 'We have marched a Red Army into the capital of the Empire. We marched through 2,200 metropolitan policemen who were too terrified to raise a finger,' and thus get their gold from the Soviets.

On 22 November all the newspapers, except the *Daily Herald*, published a list of the leading marchers with details of each one's police record and past activities. According to this Wal Hannington had been sentenced to twenty-eight days' imprisonment for creating a disturbance, released after two days, and bound over. Tom Dingley, formerly a paid organiser of the Red Trade Union International, had had two spells in prison for political activity. Gordon Currie was 'an indefatigable revolutionary propagandist'. Tom McKay had been 'mainly instrumental for dividing the unemployed into contingents of eight in order to cope with the police. He had disciplined the unemployed on the march with a view to making them into a Red Army.' Altogether twenty-one leaders found their names in bold type. In fact many of them had been imprisoned for seditious speech and riotous assembly. Here, every detail which could discredit them had been scraped together. One Scots leader was described as having lived for years on the savings of his mother, a charwoman. The leader of the Walsall contingent had been reported by the poor law relieving officer as 'a man of low type and very insolent'. Other names on the list had the simple comment 'no trace'.

In order to discredit the marchers the prime minister's office had obtained from the Special Branch in Scotland Yard records of the march leaders and had issued them to the newspaper reporters who had been summoned to Downing Street, together with details of a plot to raise rebellion. It was intended that the Special Branch records should be used with discretion but the *Daily Mail* printed them verbatim. In the Home Office there was sharp criticism of the way the thing had been done, by giving out information which was inaccurate, vague and based on surmise, and in any case improper to disclose – 'a deplorable business' it was thought. The view among the marchers, preparing to move off for Trafalgar Square, was that the disclosure showed that Bonar Law had 'got the wind up'. What disgusted them was that the names included three men with records of criminal offences, housebreaking, rape and assault and robbery, men who had no connection with the unemployed movement though they claimed to have, and it was these names that the press had seized on.[20]

By one o'clock the marchers had begun to assemble on Victoria Embankment. The East End unemployed, led by two hundred Lancashire men, arrived under police escort at

Temple Station grounded their banners and fell out. Some of the girls amongst the demonstrators were offered work as domestic servants by onlookers. The detachments from South London came over Blackfriars Bridge with the men of Kent and Devon. They sang:

> Bonar Law has got the wind up
> Bonar Law has got the wind up
> Bonar Law has got the wind up
> But he can't put the wind up us

to the tune of 'John Brown's Body'.

There was a roaring trade in red rosettes and badges. A big crowd gathered to see the expected battle with the police. It was known that the deputation would be allowed to go to the Ministry of Labour, but only the marshals knew what the main body meant to do. A wide area of streets between Waterloo Bridge and Hyde Park Corner had been prohibited. The marshals, surveying the position around Whitehall, found that the gates leading from the Embankment to Whitehall and at the entrance to Downing Street had been padlocked. They could see nothing of the 'machine guns mounted on certain buildings in readiness to sweep the streets' which had been promised in the press but mounted and foot police were on view everywhere.

At two o'clock the bugles sounded the fall-in. The deputation led by Tom Dingley moved off in the direction of Whitehall, escorted by police. The column of fifty thousand, with the band from Barrow leading, moved off westward along the Embankment towards Waterloo Bridge. It was already in a prohibited area but suddenly the marshals, by arrangement with the police, led it off to the right up Savoy Street and across the Strand for Kingsway and Hyde Park Corner and speeches in the Park. There was no clash and those who had come to see a fight went away disappointed. 'I am proud of the absence of militaristic methods, although seventy per cent of the marchers are ex-servicemen,' declared their chaplain. 'There are men with militaristic leanings, but it was speedily made clear by the majority that any suspicion of militaristic bearing would be resented.' Tom Dingley and Percy Haye, leaders of the deputation, faced Sir A. Griffith-Boscawen, Minister of Health and Sir A. Montagu-Barlow, Minister of Labour across the table. They were completely at cross purposes. The ministers explained that Bonar Law was not available. Dingley and Haye refused to put their case unless he was present. The ministers thought that everyone should behave like Englishmen do and talk all the same – 'As man to man, let us deal with your grievances in a constitutional manner'. Dingley stood firm. 'I am bound,' he said, 'to a strict mandate that there can be no interview unless we interview the Prime Minister. We are going to be as constitutional as you are. We are as well disciplined as you are, and if there is any bother it won't be on our side. I want you to have a special note of that. The unemployed have arrived at a stage when they are no longer prepared to put up with it as they have done in the past; they are demanding that some steps should be taken to alleviate their position. They have been on deputations galore, they have seen responsible Ministers, they are not particularly concerned whether it is Mr Lloyd George or Mr Bonar Law, the system under which they are existing is the same. It had simply been a talking match. They are demanding that some definite promise be made to this deputation as representatives of the national unemployed. We are determined to stay here in London and force the boards of guardians to maintain us until we do see the Prime Minister. Some of you might think that is bravado. We cannot help that. We have contingents that are waiting to come into the town and I am not here to use lies at all; I am minimising the psychology of the working class as well as the unemployed, but there will be a greater march on London if we do not get something tangible to relieve the situation. We have proposals regarding the National Debt and a trading agreement with Russia, and we know that these are outside the scope of the Ministry of Labour and the Ministry of Health. The only thing we can do is for us to retire and we will have to report back to the men and they will have to decide in the near future what they are going to do.'[21]

'Comrades, this is the first round,' Wal Hannington told the multitude in Hyde Park. 'Now for Round 2. Don't take any notice of public statements in the press or anywhere else as to what you are to do, unless they are over the signatures of Tom Dingley, Percy Haye or myself. The capitalist press are spoiling for a fight. You have not had a fight, but you have displayed your solidarity and your strength and the opposing forces do not know how we stand. If there had been a fight today we possibly should have been defeated as an army, and the opposing force would have laid down the condition on which we could work in the future. But there has been no fight and there is no defeat. The position is now to make arrangements for Round 2.'

The Committee of Ways and Means which met that night decided on their second course of action, to call up reinforcements until Bonar Law gave in.[22]

The new campaign opened the next day. As the marchers began a sandwich-board parade round the Palace of Westminster, the Reverend Pickering was arrested for obstruction. When ordered to be bound over, he refused. 'I don't require binding over, I always keep the peace. We are not leaving London, we are going on, not with shot and shell, but with faith, and nothing can stand against that, not even the power of militarism.' He was bailed out and carried shoulder-high from the court.

Inside the House of Commons Lieutenant-Commander Kenworthy asked the Prime Minister whether his secretary summoned the reporters of certain selected newspapers and gave them details of an alleged plot by certain unemployed workers to raise His Majesty's subjects in rebellion against the Crown, but he received an evasive reply. Persisting, he moved the adjournment, seconded by George Lansbury, on the issue of interference with freedom of the press, only to be defeated. In the meantime the operation to summon reinforcements got swiftly under way. By the last day of November fresh contingents had already started in response to a call to all branches from the Council of Action; thirty-five men from Dundee, fifty from Barrow, thirty from Sheffield, and others from Plymouth, Birmingham, Great Yarmouth and Brighton.[23]

This move was taken more seriously by ministers and civil servants. At the Ministry of Health the attitude hitherto had been that Boards of Guardians must deal with each application from the marchers on its merits but now a policy was required and, after conferring with the Home Office and the Ministry of Labour, it was decided to issue instructions calculated to discourage the reinforcements as strongly as possible. In the first place the view was that the knowledge that the marchers in London were having to put up with a good deal of discomfort would deter recruits from the provinces. But there was also the fact that during the initial march the Guardians had, in the Ministry's view, indulged in extravagant expenditure under political pressure, and this made it imperative that they should now be told that anything beyond the limits of the regulations for casual wards was strictly illegal. A confidential memorandum went out to all the General Inspectors of the Poor Law in their districts: 'It is of course most desirable that the marchers should be discouraged as far as practicable and it is anticipated that the limitation of relief to the Casual Wards may be effective specially in the early stages of the march when the numbers are small. The attitude of the police has resulted in specially favourable treatment of the marchers but this question is under discussion with the Home Office.'[24]

This policy, of which the reinforcements soon became aware, only hardened their intention of getting to London, but the marchers in London also had to face it. Some guardians sought to get rid of them by reducing their food and accommodation to the bare legal minimum, and those who did not were corrected by the inspectors. In Willesden when twenty-five men in the Salvation Army hostel applied for outdoor relief the guardians resolved that 2s a day was too much and stuck at 1s 6d. Two hundred and fifty men sleeping in Battersea Baths applied for food to the guardians and were told they must enter the workhouse. They refused and tried to live on the proceeds of street collections. In St Pancras eighty-four men from Erith and seven from Sheffield were told that the guardians could do no more for them and after breakfast on 27 November they were given some bread and cheese to start marching home. When a hundred and twenty men applied to the Wandsworth casual ward: 'We were offered a slice of bread each with a square of margarine. Next day we had the same with the addition of cocoa. We refused the cocoa, and some policemen outside whom we asked to take a sip said it was unfit for pigs.'

In these circumstances some of the marchers wanted to go home. Some, even of the marshals, disagreed with the decision of the Council of Action to stay in London. One of them wrote home:

> As for the position down here everything would be all right but for the bad leadership of the National 'limelighters'. The Communists are in the majority. I maintain that if the right tactics had been used it would not have been necessary to call for more reinforcements. A great tactical blunder arose. Personally I don't think Law will climb down. After all we have got out of the march what we intended and expected.[25]

Others were disturbed by letters from their wives and dependants. At the Ministry of Health officials were discussing whether the poor law inspectors might be able to stop outdoor relief being given to marchers' families, or at least to see that it was given only in kind. A few marchers tried to make their own way home. Two South Wales miners reached Farnham, Surrey, in a state of collapse. One of them, a lad of eighteen who had left his job to join the march, broke a confectioner's window and took some chocolates in order to get locked up for the night; he was bound over and given a railway-ticket home. The other, aged twenty-four, was found sleeping in the cattle-market; he was given one day's imprisonment and also sent home. Both had to have several days' treatment in the workhouse infirmary. Also on his own way home, one of the criminals with a record of rape and housebreaking, whom the Government had named as a march leader, was charged at Highgate with begging on the Great North Road. When he told the Court that he was returning home because he had found that the marchers were controlled by Communists and not by genuine unemployed leaders, and that he had done with the unemployed organisations, he was discharged: the Court was not told that he had been expelled from the March because he would not obey the rules for street collections.[26]

Most men who wanted to get home went to the guardians. These authorities were in a dilemma. They wanted to get rid of the marchers as quickly as possible but they were not inclined to pay their fares home without authority from their counterparts elsewhere. At Edmonton they would have done even this if their clerk had not objected. One way or another a large number did return by train. The Willesden guardians bought railway-tickets for twenty-seven men to Newcastle, Lincoln, Jarrow and Luton. One hundred and six marchers including seventy-nine from Manchester, sixteen from Ashton-under-Lyne and eleven from Bury were seen off from St Pancras station early on 7 December by the chairman of the Edmonton board of guardians. In that group it was the end of long and heated arguments. The majority had been persuaded by the Council of Action to stay, but the argument swung the other way converting all but nineteen. All the rest followed their own leaders whose view was that they had come for 'an honest unemployed demonstration, not to be exploited by the Communists; they had kept their men out of trouble and now that the guardians would pay, they were going to get them home safely'.[27]

The argument, whether to stay or go home, raged in all contingents. Seventy marshals at a special meeting voted by a small majority for going, but the Scots, with most mileage at stake, declared that they would leave the national organisation if the men were sent back immediately. The fact that reinforcements were already on the road complicated the issue. Percy Haye wrote to the Midlands organiser of the Communist Party:

> With reference to your remarks concerning a strategic retreat, the question is being discussed along these lines at this end. Personally I am not in favour, as considering the fact that there are 1,000 or more men on the road from different districts, it is an item which has got to be dealt with, and if we are to tell these men they have got to go back after accomplishing half their journey, it is just as likely to cause disorganisation as anything else. At any rate things will soon sort themselves out, I suppose, and we must await developments.[28]

The tactical device agreed upon was a relay system in which the reinforcements would, as far as possible, take the place of the men who had departed. The departures could be seen as a considered move, those that remained being the staunch and true while it was the worn out, the dispirited, the worried and the disgruntled who had gone home.

In Parliament, George Lansbury so irritated the Prime Minister with the marchers' demand to see him that Bonar Law was provoked to burst out: 'I am sick and tired of hearing about the unemployed marchers and do not want to have anything more to do with them.' Encouraged by the efforts of George Lansbury, Jack Jones and Will Thorne in the Commons, the Council of Action had a petition presented requesting to be heard at the bar of the House. It was accepted and duly laid on the table. A demonstration followed it. On 12 December a hundred picked marchers gathered gradually by twos and threes in the outer lobby and while they were talking with their Members, on a signal from Wal Hannington, displayed posters – 'Work or Full Maintenance' – and, bursting into 'The Red Flag', supported by several members of Parliament, carried its strains into the Chamber before the police could act. Three days later when, in spite of strong protests from Labour members, Parliament rose until February, the Council decided to present a petition to King George that he should recall Parliament. From a demonstration in Trafalgar Square, a somewhat thinner one than before, members of the Council were permitted to go through Admiralty Arch as far as the gates of Buckingham Palace. There they were stopped and told that the King could not receive a petition; it must go to the Home Secretary. The marchers waiting in the Square sang, as the Wobblies had sung long before:

> You will eat bye and bye
> In that glorious land above the sky.
> Work and pray, live on hay,
> You'll get pie in the sky when you die.[29]

By this time the first reinforcements had arrived, ten men from Brighton, twenty from Erith and twenty-seven from Oxford. Many more were on the road, forty from Barrow, forty-four from Dundee, fifty from Edinburgh, fifty from Glasgow, thirty-five from Greenock, thirty from Great Yarmouth, fifty-two from Liverpool, fifty from Salford, thirty-two from Sheffield, and other groups from Birkenhead, Blaina, Castleford, Derby, Gateshead, Ipswich, Lincoln and Wigan. These men met the impact of the new policy on the poor law regulations at every resting place. At the same time they received even more generous hospitality from local citizens, labour clubs, and churches than the first marchers had had. Sometimes they tried their friends too hard, for – unlike the first contingents – these men came along in smaller bands of thirty to fifty, arriving one after another at the same places. The Glasgow men strained the hospitality of Bradford where the Trades and Labour Council provided a hundred, in parties of twenty-five on successive days, with a good tea, a hot dinner, a proper bed and breakfast of bacon and eggs. The effect on the council's funds was such that it was decided to ask Glasgow to give credentials to all marchers in future; the council would, however, continue to help.[30]

The task of the poor law inspectors, to see that the regulations were observed, was not always possible to fulfil. At Ipswich the inspector told the clerk to the guardians that the marchers were to be treated as tramps and detained the full time, i.e. two nights. His view was: 'Most of these misguided men are taking it more in the way of a picnic than otherwise and they intend to maintain themselves by picking up on the way as much as they can induce a benevolent public to throw them in return for wayside entertainment.' At Derby the inspector reprimanded the clerk for paying the Co-op to feed twenty-three men from Bootle. At Leeds he told the workhouse master to inform the marchers that instructions had gone to the workhouses not to welcome them, and asked the city police to discourage the thirty-two men who were already there. As the police were unwilling to act without instructions from London, he instructed the master to 'treat them just as strictly as he could according to the regulations but without being quite strict enough to provoke a row'. At Barrow-in-Furness, where the guardians had already been in trouble for supplying the first marchers with boots, when Scottish reinforcements from Govan arrived, made a good collection, and had a substantial tea in the town, the guardians refused to treat them as vagrants but put them in the workhouse, actually moving inmates out of the workhouse into the casual wards in order to make room for them, and then gave them a hot supper, eggs for breakfast and meat and cheese sandwiches to take for lunch. The inspector could only report this to the Ministry as extravagant treatment of what he described as 'a rougher lot than most'.[31]

The new marchers were always ready to resist the regulations, refusing to be treated as vagrants and to go into the workhouse as casuals and suffer the indignity of being searched on entering. Twenty-seven Newcastle men refused the workhouse at Leeds for that reason and prepared to spend the night on the steps of the town hall until the police put them inside. On reaching Leicester they again rejected the workhouse and were able to get in the club-room of the Workers' Union. 'If we had not got in there,' their leader said, 'we would have slept in the market square. We are sticking together even if it means some of us die from hardship. Only three times during the past fortnight have we been in bed, and some of us have fearful colds. But we shall go on to Market Harborough, though we don't know yet whether we shall sleep indoors or out.' These men were five or six years younger than those who had marched in October. Led by Sam Langley, the group was composed of six miners, eleven skilled men and ten labourers.[32]

The attitudes of the guardians varied from place to place. The guardians at Berwick, anticipating the arrival of fifty-three men from Edinburgh, instructed the workhouse master that they were to be dealt with strictly as ordinary vagrants. Any man who had enough money for a bed was to be turned away; every man admitted was to give up his tobacco and submit to be bathed. The marchers ignored the workhouse; the Salvation Army took them in. At Newcastle they found that they were not to be treated as vagrants but to have the better dietary of the workhouse inmates. They rested there for two nights and were entertained to tea by the Socialist Society in the Royal Arcade. The member of Parliament, Charles Trevelyan, assured them that Labour was making every effort in the Commons to help them. All the Scots did not take such a favourable view of the situation. A group of twenty-seven from Glasgow, arriving in Newcastle a few days later, after also having tea in the Socialist Hall, rejected the Lord Mayor's offer of the workhouse. They felt that the sum collected for them was quite inadequate – 'That for twenty-seven! That is not 7s 6d a night!', and late in the evening they were still rattling their collecting boxes in the Cloth Market – 'Assist the Glasgow hunger marchers!'[33]

As well as the shared hardships, a self-imposed discipline held groups together. By the time the Edinburgh men had reached Newcastle they had already sent home six of their number for the crime of begging without permission. This was the heaviest penalty for misbehaviour. At Leicester a Newcastle group held a trial of a marcher who had broken the rules.

Judge, jury, counsel and officials, chosen from among themselves, assembled in the club-room of the Workers' Union and the usher declared the court in session in the name of the Soviet Republic of Great Britain. The charge against the accused was that he deliberately absented himself from a certain place at Nottingham where the marchers had slept, thereby incurring them in the expense of hiring a bed which had not been used, also absenting himself from a meeting, and not joining in the march to Loughborough on the following morning. He pleaded not guilty. After taking the oath he admitted under examination by counsel that he met a chum and went with him to sleep because he wanted to get clean. He was found guilty and sentenced to 'push the barrow every day until we get to Tottenham and tobacco allowance stopped for three days'.[34]

In London the Council of Action, on the crest of a campaign of publicity for the unemployed, approached the Trades Union Congress to support it as Labour members had done in Parliament. The General Council of the TUC agreed to hold a national demonstration on Sunday 7 January to be called Unemployed Sunday. It went further by forming a joint committee with the National Unemployed Workers' Committee Movement, to which the London Labour Party and the London Trades Council adhered. This news had only just been announced when the last reinforcements of three hundred Scots reached London on 30 December.

These hardy men, on the march throughout December, had met with a mixed reception on the way. More often than not they had had to accept the casual wards, and even sometimes the regulations, though not without vigorous grumbling. All Scots groups were ordered to concentrate at Luton so as to make an impressive entry into London.

They descended on that town, arriving in parties of thirty or forty each day in the week before Christmas, and taking the authorities by surprise. The first two groups were put in the workhouse where they had the inmates' fare and were not required to observe the rules strictly, but when it became overcrowded the borough council gave the use of the Plait Hall where the guardians sent food and straw to sleep on. The marchers, finding that the Sunday dinner, on the day before Christmas, amounted to pressed beef and bread, demonstrated to the board of guardians, so that the Chairman, after a sharp argument, had potatoes and carrots sent in. For Christmas dinner there were vegetables with the pressed beef, and as each contingent came in, the Co-op was stripped of all its bread. The guardians, the Co-op manager, the assistant relieving officer, the guardians' investigation officer, and the chief constable spent their Christmas holiday on the alert; but the peace in Luton was not disturbed until the last group of Scots, having had a hard time on Christmas Day, arrived in the town on Boxing Day. Defying the marshals' orders to stay in the Plait Hall, they sallied out to the public houses. Only two men, from Glasgow and Dumbarton, were brought to court, bound over for fighting and sent to prison for using obscene language. That day Gordon Currie and George Wilson from the national executive in London took over command. At the next stop, St Albans, where the marchers spent the night in the riding-school and received the bare casuals' diet, one of them, charged with being drunk and disorderly and fined 10s from the 16s 9$\frac{1}{2}d$ he possessed, declared: 'We are not getting treated as men; we are getting treated as dogs on the road.' Barnet put the marchers in the barracks again and, after Edmonton had refused to accept them, they ended up on 29 December at Islington in a school lent to the guardians for the night.[35]

The Council of Action had decided to make an issue of accommodation in London. It was determined that the Scots should not have the bare diet of the casual wards. After being referred by the Ministry of Health to the Metropolitan Asylums Board as the body controlling the casual wards in London, the Council got the Board's agreement to lift the regulations as to bathing, searching and detention. But there was a misunderstanding. The Council understood the concession to include adequate food instead of the casuals' dietary. This was not so, however, and when the Scots found themselves on bread and margarine for breakfast the Council marched them all out from St Pancras, Paddington, Holborn and Hackney to the Board's office on Blackfriars Embankment. A deputation of nine, led by Wal Hannington and Tom Dingley, demanded bacon or egg for breakfast, meat and two veg for dinner, jam or celery for tea, and broth or soup for supper, but was told that the Board had no power to vary the diet without the sanction of the Ministry.

The nine repeated their demand at the Ministry in Whitehall while the three hundred waited in St James Park for the result. The answer, that the fit men must have casual diet and the unfit could see a doctor, was shouted down by the three hundred, and the nine settled down inside the Ministry. At 4 p.m. no agreement was in sight; the marchers would not give way though none had eaten since early morning. George Lansbury, summoned by telephone, after arguing with the permanent secretary in the Ministry, arranged for sympathetic guardians in Poplar, Shoreditch and Southwark to take in the marchers. Those fared best who went to Poplar where the guardians were not disposed to take much notice of the Ministry, and after the relieving officer had bedded them down in Bow Baths Hall he took them in batches to the various cookshops, giving them tickets for meals to the value of 15s a week.[36]

On 7 January, Unemployed Sunday, Trafalgar square had rarely seen such an enormous demonstration of the combined forces of employed and unemployed, to demand that Parliament should be recalled and made to act. The Council of Action realised that if the pressure was to be maintained it must think of getting still more reinforcements. There were now fewer marchers in London than at any time, about twelve hundred. There was also the likelihood that more men would go home as the conflict over accommodation sharpened because of the cost to the guardians. Even the guardians at Southwark and Shoreditch were getting tired of the Scots, and prepared to get rid of them. Philip Curran and Sam Langley were charged at Tower Bridge Police Court with the offence 'that both being pauper inmates of Christchurch workhouse at Southwark did refuse to be removed to another workhouse', a test case for which both men had volunteered.

The workhouse master said that the men were admitted as destitute wayfarers to an institution which was for the aged and infirm and when they were requested to move to Belmont Institution they refused and locked themselves in. The magistrate said that there was no defence and the men must not imagine they could dictate to the guardians; they were liable to one month's imprisonment but in view of their good character he would send them to prison for seven days without hard labour. While their comrades in the workhouse behaved in an exemplary fashion, scrubbing out their ward and keeping strictly to the rules, the Council of Action tried to negotiate with the guardians, but to no avail. After giving a vote of thanks for the kindness they had received, the men marched out to the Brotherhood Church in Finchley where, although they would get beds, they would have to depend on collections or outdoor relief. A week later the Shoreditch guardians told a hundred Scots to leave the workhouse or be treated as vagrants in the casual wards.[37]

In these circumstances the Council of Action decided to carry out two recruiting marches from London, one to Birmingham, and the other south and along the coast. On the day they started out, 24 January 1923, the question of how to deal with the marchers effectively was discussed in Whitehall. The Ministry of Health asked the Home Office if the police could give more help to the guardians; if not, the matter would have to be taken up in the Cabinet. The Ministry's view that the marchers were not a matter for the poor law, but one for the police to deal with, was not acceptable to the Home Office – on the grounds that the marchers could not be treated as unlawful assemblies, and if the police were to stop or break up processions more serious difficulties would arise. The Home Secretary reported to the Unemployment Committee of the Cabinet: would it not be possible, he suggested for the guardians to refuse the workhouse to organised bodies and for the police to warn the marchers accordingly and so persuade them to stop, dealing with any consequent disorder? This, was more than the Cabinet was prepared to do and the final instructions were less drastic – as before, strict enforcement of the regulations for vagrants in the casual wards but now strengthened with the promise of police action to ensure such action. The marchers' recruiting parties, led by Wal Hannington and Tom Dingley, pledged themselves to break down the instructions from the Ministry of Health.[38]

The recruiting marches, which were carefully planned, were to be the last effort. Hannington's column of a hundred and thirty-five, mostly Londoners, was to arrive at Birmingham on 3 February and return via Oxford to Maidenhead where it would meet the second column, and so back to London. The second column from London of one hundred and sixty north countrymen was to divide at Brighton, one half marching via Winchester and Reading under the Reverend Pickering while the other went eastward led by Tom Dingley through Dover, Canterbury and Chatham. The main success was against the poor law authorities.

When the northern column arrived at Luton it refused the casuals' diet of bread, margarine and tea, went out in to the town, had meals in the cafes, sent the bills to the board of guardians which eventually paid them, and earned the name of 'The Poached Eggs Brigade'. At Rugby, faced with the same diet in the drill hall where they were billeted, Hannington and thirteen others raided the workhouse and took twenty-eight large pots of jam from the stores. They returned the empty jam pots to the workhouse and thanked the master for 'the jam which we have so much enjoyed at breakfast'. When the police in Coventry tried to effect a warrant for Hannington's arrest, there was a stand-up fight. William Hunter was sentenced to two months' hard labour. On being asked if he had anything to say he replied: 'Absolutely nothing.' Hannington, who gave himself up to avoid a major conflict, told the court, after being remanded in custody for five days and taken to and from Leicester gaol in handcuffs: 'If you treat men like dogs you must accept that men will act like dogs. Our motive was to break down the callous and brutal orders of the Ministry of Health which branded these men as tramps and vagabonds by issuing instructions that they should only be served casuals' diet, an instruction which the marchers have always succeeded in getting set aside until they got to Rugby. The taking out of the summons and the way in which bail was opposed by the prosecution convinces me that vindictiveness and spite are behind these proceedings.' His punishment for 'feloniously stealing twenty-eight pots of jam' was £5 or twenty-eight days in prison. When he refused to pay, a Quaker member of the guardians who had had him arrested met the fine.[39]

At this point the police issued a warning to all the recruiting groups:

At places to which the marchers are proceeding the Guardians' accommodation is strictly limited and no more men will be taken in by the Guardians than there is room for. They must not expect to receive relief except on the same conditions as any other vagrants, under which each man admitted may be searched and required to have a bath; supper to consist of bread and margarine or dripping and a hot drink; and breakfast the same. They may also be required to perform a task before leaving.[40]

The southern column tried on the Luton tactics at Brighton, but ten marchers were arrested and fined. When the Reverend Pickering's company, having split off as planned, reached Southampton they had no need to battle. The guardians put them in the Atlantic Hostel at Eastleigh – hutments used by the shipping-lines to house emigrants – and the Transport and General Workers' Union arranged a meal of Irish stew and a breakfast of sausages and mashed potatoes. It was otherwise at Winchester; they had to accept the casuals' diet in the workhouse after arguing among themselves until two o'clock in the morning whether to march out in force into the city. That round was lost but at Reading the guardians gave them a good deal more than the legal diet, and again at Wokingham they could refuse to enter the workhouse as the Church provided a school and supporters gave food.

The second southern company, ninety strong, were met at Canterbury by the chairman of the board of guardians who marched at their head to the workhouse where they were given a good dinner, and cigarettes from the chairman. At Sittingbourne the guardians had resolved to obey the Ministry to the letter. Tom Dingley replied that they were not going to be treated as casuals and if the guardians did not give them a better reception they would raid the town. Asked if he meant that as a threat, he answered: 'You can take it as such if you like and you may expect trouble, for there are many ex-servicemen with us and they can use their fists as well as the police can use their truncheons', and police reinforcements were hastily summoned. The column marched on the workhouse but refused to enter on the conditions laid down by the master, and at last found refuge in the parish hall. Later, at an open-air meeting, Tom Dingley spoke:

We are only the nucleus of the red army. We are feeling the country. Wherever we have been we have been treated as we should have been, but here we are being treated by the guardians as vagrants, this is the sort of place we are out to find. We are not strong enough today, they have drafted charabanc loads of police here and it is their turn but, by Christ, when I get to London and report how we have been treated here, we shall come again, not ninety strong but nine hundred strong. Today it would have cost the Guardians £4. 15s od to feed us, but it has cost the ratepayers £85. 16s 6d for cost of extra police today, good luck to them. I know, I have worked it out, but when we come again it will cost £200 for extra police. I know something about the secret work of the police, I was their pal in the police strike and went to prison for four months. We have got men who were members of the Force and got the sack through the strike, on our side, and they are teaching us some of the secrets of the CID work.

I am a rebel, my comrades are rebels, I am an extremist, my comrades are extremists, because we have been driven to it by extremist conditions. Don't think we are anything to do with the Labour Party, we have had some of those bleeders, they dope us as bad as the Church dopes you. There is no Christianity, during the 1914–18 war the clergy was praying for you to kill the Germans, is that Christianity?[41]

Hannington's column, temporarily without its leader, had lost a dozen Scots who had decided to go home. George Cook had pleaded with them: 'I know you have good reasons for leaving but I beg of you to remain loyal to the Movement, and I hope you will go as recruiting agents wherever you go and not let people think that you have returned home because you are fed up.' The Birmingham police found them, apparently in a distressed state, in a cellar known as The Dugout used for unemployed meetings and, satisfied that they had deserted from the column, paid their railway fares home, which they promised to refund. Almost on the same day eleven men arrived at Canning Town by cargo boat from Edinburgh; their object, they said, was to show that Edinburgh still supported the hunger marchers.

The column avoided Birmingham, as there was news of a strong concentration of police there, and turned south to Banbury. This unplanned move meant that the poor law inspectors were unable to warn the boards of guardians concerned in time. At Southam the marchers went into the workhouse, but the guardians fed them in the local inns. Banbury, where the news of an approaching horde closed the public houses for twenty-four hours and cleared all the goods out of shop windows, added jam to the diet, and Buckingham supplemented it with soup and bully beef. At Bicester, where Hannington caught up with his troops, the guardians gave soup and jam as extras in spite of the presence of the poor law inspectors who tried to insist on the bare legal diet. Their chairman said, 'We do not want any trouble in this town.' The marchers told Hannington that 'they had been living like lords'. At Maidenhead, where the column joined the Southern company, the whole battalion was cared for by a committee of ministers, Labour Party members, and the mayor who was also clerk to the guardians. The marchers were well pleased with their success so far, though as they came nearer London they found that the contest was not yet over. At Brentford a strong force of police was hidden in the workhouse and the marchers accepted the casuals' diet.[42]

The marchers felt that they had won one battle. The poor law inspectors had to admit defeat:

> On the whole therefore the marchers have had a fairly triumphant progress through Oxfordshire, Bucks and Berkshire and have successfully upheld their claim that they are not vagrants and must not be treated as such. There are only two points on which it is possible to find any satisfaction. The marchers have attracted no recruits since they left Warwickshire where they picked up nineteen from Birmingham and the North, and abandoned their express intention of passing through Warwick and Oxford, places where they could have been properly handled. The guardians and the police must share the responsibility for the failure to make the marchers amenable to the law.[43]

On 13 February, as Parliament assembled at last, the two recruiting columns met in Hyde Park as planned, but little larger than when they had set out. Wal Hannington, greeted with cries of 'Who pinched the jam?', addressed encouraging words to the meeting. The position was, however, that the number of marchers in London was lower than ever. Bonar Law again refused to see them. The struggle seemed to be petering out. The Council of Action agreed that all should return home on 20 February. The campaign had been sustained in London for two months but now energies were exhausted. There was another reason. It was necessary to concentrate on preparation for a national conference which was long overdue. At the farewell demonstration in Trafalgar Square, Wal Hannington declared that a greater march would take place after the conference, and the thousands present pledged their support for it. However, it was to be seven years before the unemployed again marched on London.[44]

REFERENCES

1. PRO HO 45/11275.
2. PRO HO 45/11275; *Daily Herald*, 1.11.22.
3. *Aberdeen Evening Express*, 16–19.10.22; *Daily Herald*, 23/24.10.22; *Dumfries Standard*, 21.20.22; *Out of Work*, Nov. 1922.
4. *Out of Work*, Oct. 1922; Nov. 1922.
5. *Bolton Evening News*, 31.10.22, 1.11.22; *Daily Herald*, 28.10.22, 31.10.22, 2.11.22.
6. *Staffordshire Sentinel*, 3.11.22; *Daily Herald*, 17.10.22; *Derby Telegraph*, 6.11.22.
7. *Leicester Mail*, 7.11.22; 8.11.22.
8. *Western Mail*, 6.11.22; *Daily Herald*, 4.11.22.
9. *Daily Herald*, 9.11.22, 13.11.22; *Reading Mercury*, 18.11.22; *Western Daily Press*, 7.11.22.
10. *Daily Herald*, 14.11.22; *Leicester Mail*, 8.11.22; Northants CRO PL Nov. 1922; *Northampton Herald*, 10.11.22.
11. *Out of Work*, Nov. 1922; *Birmingham Mail*, 8.11.22.
12. *Doncaster Gazette*, 3.11.22; *Lincoln Echo*, 6.11.22; *Daily Herald*, 9.11.22, 13.11.22, 14.11.22.
13. *Daily Herald*, 9.11.22, 13.11.22; *Western Times*, 10.11.22.
14. *Barnet Press*, 28.11.22, 20.11.22, 25.11.22; PRO HO 45/11275.
15. *Daily Herald*, 17.11.22.
16. *Daily Herald*, 18.11.22.
17. PRO HO 45/11275.
18. PRO HO 45/11275.
19. PRO HO 45/11275; *Daily Herald*, 20.11.22.
20. PRO HO 45/11275; Hannington, *Never On Our Knees*, 1967, p. 143; *Pall Mall Gazette*, 20.11.22, 21.11.22; *Daily Mail*, 22.11.22.
21. *Daily Mail*, 23.11.22; *Daily Herald*, 21.11.22, 23.11.22; Hannington, op. cit., p. 146.
22. PRO HO 45/11275; *Daily Herald*, 27.11.22; Hannington, *Unemployed Struggles*, 1936, p. 87.
23. *Daily Herald*, 29.11.22, 1.12.22; Parliamentary Debates, Vol. 1. No. 6; PRO HO 45/11275.
24. PRO MH 57/105.
25. PRO MH 57/105; *Daily Herald*, 14.12.22.
26. *The Times*, 1.12.22; *Daily Herald*, 30.11.22.
27. PRO MH 57/106.

28. PRO MH 57/105.
29. PRO HO 45/11275; *The Times*, 18.12.22; Hannington, *Unemployed Struggles*, pp. 88–92.
30. *Yorkshire Post*, 15.12.22; PRO MH 57/105.
31. PRO MH 57/105.
32. PRO MH 57/105; *Leicester Mail*, 19.12.22.
33. *Newcastle Mail*, 12.12.22.
34. *Leicester Mail*, 19.12.11; *The Times*, 21.12.22.
35. *Luton News*, 28.12.22; *Daily Herald*, 28.12.22; *Herts Advertiser*, 30.12.22; Hannington, *Never On Our Knees*, p. 155.
36. *Daily Herald*, 1.1.23–3.1.23; PRO MH 57/105; Hannington, *Unemployed Struggles*, pp. 94–6.
37. *Daily Herald*, 8–13.1.23, 20 and 23.1.23; *Evening Standard*, 13.1.23, 19.1.23.
38. PRO HO 45/11275.
39. *Birmingham Mail*, 3.2.23, 6.2.23; Hannington, op. cit., pp. 100–4.
40. PRO HO 45/11275.
41. PRO HO 11275/438775.
42. GLC. BG/B193; Hannington, op. cit., pp. 105–6.
43. PRO HO 45/11275.
44. Hannington, *Insurgents in London*, 1923; *Daily Herald*, 14.2.23; 16.2.23, 19.2.23.

3

Only the Miners Marching, 1923–8

There was no marching activity between February 1923 and the march of three hundred South Wales miners in November 1927. The NUWCM stayed in existence, but for some years there was a low level of activity. At its fourth national conference in December 1924 the chairman reported 'an apathetic tendency throughout the Movement'. One reason was that unemployment had been falling – from over two million at the beginning of 1922 to barely one million in mid-1924. Other reasons can be found in the political attitudes of various sections of the labour movement, and the conflicts between them.

The Communist Party had the decisive voice in the leadership of the NUWCM, and there was no major march in the interwar years, with the notable exception of the Jarrow Crusade, without Communist leadership. When and why marches were embarked upon was necessarily influenced by the policy of the Communist Party at any given time, and the relationship of that party to the Labour Party and the trade unions.

In Communist eyes, solidarity between employed and unemployed was a paramount issue. As Hannington and his Communist colleagues were only too well aware, unless such unity could be established, there was a grave danger that the unemployed would be used as blacklegs in disputes and as cheap labour undermining wage agreements. With this in view, it appeared essential that an unemployed organisation should be closely linked with the existing trade union movement.

Initially this strategy met with some success; it was agreed by the 1923 TUC at Plymouth that a Joint Advisory Committee on unemployment should be established by the General Council of the TUC and the NUWCM. This Committee remained in being for some years, and was responsible for the adoption of a six-point Unemployed Workers' Charter calling for work or effective maintenance at £3. 18s per week for man, wife and two children, to be administered by the trade unions instead of by the Poor Law authorities; government schemes to provide work at trade union rates; state workshops to supply government departments; hours of work to be reduced generally to six per day; occupational centres for the unemployed; and at least a million new homes at rents within the means of wage earners. These demands were amplified in leaflets, 700,000 of which were distributed by NUWCM members and Trades Councils.

Also associated with the NUWCM was the National Minority Movement formed on Communist initiative in 1924. Its object, initially, was to coordinate the activities of militant trade unionists who were dissatisfied with what they regarded as the policies of class collaboration of the existing trade union leaders. It had its origin in two post-war developments: the formation of a British Bureau of the Red International of Labour Unions, and the rise of rank-and-file movements, known as 'minority movements' in various industries, including mining, engineering and shipbuilding. The importance with which the Communist Party regarded this work was exemplified by the temporary transfer of Wal Hannington from the NUWCM to the NMM to take charge of the metal workers' section in August 1924.

At the 1925 TUC it became clear that the activities of the National Minority Movement were bearing fruit. But subsequently, after the 1926 General Strike, the atmosphere changed. Attacked by Communists for betraying the strike, the trade union and Labour leaders launched a determined campaign to 'outlaw' the Communist Party. And although the main drive was to complete the expulsion of Communists from the ranks of the Labour Party, and to destroy the influence of the Communist Party and of the Minority Movement within the trade unions, various steps were also taken to isolate the NUWCM from the trade union movement, and to break any link between it and the local trades councils. These moves had already begun by the time of the 1927 miners' march.

But meanwhile, in the months following the first (1922) hunger march, relations between the NUWCM and the General Council of the TUC were not unfriendly.

Bonar Law had been succeeded as Prime Minister by Stanley Baldwin in May 1923 without any noticeable change in Conser-

vative policy. Two of Baldwin's problems were, the need to re-
unite his followers, some of whom were drifting towards the
Liberals, and unemployment. The unemployment rate
(though lower than that of 1922) rose from 11·2 per cent in May
1923 to 11·7 per cent in October. The engineering, shipbuilding
and textiles industries were depressed. Baldwin saw a solution
to both problems. He announced: 'The unemployment problem is the most crucial problem of our country . . . I can fight . . .
I am willing to fight it. . . . I have come to the conclusion myself
that the only way of fighting this subject is by protecting the
home market.'

However, at the general election in December protection was
rejected and the Liberals helped the Labour Party to defeat the
Government. The first Labour Government, headed by
Ramsay MacDonald, took office, a Government which, in
Neville Chamberlain's words, 'would be too weak to do much
harm but not too weak to get discredited'.

Socialists and Communists greeted the new government as a
triumph for the working class, although the Communists
warned that immediate results could not be expected from a
minority government and that the workers must have patience.
The Government's achievements during its short life of barely
nine months were, in several respects, in line with the demands
of the Movement. In June the 'gap' between benefit periods
under unemployment insurance was abolished. In August an
Act of Parliament increased the benefit for an adult man to
eighteen shillings, for a woman to fifteen shillings, for a
dependant wife to five shillings and for each dependant child to
two shillings, and took a further step in making extended or
uncovenanted benefits (beyond those covered by contributions) as much a statutory right as standard benefits. These
were substantial improvements for the unemployed. They were
still a long way off the Charter but some way towards it. Little
was done, however, to increase employment, and that too late.
In July the Chancellor of the Exchequer announced various
schemes, inherited from the Conservatives, for road-making
and municipal works. There was at least the promise of more
employment from Wheatley's Housing Act, and its provision
for large-scale subsidised building of council houses at controlled rents won the full approval of the Movement. It eventually

provided, not the million homes demanded in the Charter, but over half a million in the next ten years.

The Movement pursued its aim of alliance with the TUC and the Labour Party. At the Trades Union Congress in September 1924 a motion to affiliate it to the TUC was defeated in spite of the existence of the joint advisory committee. This was not surprising; the proposal was a highly controversial one from the point of view of the trade unions. When Hannington addressed Congress, after the event, he still hoped that the decision would be reconsidered at the next Congress. He was able to show how the unemployed had helped workers in the numerous industrial disputes during the Labour Government; in particular he quoted with effect a letter from Ernest Bevin, general secretary of the Transport and General Workers' Union in which Bevin sent his best thanks for the 'splendid and valuable assistance' given by the Movement during the dockers' strike in February. Congress also rejected another proposal intended to make a closer relationship, a scheme by which members of the Movement would have been able to transfer membership to that of a trade union when they obtained work.

When Hannington addressed the Labour Party Conference in October on behalf of the Movement he had prepared a speech which criticised the Government harshly for its failure to reduce unemployment. But when, during the conference, the news broke that the Government was about to fall, he quickly altered his remarks to centre not only on the grievances of the unemployed but also on the coming electoral struggle and the support which the Movement would give. In fact it issued 100,000 manifestoes for the general election in that month.

The end of the Labour Government in November 1924 showed the effects which the hopes pinned on it had had on the Movement. At its fourth national conference, the chairman Jack Holt, could only report that, instead of progressing, it had retrogressed. Headquarters had had a continual struggle for existence owing mainly to lack of funds, and had it not been for donations from the executives of various trade unions, the Movement would undoubtedly have closed down. Wal Hannington underlined this: 'The advent of the Labour Government had caused a wave of indifference to sweep over the unemployed, as many thought that their requirements would be attended to without effort on their part.' The record showed that this was only too true. An attempt to start a national movement against evictions from homes had failed. Repeated efforts to call a national conference within a year of the previous one had been abandoned because of the poor response from local committees. *Out of Work* had ceased publication because of a debt of £200 to the printer. It had been restarted as *The Unemployed Worker* but this had lasted for only three issues. Now, however, conference was told things were bound to change. The Conservatives would surely attack the unemployed and the Movement would come to life again and be able to confront the Government. The best defence was attack and a resolution to organise a campaign jointly with the TUC and the Labour Party for the six points of the Charter was carried nem con.[1]

In 1925 all industrial issues were subordinate to the miners' conflict culminating in Red Friday, 31 July, when Baldwin gave way to the threat of a strike of all transport workers and railwaymen to defend the miners against wage reductions, and gave the coal industry a temporary subsidy and a royal commission of inquiry. The Movement had been able to continue friendly relations with the TUC until that time. Meetings of the joint advisory committee were held regularly. In March there was a great demonstration in London, in which fifteen Members of Parliament joined, against the unfair treatment of the unemployed at the labour exchanges. On 1 June a second Unemployed Sunday was organised by the committee with such massive support that the TUC and the Labour Party were encouraged to hold a special national conference on 24 July. The Movement proposed that the conference should consider a twenty-four hour general strike against unemployment, but without success. The Movement resurrected the idea of a national march on London but this also, along with seven other specific proposals, was too much to be accepted, and the result was no more than a general condemnation of the Government's inaction. Thus far the Movement's aim of closer relationship with the TUC and the Labour Party had had only moderate success. Thereafter there were no more meetings of the joint advisory committee although the Movement continually requested them. The conflict between the miners and the Government now over-shadowed all other issues.

While the royal commission on the coal industry sat throughout the last three months of 1925 and the first three of 1926 the Government prepared for the possibility of a general strike. The country was to be organised in ten regions each governed by a civil commissioner, supported by the Organisation for the Maintenance of Supplies, a voluntary strike-breaking body. The TUC placed its faith in the royal commission and the power of negotiation while the National Minority Movement and its parent, the Communist Party, urged that Labour should also get ready for a conflict. The Minority Movement had in fact attracted much great support in the trade unions. Nearly seven hundred delegates representing three-quarters of a million workers attended its conference in August 1925 when the slogan was – 'Prepare for the Coming Fight', and a call went out from Tom Mann for propaganda in the armed forces. This resurgence had an effect at the TUC in the following month which, among other decisions in line with the policy of the Minority Movement, agreed to establish shop committees as 'indispensable weapons in the struggle to force the capitalists to relinquish their grip on industry'. Within six weeks, however, came a counter-attack. The Labour Party Conference at the end of September not only decided to expel Communists from membership but began moves to debar them from acting as delegates even when elected as such by their trade unions.

In October the Government had twelve leading Communists arrested under an Act of 1797 and tried at the Old Bailey for seditious libel and incitement to mutiny. Seven of them were sentenced to six months' imprisonment, and five to twelve months, who would thus be out of the way during the General Strike. As one of these was Wal Hannington, the Movement was again without its national organiser and this time for a longer period. It was probably hardly a coincidence that, at the same time, the Special Branch raided the headquarters of the Movement on the top floor of 105 Hatton Garden and took away the minute book of its National Administrative Council, its cash account book, and its file of addresses.

There was new life in the Movement at the fifth annual conference in January 1926. The attendance of nearly a hundred delegates from fifty-three local committees and district councils was an encouraging advance on the low-water mark at the end of 1924. Conference accepted the lesson of the failure to continue *Out of Work*; instead news of the unemployed would be published in the Minority Movement's *Worker* and in the *Sunday Worker*. There were positive proposals for increasing employment – electrification of the railways and the construction of light railways, widening and deepening of canals and waterways. In the existing relief schemes for giving employment it was still necessary to fight for full trade union rates. Some local authorities continued to pay only 75 per cent of the standard wages. Authorities, therefore, must be made to employ only trade union members as has been done at Battersea, Bethnal Green and Barnsley. Clinging still to the aim of working with the TUC, the conference voted unanimously once again to pursue affiliation and, less hopefully, also to the Labour Party. The Minority Movement could be relied on to help with the TUC.

A national march on London was discussed. Beecroft of Lanarkshire moved and Tripp of Lincoln seconded that 'This Conference congratulates the National Administrative Council on reviving this project and hopes that the March will not be unduly delayed, and that when launched, be split up into contingents, each area, in the interests of discipline, being responsible for its own contingent.' There was opposition from Tredegar, Gateshead, Burnley and Camberwell. On a show of hands this tentative motion was narrowly lost; on a card vote it was carried but by only nine votes. Perhaps the motion would have received much more emphatic support if Hannington had not been absent in prison. A suggestion by a delegate that he had gone to the Minority Movement for a superior position which had first claim on his services was brushed aside; the local committees had already collected £50 for his dependants. A letter from him written during the trial at the Old Bailey was read to the conference: 'The Attorney-General Hogg is now replying to the defence. Listening to Hogg roll out lie after lie against us, it sounds as though we are going to get a stretch. My one hope is that our incarceration will give impetus to the Movement. I shall think of the Movement all the time and I trust that they will think of the lads behind bars and act accordingly. On with the fight lads. NO SURRENDER.'[2]

The history of the General Strike is not a subject for this book, but one effect may be noted. The TUC abolished early in 1927 the joint advisory committee and ended the Movement's long-sustained hope of joint action. After the Trades Disputes Act in May 1927 the TUC ended the year with a new policy of collaboration with the employers.

During the greater part of 1927 the Movement was taken up with campaigns against two proposed reforms, of the Poor Law and of Unemployment Insurance, both of which seemed likely to restrict it and to worsen the lot of the unemployed. The Ministry of Health was working on a change in the administration of poor relief. From the Ministry's point of view many of the boards of guardians, elected locally, by unemployed and employed alike, had shown themselves to be too sensitive to the electorate and too generous in handing out relief. They were by no means all Labour. Conservative boards knew that it was useful to the shop-keepers and publicans to maintain purchasing power among the unemployed. The pressure of the agitation organised by the Movement had had its effect on the guardians. They were to be abolished and their responsibilities transferred to new committees of the county councils or county boroughs, to be called public assistance committees. These bodies, which would be fully controlled by their parent bodies, would be composed partly of elected councillors and partly of persons with experience in the tradition of the poor law. For Neville Chamberlain, Minister of Health, the proposal was a long overdue administrative reform of the Poor Law, though his intention was also to remove, in his own words, 'the effect on sound local government of a continuation of elections turning on the one issue – whether out-relief is to be administered on a higher or lower level'. As the Movement saw it, this proposal would move poor relief further away from the pressure of public opinion. The Movement led a vigorous campaign of opposition until the reform became law in the Local Government Act of 1929.

The other Government reform to engage the Movement, affected the unemployed more closely. The Blanesburgh Committee, appointed by the Baldwin Government to inquire into unemployment insurance because of the insolvency of the scheme and alleged frauds under it, completed its work in

January 1927. The recommendations caused an uproar in the Labour movement, both inside and outside Parliament, for they involved a serious worsening in benefits. On the one hand, the extended benefit which had been received by men who had exhausted the standard twenty-six weeks' benefit would be replaced by a new type of payment to be called transitional benefit to which they were to have a statutory right. But on the other, there were to be changes in the scale of payments – less for an adult man, more for his wife, but less for young people under twenty-one and for boys and girls under eighteen, so that the income of a family which had unemployed children would be drastically reduced. Moreover, the claimant would have to have made thirty contributions during the previous two years, a more stringent condition than before. He would also have to prove with some tangible evidence such as a note from employers that he had been 'genuinely seeking work'. This last item was not new but the recommendation was that it should be more strictly applied.

The Movement as well as the Labour Party and the TUC conducted a strong campaign against the report throughout the year and when the Government's Bill was presented in the autumn it was passed only after the use of the guillotine in the House of Commons and the suspension of four members of Parliament. When the Act came into operation in April 1928 certain concessions had been made. An adult man's benefit was cut from eighteen shillings to seventeen shillings, while an adult woman's remained at fifteen shillings, but a dependant wife's rose from five shillings to seven shillings and that of a man, wife and two children went up one shilling to twenty-eight shillings a week. The rule of thirty weeks' contributions was postponed for a year. But the drive to operate the 'not genuinely seeking work' clause continued so that thousands became disqualified for benefit.

There was a slight improvement in employment in general during 1927 and 1928, but the miners were the exception and it was the special plight of the coal industry which produced the marches on London by the Welsh miners and on Edinburgh by the Scots in those years. The demand for coal exports had continued to fall. After the General Strike the miners remained out for another six months until they were forced by starvation to accept a longer working-day of eight hours and cuts in wages. Employment increased up to May 1927 because of the replenishing of stocks used up during the Strike, but then there was a sharp fall, and by July a quarter of a million miners were registered as unemployed and in addition there were scores of thousands who had exhausted their benefit and many others working short time. South Wales was the worst hit area; it alone had sixty thousand out of work. Local councils and boards of guardians, often strongly Labour, no longer able to raise an adequate income from the shrunken rates, became dependent on loans which were stringently controlled by Government departments. It seemed that nothing could be done, but a protest had to be made. When A. J. Cook, general secretary of the Miners' Federation, suggested at a hillside meeting in the Rhondda on 13 September that the miners must 'go to the fountainhead of the trouble' and march to London, the response was immediate and whole hearted.[3]

The march of the South Wales miners – which started on 8 November 1927, arrived in London on the 20th and returned on the 27th – owed a good deal to the national march of the Movement five years before. There was the same combination of Communists and socialists in its leadership. The march committee consisted of A. J. Cook, Arthur Horner, check-weighman at Mardy and member of the executive of the South Wales Miners' Federation, S. O. Davies, miners' agent at Merthyr and Dowlais, J. Hughes, miners' agent in Llwynypia, Noah Rees, miners' agent in Clydach Vale and also one non-miner, Wal Hannington, chosen as the man with the experience necessary to make the march a success. He was still both a leading figure in the Minority Movement and national organiser of the National Unemployed Workers' Committee Movement. Much followed from that, in the character of the march, in behaviour, in support for it and in opposition to it. The basis was the Rhondda No. 1 District of Miners and the NUWCM. There was no support from the miners' leadership either in South Wales or nationally but some came from Lanarkshire and Yorkshire. However, Walter Citrine, General Secretary of the TUC, intervened. Having ascertained that the march had not got the official support of the Executive of the Miners' Federation, he circularised trades councils on the route informing them that the TUC General Council was unable to recommend support for the march. The result was that some trades councils, notably London and Bristol, who had at first given encouragement, backed down. The London Trades Council withdrew its initial support at a special delegate conference at which a march organiser protested, 'This is the most disgraceful exhibition I have seen from any section of the labour movement. You have passed a vote of confidence in Baldwin.' In the newspapers the march was described as a communist manœuvre.[4]

The lack of support from Labour leadership was no surprise at the time and it may now be seen as a symptom of changes in the TUC and the trade unions which may be ascribed to the effects of the General Strike. While the Minority Movement grew from 1924 onwards its militancy did not cause conflict with the TUC at first. According to Macfarlane: 'The TUC was moving more and more on lines supported or initiated by the Minority Movement.'[5] This was particularly so in the case of the miners amongst whom there were two hundred Minority Movement groups in 1925. A large number of these remained within the South Wales Miners' Federation until the end of the miners' lockout in November 1926. The aftermath of the General Strike brought about a different situation. At the Trades Union Congress in September 1926 the secretary of the Garment Workers pointed to the danger of the Minority Movement becoming the majority unless the General Council told trades councils not to affiliate to the Movement.[6]

By the end of the year the National Union of General and Municipal Workers had declared membership of the Minority Movement (MM) or the Communist Party to be inconsistent with loyalty to it, and in February 1927 the TUC General Council withdrew recognition from trades councils associated with the MM. Meanwhile the Labour Party was disaffiliating local parties which had refused to accept the ban on Communists. The Minority Movement fought back with a proposal for a general strike against the Trade Union Bill only to be rejected by the TUC, which at the same time, confirmed the General Council's decision of February.

The Communist Party had not as yet changed its basic line towards the TUC and the Labour Party, although it felt impelled to declare war on those trade union leaders who were advocating industrial peace. The aim was still to bring about a militant leadership of these organisations. It was the desire to resist such a challenge that resulted in the refusal of official support for the miners' march. For the association of its leadership with the Minority Movement and the Communist Party was well known.

Much of the march organisation was on the lines of 1922. Marchers were told they must be ready to accept hardship and strict discipline on the road. The march committee was 'anxious to enlist ex-servicemen for efficiency and discipline on the march'. Each village had its committee to provide boots and clothing and the women made house-to-house collections. Hundreds of volunteers came forward, most of whom had to be rejected in order to limit the total to three hundred. Only those who were medically fit were chosen, and those who had exhausted their benefit, in case they should jeopardise their rights to it. The men from the valleys assembled on the appointed day, from the Rhondda, Ferndale, Tylorstown, Tonyrefail, Porth, Gilfach Goch, Caerau, Maesteg, Ogmore Vale, Aberdare, Aberaman, Cwmaman, Nantyglo, Brynmawr, Blaina, Caerphilly, Abertridwr, Llanbradach, Dowlais, Merthyr, Abercwmboi, Treorchy, Cwmparc, Cymmer, Glyn-corrwg and Neath. Sixty per cent were ex-servicemen. Each detachment of twenty had its leaders, two detachments forming a company each also with its leader. All leaders were ex-servicemen; one, two or three red stars on armbands indicated their rank. First aid was in charge of an ex-RAMC sergeant; there was a lorry with field-kitchens and a motorbike for the scouts. A disciplinary tribunal of four had power to expel any man guilty of disorder. Each miner carried his safety-lamp and lit it at dusk. The thousands who turned out to meet them on the way saw first, in the distance, three hundred lamps swinging along in the dusk.[7]

At the end the miners talked to *Workers' Life*:

At Bristol two thousand unemployed came out two miles to meet us. A. J. Cook walked with us part of the way and showed himself a man by refusing ham and eggs for dinner in Swindon and having 'jipo' with the boys and sleeping with us on the boards. Postman W. Bryant did good work for us too, so did bugler A. Rhys, and our cook, 'Long John Silver', and we shan't forget the fine concerts we had on the way. We shall never forget the welcome at Chiswick. We slept in the schools, got a hot supper and breakfast, sandwiches and meat pies when we left. We have been going now for twelve days and we are pretty well hardened to it. But still we shall want new boots to go home again.

The editor of *The Miner*, the organ of the Miners' Federation of Great Britain, who was with the marchers at Swindon, described their anger at the newspaper lies about them. They had read in the *Daily Mail*: 'To the satisfaction of well-fed Red politicians sitting in comfortable offices in London a pathetic contingent of pale and mostly thinly-clad men are tramping across Southern England in bitter weather. After four agonising days two hundred and sixty unemployed miners, who have been forced to make the hardship march to London, reached here tonight.' Outside the town hall, with due ceremony, they made a bonfire of the *Daily Mail*, each detachment leader stepping forward in turn to throw his copy on the fire. They knew well that for a young miner from Ferndale, where 70 per cent were on the dole, life on the march with meat once a day and any amount of bread, cheese and tea, was a great improvement on living at home with mother on fifteen shillings a week from the guardians, of which ten shillings went on rent.[8]

Although this march was made in a very different situation from the march of 1922 and with more limited objectives, by a homogeneous and more disciplined body which earned compliments from the police on its behaviour, there were similarities. In all the towns and villages on the way the trades councils and Labour Parties helped them generously in spite of the warnings from the TUC. The cottagers made their contributions and the labourers' children gave them food. In London all were housed and fed in Bethnal Green town hall for a week, with free cinema seats and haircuts. Similar also were the Prime Minister's refusal to see a deputation, and the substitute interview with the Minister of Labour, Sir Arthur Steel-Maitland. The deputation demanded that the thousands of miners who had been struck off benefit should be placed on it again, that special help should be given to elderly men who were disqualified from benefit and were unlikely to be re-employed and to lads for whom there were no prospects in the industry, and above all that the Government should recognise that the situation in South Wales was too serious for the local authorities to deal with. During long and heated exchanges the Minister declared: 'You are asking me to break the law', to which they retorted: 'It's not a question of breaking the law. It's a question of human life.' Finally he revealed his offer, the provision of training centres at which the miners could acquire the nimble use of their fingers. In the following weeks many Welsh miners were placed back on benefit and received more generous poor relief. Charitable feelings were stirred and the Lord Mayor of London opened a million-pound fund.[9]

Two marchers died. Arthur Howe of Trealaw, one of the cyclist scouts, was knocked down by a bus. The medical opinion was that he had been undernourished for many months. John Supple of Tonyrefail, a married man with seven children who had been unemployed for two and a half years, developed pneumonia after a meeting in Trafalgar Square in pouring rain. He left a letter to his wife: 'Don't worry about me. Think of me as a soldier in the Workers' Army. Remember that I have marched for you and for others in want.'[10] When the miners returned home the bodies of both men were taken with them and buried in their own villages.

The Movement continued to grow as new branches were opened as a result of a campaign after the march of the Welsh miners. At the same time, when the Unemployment Insurance Act came into operation in April, the 'Not Genuinely Seeking Work' clause was applied more rigorously and thousands were refused benefit because they could not provide evidence that they had been looking for work. This stimulus to the Movement led it to demonstrate to the Trade Union Congress in September 1928. Two thousand miners, led by Wal Hannington, marched from the West Wales coalfield to the Congress at Swansea to protest against the evil effects of industrial rationalisation, only to find their deputation barred from making itself heard.

Undeterred by this rebuff the Movement immediately organised a march in Scotland. Unemployment, particularly in the old coalfields, was as chronic as in Wales, and poor relief was stringently administered by the parish councils. Some two hundred and fifty men went from Lanarkshire, Stirlingshire and Fifeshire, led again by Hannington, with their banner – 'The Miners' Hunger March to Edinburgh'. Along with them were jute workers with the banner of the Dundee branch of the Movement and shipyard workers from the Clyde. All through West Lothian they were met by groups of supporters. The leaders with their whistles and red armbands with red stars were in complete control. The silver band of the trades council met them in Edinburgh and led them to a reception by the council. The interviews with authority were productive. The Scottish Board of Health agreed to investigate the cases of harsh treatment under the poor law which the marchers presented and to look into any future ones received from the Movement. Ministry of Labour officials were also willing to take up the numerous complaints of unfairness over unemployment benefit.

The Scots miners felt well satisfied with their march. Many wanted to make a march on London, and to start right away. Hannington and the other leaders were all in favour but they had to point out that considerable preparations would be necessary. The march was also a financial success. So much money had been given that there was a surplus. Part went to the Miners' Relief Fund, part to the Movement to organise a national hunger march. During the next month, October, the Movement began to use it.[11]

REFERENCES

1. NUWCM, *Report of Fourth National Conference*, 6–8.12.24.
2. NUWCM, *Report of Fifth National Conference*, 23–25.1.25.
3. *The Miner*, 8.10.27.
4. *The Miner*, 15, 22 & 29.10.27; *The Times*, 7.11.27.
5. Macfarlane, L. J., *The British Communist Party*, 1966, p. 155.
6. Macfarlane, op. cit., p. 172.
7. *The Miner*, 5 & 12.11.27; *Workers' Life*, 10.11.27.
8. *Workers' Life*, 25.11.27; *Swindon Advertiser*, 18.11.27; *Brentford & Chiswick Times*, 19.11.27; *The Miner*, 19.11.27; Hannington, *Unemployed Struggles*, p. 156–63; Hannington, *Never On Our Knees*, pp. 204–10.
9. *Reading Standard*, 19.11.27; *Sunday Worker*, 13 & 27.11.27; Hannington, W., *March of the Miners*, 1927.
10. *Sunday Worker*, 4.12.27; *The Times*, 28.11.27.
11. *Edinburgh Evening Despatch*, 22 & 24.9.28; *Edinburgh Evening News*, 21 & 25.9.28.

4

'Not Genuinely Seeking Work', 1928–9

In February 1929 an unemployed man of Birkenshaw, W. Bamforth, wrote to the *Bradford Telegraph*:

> I happen to be one of the unemployed and had to go before the committee. The questions you had to answer were enough to make one's blood boil, especially those who had done their bit in the late war. It is all very well asking a man to go and find a job but why don't they find you one themselves? I was always given to understand that was what the Labour Exchanges were for. I and my fellow workers are only too willing to work if anything can be found to do.

In Derby the guardians were aggravated by the same situation. They argued that the Labour Exchange was too strict in depriving the unemployed of benefit because they were, in the official phrase, 'not genuinely seeking work'. When a man was refused national benefit he had to come to the guardians for local relief. Their concern was that the cost of keeping the unemployed should not fall on their rates but on the national exchequer. There is no record of the questions which angered Bamforth. His trades council, however, wrote to condemn the practice of the interviewing officer at the Exchange in giving his opinion of the character of an applicant to the insurance officer, the man who decided whether benefit should be given or not.[1]

The experience of Bamforth and of the Derby guardians was multiplied many times over. The letters NGSW, standing for 'not genuinely seeking work', were the bane of thousands of unemployed who trudged miles from their homes to get from an employer the evidence – a scrap of paper certifying that they had asked for work – sufficient to satisfy the Labour Exchange. The onus was on them to prove that they could not get work. Hundreds of thousands of claims for benefit were disallowed because men could not give such proof. They were judged guilty of being idle unless they could show otherwise.

Resentment at the NGSW clause of the 1927 Unemployed Insurance Act was the first cause of the march of 1929. The second cause was the threat of worse to come embodied in the same Act. The rule of the 'thirty stamps qualification' was due to come into force in April of that year. It provided that a man must have made thirty contributions to insurance during the preceding two years before getting benefit. The official figures showed that about a third of all applicants had worked for less than thirty weeks over that period. The effect would be to strike a quarter of a million men off benefit. From the Labour Government's Act of 1924 onward, successive Acts had contained the thirty stamps qualification, but each time the date of operation had been postponed; each Minister had said 'not yet', until there were better times. Now, when operation seemed imminent, better times were no nearer. Meanwhile the old rule still applied, that a man must show that he had eight stamps on his cards in the preceding years and thirty stamps over any period since he started. Only postponement of the new rule kept hundreds of thousands of unemployed in benefit and out of the poor law.

These two measures, NGSW and the 'thirty stamps qualification', were the chief targets in the marchers' Charter of Demands. Not only should the NGSW clause be abolished but the onus should be placed on the Labour Exchange to show that a man had refused suitable work. The Charter also covered a wider field. As in 1922 it put forward the 'right to live' and a definite scale of benefits. These were on the same level as in 1922 except that the amount for man and wife was now 40s instead of 36s while the demand for supplements for rent and fuel of 1922 were not now included. Whereas the demand in 1922 had been the general one of work or full maintenance now it was more specific. Unemployment must now be considered as a national crisis and the Government must take full responsibility for relieving distress. Until such action could be taken the Boards of Guardians must be retained and given ample help. Positive steps must be taken to reduce unemployment; national schemes of work at trade union rates, reduction of the working day to seven hours a week, old age pensions to be payable at age sixty and increased to 30s a week, the school-leaving age to be raised to sixteen with a child's allowance of 10s a week.

The march started on 22 January 1929 when the Scottish contingent left Glasgow; all contingents arrived in London on 24 February and returned home on 4 March exactly as planned.

Wal Hannington, released from the Minority Movement, was again in command and the stamp of his organising ability, energy and courage was as evident as in 1922. There was the same obstruction in the shape of the regulations for casual wards activated by the Ministry of Health poor law inspectors, the boards of guardians and the masters of the workhouses.

The attitude of the TUC and the Labour Party to the march was as in 1927, only more so. The changes in the labour movement which lay behind the lack of support then had by now intensified to produce hostility.

During 1928 the TUC continued its search for industrial peace, one aspect of this being the Mond-Turner negotiations, the other being an investigation into so-called disruptive elements in the trade unions. In line with this, the executives of the National Union of Railwaymen, the Transport and General Workers' Union, the National Union of General and Municipal Workers, the Shop Assistants', Boilermakers', and Painters' unions took steps to exclude the Minority Movement or to prohibit Communists from standing in elections for union positions. There was some opposition to this trend, but it was not very successful. A manifesto by A. J. Cook, Secretary of the Miners' Federation and a prominent figure in the Minority Movement, and James Maxton, chairman of the Independent Labour Party, denouncing the policies of 'peace with capitalism' did not win enough support to cause problems for the Labour leaders. The latter were busy with preparations for the 1929 General Election, bringing to birth the statement entitled 'Labour and the Nation'. At the 1928 annual Labour Party Conference, new rules were adopted under the heading 'Party Loyalty'. These were designed to stop joint activity of any kind between Communists and Labour Party members, either nationally or locally, while Communists were finally prohibited from election as delegates from trade unions to Labour Party meetings or conferences.

This process of excluding Communists, which the latter had tried unsuccessfully to resist all through 1927, was in the end made easy for the Labour leaders by a change in Communist Party policy which began in 1928. The change emanated from the Communist International (CI) which had been reconsidering its attitude to social democratic organisations in Europe. In

February 1928 the CI held a Commission on the British situation in Moscow at which the view was expressed that, since the Labour leaders had betrayed the workers and were, moreover, in process of transforming their organisation into an auxiliary apparatus of the capitalist state, the time had come for the British Communist Party to adopt sharper tactics of opposition to the Labour Party in order to win the leadership of the working class in the struggle against capitalism. After much argument, the British representatives agreed to a turn in policy, and this was subsequently endorsed by the British Party as a whole. The new policy, which became more extreme as time went on, eventually became known as 'Class against Class', under which the Labour Party was characterised as the 'third capitalist party'; in the 1929 election, workers were in fact urged not to vote Labour even where no Communist was standing.

The hunger march of January 1929 took place a few months before this election, but at a time when relations between Communists and members of the Labour Party had deteriorated.

Whereas in 1922 the Hunger March Programme had been signed by three comparatively unknown unemployed engineering workers, now the Manifesto signed in March made an appeal to all trade unionists, and to it were appended the names of twenty-one men and one woman; some of them held office in trade unions and many were widely known in the union world. From the miners there were not only A. J. Cook, Arthur Horner and William Allan, General Secretary of the Lanarkshire Miners' County Union, but also Will Lawther, executive member of the Durham Miners, and miners' agents from South Wales and the Forest of Dean; from engineering, as well as the veteran Tom Mann, who was also president of the march, Jack Tanner of the AEU National Committee also signed. The Furnishing Trades Association was represented by its president, Alex Gossip, also treasurer of the march, the Tailors and Garment Workers were represented by their London organiser, Sam Elsbury, the Iron and Steel trades by R. Purcell, and Parliament by Shapurji Saklatvala of Battersea. It was an impressive list though those in the know could easily tell that most of those on it were either Communists, or prominent in the

Minority Movement, or both. The TUC General Council made it clear to the press that it had no connection with the march and condemned it on the grounds that it would cause hardship to the marchers. It promoted the hardship by telling all trades and labour councils on the routes of the marches not to help them. Another effect of the TUC enmity was that, in contrast with 1922, the *Daily Herald*, still owned by the TUC, excluded all news of the march from its columns because it was 'unofficial' and 'communist-inspired'.

When the 1929 march took place, unemployment occupied the thoughts of politicians and electorate alike, whereas in 1922 it had been regarded as a temporary nuisance. Perhaps this was why the march was started in deep mid-winter with its inevitable hardships. If it had been left until the spring it would have come into the period of the general election and local Labour parties would have little time or sympathy to spare for the marchers. The Movement was growing and was more firmly based in industrial districts; contingents from Sheffield and Derby took the place of the groups from Southern England and East Anglia in 1922. The Welsh miners' march had been a fillip, the Scots had pressed for a national march, public opinion was becoming stirred. There was no lack of men eager to go. The first number of six hundred was raised to a minimum of eight hundred and a maximum of one thousand, because of the press of volunteers. Some had marched from Wales in 1927 and others in Scotland, but hardly any had had the experience of 1922. Only two names besides Hannington's seem to appear on both national marches – Sid Elias who led the Cardiff contingent in 1922 and the North-East coast contingent in 1929, and John Quinn, a leader of the Scots in both years.

The Scots, the men of Devon from Plymouth, and the Welsh, were worst hit by the hard weather. One hundred and sixty-four Scots – miners, shipyard workers and dockers – assembled in Blythewood Square, Glasgow, to start their five-hundred-mile trudge to London. Engineering worker George Middleton, their leader, described the scene:

> A finer sight for inspiration has never been seen than those men assembled in company formation, properly dressed in sections of fours, fully equipped, with valise and haversack, containing their requirements for the road, and carrying seven splendid banners,

each with an appropriate slogan written thereon. Thousands of Glasgow workers gathered to cheer the marchers off on their noble, heroic way, and when the whistle sounded, and the command went forth to march, a mighty hurrah was heard from thousands of throats, followed by 'Good Luck, Give Baldwin Hell' and many other expressive working-class sentiments.

They followed the same route as in 1922 as far as the West Riding but then went through Manchester and Staffordshire instead of via Sheffield and Derby. Early on they needed all their determination. George Middleton continued:

We awoke from our slumbers on Sunday morning to find the snowflakes quickly falling and the ground looking lily white. A very pleasing sight for the artistic temperament but not very welcome to those with a fourteen mile tramp in front of them. Thornhill was our destination that day, and we started off with our feet sinking two inches deep in the snow-covered ground. The going was exceedingly heavy, particularly for those whose boots were 'the ware o' the wear', but with grim, dour, set faces we plodded on. Only men actuated and inspired with a great ideal would have been prepared to continue under such trying circumstances. Compensation was forthcoming after we had gone about nine miles. A magnificent hot dinner of mince, onions, turnip and potatoes was served from our field kitchen. Thornhill, a small village, was reached about 6 o'clock, and accommodation found in an old barn, which made a passable billet. That day's march had been a severe test for the men. We had been marching through open country in a blinding snow-storm. Every man was dead beat and the heavy snow on the roads had made the marching very hard and difficult.[2]

Fearful that these conditions would affect the start of the North-East coast army, the Scots sent a telegram to Newcastle, and received the reply: 'Greetings to courageous Scottish contingent. NE Coast contingent assembling ready for the road.' The men from the North-East also had to face snow, rain and slush deep on the roads. Snow caught up with the Plymouth men on 11 February. George Tremaine, their leader, described their struggles:

We left Exeter for Honiton next day in a heavy downpour of rain. When we had tramped five miles the rain turned to snow, driven by a north easterly wind, and into the North East we marched. On, on, we marched, the remaining twelve miles to Honiton being accomplished without a single halt. We were met by the workhouse master, who had prepared for our coming. Bread, beef and margarine for tea, laid in rooms in which large fires had been lighted. We were presented with the difficulty of drying our wet clothes – not only the clothes we were wearing, but also the change of clothing which many of us were carrying in our packs. The workhouse master consented to dry our clothing during the night but the conditions in the 'spike' at Honiton are so primitive that on Tuesday morning, Feb. 12th, we were compelled to get into clothes still wet from the soaking of the previous day. Nine-thirty a.m. saw us on the road for Chard, sixteen miles away. The snow had ceased to fall but the temperature was below zero, a circumstance which caused our clothing to freeze stiff as we marched. The further we marched the more difficult became the roads.[3]

For the marchers what mattered was the kind of food they had and where they slept, the comradeship that developed, the pride of a contingent in its performance, the sense of striking a blow for a better life. The material comforts depended on the sympathy of local trades councils and labour parties and the extent to which they would defy, officially or unofficially, the TUC, and on the laxity or humanity of boards of guardians and workhouse masters. If the first was lacking, the marchers had to depend on the second. In their progress, wittingly or unwittingly, the marchers promoted conflict, or at least disagreement, between the Labour leadership and the local trade unionists and party workers, and also, though to a less extent, between the Ministry of Health and local boards of guardians. Both kinds of local protagonist were informed well in advance by the march organisers of the coming visitation by the marchers and so had time to decide on their attitudes.

As the marchers progressed along the nine scheduled routes – from Scotland, the North East, Sheffield, South Wales, the South West, Lancashire, the Midlands, Derbyshire, and Nottingham – it became clear that the great majority of trades councils, local Labour parties and Co-operative Societies were sympathetic. Accommodation and food for about a hundred and twenty nights had to be organised. By the time the marchers reached London, about 40 per cent of the nights had had to be spent in workhouses. Of the remainder over half had been wholly cared for by local Labour organisations and many others partly, when, for instance, food was taken into the workhouse. The trades councils and Labour parties which provided for the marchers in one way or another outnumbered those who refused help by two to one. The attitudes in the localities were seldom as clear-cut as that suggests. The marchers met with many different degrees of sympathy, generally greater in the large towns, but not always predictable. Sometimes there was an official welcome from the trades council, sometimes it was an unofficial one, when there was a compromise between loyalty to Labour and feelings for the marchers. Even a refusal to help revealed quite often a schism within the local body, which resulted in the marchers receiving comfort from a sympathetic minority.

The Scots experienced all these varieties of support, beginning on the first day out. George Middleton reported:

> Kilmarnock was our destination that day, a distance of 21 miles. We arrived at 5.30 p.m. and a fine reception awaited us in the Town Hall, organised by a band of local comrades connected with the Miners' Relief Committee. The Trades and Labour Council had decided to give us their moral support but that was as far as their assistance extended. The Kilmarnock Co-operative refused all assistance but the local co-operative of Galston, Hurlford and Darvel responded magnificently with generous gifts of foodstuffs.

Then coming into England after a week's hard going they met the unofficial reception:

> The men were early astir, and many of them talking agitatedly about what was in front of them that day. We were going to march over the Border into Carlisle. Many of the men in our contingent had never before been over the Border, had never seen England. Men, many of them middle-aged, who had toiled and wrought in the mines and factories, giving the best of their lives in piling up wealth for the bosses, men who yearned to see the world, and now for the first time in their lives they were going to see England, though they had to walk it.... We went 'over the Border' shortly after noon. A halt was made and the marchers gathered in a circle to sing the old Scottish rebel song, 'MacGregor's Gathering'.... We reached Carlisle at 7 o'clock that night. Our advance guard had fixed us up at the Trades and Labour Council rooms. A fine tea was provided by the T & LC and the women's section rendered very

valuable assistance. Although the T & LC had decided that in view of the TUC General Council's policy towards the march, they could not give us their official blessings, they nevertheless gave us an excellent 'unofficial' reception.[4]

Some observers thought the marchers were having it too good. Was it right, that, as reported from Scotland, men had been seen in the public houses? 'We are demanding the right to live, and we are entitled to our pints of beer as much as anyone else,' was their reply. Next day, 'the Penrith Labour people gave us a splendid welcome. Shepherds' pie, as much as we could eat, was served up to us, and the men did it justice.' Two days later at Kendal women members of the Labour Party admitted them unofficially to the party rooms. Generally, when the men of the party hesitated to help, if there was a women's section the marchers could feel sure of a good reception. Warmth, together with some coldness, continued on the way south:

What a wonderful reception we received when we reached Preston. At the Trades' and Labour Council Hall, where we were to be billeted for the night, thousands of people had assembled outside awaiting our arrival. I formed the men up compactly to sing to our audience 'MacGregor's Gathering' and a very impressive sight they made as with sticks in the air they sang that famous chorus.

> Then gather, gather gather,
> Gather, gather, gather;
> While there's leaves in the forest
> And foam on the river,
> MacGregor despite them shall
> Flourish for ever.

I do not know whether the workers of Preston had ever heard it before, but they cheered it to the echo. We trooped into the Hall and there before us was a wonderful spectacle. Tables laden with dishes of Lancashire 'hot pot'. It was great stuff and never more relished than it was that night. Again our reception was 'unofficial' but a word of thanks and praise is due to Councillor Taylor and his colleagues, who gave us splendid assistance and told the marchers that what they were doing was contrary to official instruction but 'they could not stand aside and see these brave men passing through Preston without rendering what help they could'.[5]

At Burnley on the fifteenth day the trades and labour council would not help but the old Social Democratic Federation gave the use of their club hall. Another two days later in Bolton a reception committee had already been busy, and the marchers slept on the floor of the West Ward Labour Club. Labour would not be involved officially although the marchers disclaimed any political allegiance. 'We are not Red', one said. 'We're not Communists. We're simply unemployed. This isn't a political matter at all. We're out of work and anybody who talks about us being Reds is talking rot.'[6]

Most contingents had a similar mixed experience. The Plymouth men, marching through country where Labour was weak, had more nights in the workhouse than most. The North-East coast contingent, a hundred miners and shipyard workers, fared pretty well. Their leaders, Elias and Thurlbeck, described what happened:

> That night in the Bigg Market, Newcastle, a mass rally was held, close on 6,000 workers, in a bitter cold night, turned out to give the marchers a send off. An appeal for overcoats met with a ready response, workers in the audience taking off their overcoats and tossing them on to the platform. From Durham we proceeded to Bishop Auckland where a by-election was in progress, and on these grounds the Labour Party refused us all assistance. It was left to one old Labour Party stalwart, Comrade Wordsley, to provide everything. This comrade, a one-time associate of Keir Hardie, showed indeed that he had not forgotten the principles of the movement, even if the opportunist career-hunting bunch, who now dominated it, had.

Matters improved as they moved into Yorkshire:

> Here a fine hot supper was provided by the Leeds Trades Club, followed by a social. This was an official welcome from the Trades Council, one of the few trades councils that broke through the sabotage of the General Council and by vote of their delegates decided that our visit would meet with their official recognition and support. They welcomed us magnificently and gladly provided facilities for us to remain for an extra day's rest, during which time our road fund was augmented by £30 in various donations from the workers of Leeds. The town council gave us the free use of the baths and wash-houses so that every marcher started on the morning of February 7th spick and span.

Two days later Doncaster rivalled Leeds:

... here the rank and file had shown that they did not stand for any sabotage by any local Jimmy Thomases. It appears that the Trades Council executive had refused to assist the marchers, but the trade unions demanded a special full delegate meeting to discuss the matter, and at this meeting the executive decision was reversed by the rank and file, and splendid hospitality arrangements were made for us. Hot baths for the marchers, a hot supper and a splendid breakfast.

In different country a contrast was soon apparent:

The Cambridge Labour Party had already informed us in a most contemptuous manner that 'if we came to Cambridge we did so on our own responsibility, as they had decided to do nothing whatsoever for us'. So we stayed in the 'spike'. The police in Cambridge were afraid of a clash with these snobs called college undergrads, and though we marched into the Market Square the undergrads fought shy of a conflict with these hefty north-east lads with their stout ash sticks.

The same attitude prevailed at Ware, and at Edmonton it went further:

... the local Labour Party and Mr Broad, the Labour MP, had for weeks been denouncing the march and declaring they would do nothing to assist ... as a last despairing effort to turn the local workers against the marchers, they had issued a scurrilous abusive leaflet against the march, in the name of a local 'scab' unemployed organisation which they were running.[7]

Marchers who were given the cold shoulder by their own class felt keen resentment, and at such times the workhouse seemed by comparison a friendly place. Seventy men from Yorkshire, miners and steelworkers, having fared well at the hands of trades councils since leaving Sheffield, were due to join the Nottingham contingent at Loughborough, but the trades council there felt it had enough to do to look after its own six hundred unemployed, nor would the Labour Party help in any way. The marchers halted outside the town hall and sat on their packs in the market place to eat their bread and bully-beef while the leaders, Ley and Mullins, called first at the Labour Club where they were turned away and then negotiated terms of entry into the workhouse with the master. After a long argument, the master agreed that the marchers should not be treated as vagrants. They had waited three hours in the bitter cold, singing 'The International' and 'The Red Flag', some holding the banners – 'We want work or full maintenance. Only cowards starve in silence', others dancing around to keep warm. During speeches the Reverend Pickering of Sheffield, veteran of the 1922 march, spoke – 'The action of the Prince of Wales in visiting the coalfield was only so much dope and tomfoolery after the reception we have received.' The marchers told the press:

> We have met a cold reception and colder hearts still, so far as the trade unionists of Loughborough are concerned. We are disgusted with the reception. We are the sons of respectable working parents, and willing to work if only this Government will let us. But we have met a spirit of comradeship at the Workhouse, and we are to shelter there for the night on conditions which I cannot divulge. If we had not received these conditions we were prepared to lie out in the open all night rather than allow the Labour Party to smash this march.[8]

Next day at Leicester they entered the workhouse again, but the trades council rallied round. Met on arrival by a Labour councillor, the marchers sat down to a meal of stewed steak, vegetables, pastries, bread and butter and tea in the Co-operative Cafe, and their breakfast was brought into the workhouse. David Ley pointed the contrast:

> Our reception in Leicester was a magnificent one. The reception at Loughborough was colder than the coldest day this last 200 years. The Loughborough Trades Council and Labour Party ignored us. Wild beasts fare better than men in Loughborough. Whilst we shivered in the open market-place and ate our meagre fare, wild beasts in an adjoining circus were being fed under cover. In my opinion the only human beings in Loughborough were the workhouse master and his staff. In the workhouse each man was provided with two blankets and two basins of soup with bread. The usual vagrant conditions were waived. Some of the marchers who were unwell received medical treatment before leaving.[9]

The workhouse was usually the last recourse when Labour failed, although the Salvation Army and the YMCA sometimes took its place. The poor law regulations were as formidable an adversary as the TUC. Boards of guardians were instructed by the Ministry of Health that the marchers were to be dealt with under the Casual Poor (Relief) Order of 1925. The following regulations were to be applied:

1 Every man must be searched immediately upon admission to the casual ward, and all articles must be taken away and restored to him at the time of his discharge.
2 Every man must be bathed as soon as practicable after his admission and his clothing must be taken from him and if necessary dried and disinfected.
3 The diet must consist of: supper – bread, 8 oz., margarine, 1 oz., tea, cocoa, broth or gruel, 1 pint; breakfast, *ditto*; mid-day meal – bread, 8 oz., cheese, 2 oz.
4 No man must be discharged before 9.0 a.m. of the second day following admission, nor before he had performed the work prescribed.

The guardians were told that they must not commit themselves in advance to receiving the marchers, whereas it was essential to the march organisers to plan well in advance. When the clerk to the Stoke Union complained to the Minister of Health that his board of guardians had resolved to provide food and accommodation for a hundred men he was assured that no promise of relief could be given to persons until they were in the Union and even then only if they were destitute.[10]

The marchers had every intention of breaking down the regulations whenever they had to go to the workhouse. They insisted that they were not casuals, vagrants or tramps and would not be treated as such. Memories of the 1922 march told them that the regulations could be bent to some purpose. Much would depend on the political complexion of the guardians and the personality of the workhouse master. Although the guardians were to be abolished very soon, some of them meant to do their duty. At Brentford, where they were expecting two hundred marchers on 23 February, they had been criticised by the Ministry on a previous occasion for not enforcing the regulations. It was resolved that all marchers were to be searched as casuals, to be bathed, to be detained one night and to be given only the casuals' diet. The clerk to the guardians received authority to obtain police protection and any additional help as required. As it turned out all was in vain for, since the Labour Party arranged accommodation, all the guardians had to do was to lend two hundred blankets; but the intention was clear enough. The only departure from the regulations was a stay of one night instead of two, no doubt in recognition of the realities of the situation, rather than any conscious departure from principle.[11]

Conflict of some kind there was bound to be. With the police it was rare, they were more concerned to avoid trouble. More than once they advised the workhouse master not to insist on searching the marchers. There was only one serious incident, with the Lancashire contingent of miners and textile, engineering and transport workers. Their leader described what happened:

> About two miles from Birmingham we were met by the reception committee and a procession with band and banners, which further encouraged the men. By this time we were in great form as we landed at the Digbeth Institute where a splendid meal was served, followed by a fine concert. Just before 11 p.m. we were formed up to march to the workhouse where we were to sleep that night. On moving off we were accompanied by an unusually large number of police, who escorted us the most round about way to the workhouse where we arrived somewhere about 12.15. When we found that we were to be locked in the casual cells, with no convenience for our control council to meet or for our Red Cross men to carry out their work and other such necessary things, we decided to leave the building, preferring to remain on the streets all night rather than accept such treatment. As we were getting on our packs a crowd of police, who had undoubtedly been held in readiness, rushed upon us and a serious conflict ensued. Several of our men were injured and we were finally overpowered by the force of the police and locked in the workhouse for the night, with the police also remaining. Next morning we marched from the spike to the Bull Ring in the centre of the town where a protest meeting was held.[12]

Conflict with the workhouse depended on the local situation, on the accommodation which was offered – which varied from the woodshed or the cold casual cells to the boardroom – on the weather, on the amount of local support and donations of food to supplement the casuals' diet, on whether or not the police were handy, or whether the ministry inspector was breathing down the necks of the guardians and stiffening the workhouse master. The master, in any case, had his ordinary clients to consider. At Loughborough, where the Yorkshiremen had found shelter, there had been repercussions in the casual ward.

James Wilson, a vagrant, was sentenced to fourteen days' imprisonment for striking the master and the porter when he could not obtain his clothes at the usual time. The casuals could not be issued with their clothes until after breakfast owing to the overcrowding by the marchers. He was 'perished, lying on the tiled floor with a little damp straw'.[13]

The regulation on searching was more often waived than not, as with the Scots at Berkhamsted where, according to the ministry inspector, 'searching was *not* enforced, on the advice of the police, who said if the Master attempted to search there would be trouble and the Master, who had warned the men as to the consequences of smoking, did not think that they did so. Even the seven in the casuals' wards were not searched, but the Master says there was no smell of smoking during the night and no spent matches, etc., in evidence in the morning'. (The seven were the leaders who asked to sleep in the casual wards while the main body of a hundred and thirty were in the territorial drill hall hired by the guardians.) The inspector commented that this was because 'they did not want the rank-and-file to see how the collected monies were spent'. The North-East men were not searched at Bishop's Stortford, 'the leader's' word that the men would not smoke in the wards being accepted.

The compulsory bathing and taking of clothes to be dried and disinfected was more often welcome than not, even when it interfered with the customary town meeting as happened at Bishop's Stortford: 'The threatened demonstration in the town was stopped – the Master saying that if the men wanted baths, they would have to have them at once and that there would not be time for the men to go into town. All but eighteen availed themselves of this – the eighteen went to town and returned quite peaceably. The men gave no trouble at all.' The rule about discharge was also comparatively harmless since no one thought seriously that the marchers could be detained a second night against their will. When, however, it was applied so as to limit the right of exit and re-entry into the workhouse, it was firmly resisted. The North-East coast men showed how at Thirsk:

The master had promised not to impose any restrictions but once inside the building we found an entire change of front. A police guard was placed at the foot of the stairs and we were told that no more than nine men would be permitted to leave the institution before morning. Heated meetings were held with the master but, backed by Sir Henry Bowers, Chief Constable of the North Riding, he remained adamant. Our temper was rising: they were treating us as tramps and worse, and we were not going to stand it.... Another attempt was made to reason with the master. He laughed at us – the rain was beating pitilessly against the window-panes ... we had marched ten miles that day, and many of the men had sore feet and were in no condition to fight. But he did not know the men he was dealing with. Unanimously we decided to march out of the workhouse and push on to Ripon – 11½ miles away. The decision was communicated to the master and chief constable and outside the police gathered in force. What a night to march in! Rain, rain all the time. Yet at ten o'clock, armed with stout ash sticks the marchers demanded the doors to be thrown open and marched into the village square.

They marched through the night across the moors, with motorised police escort, until they reached Ripon at half past two. There, they were taken in at the Constitutional Club where fires had been lit and tea brewed in readiness.[14]

Regulation 3 governing the diet was the most hated, not only because men were hungry and the food offered was insufficient to give strength to go on, but also because of the slur attached to it, and the vagrant status which it implied. The Lancashire men understood that it was important at the start of the march to set a precedent, a point which the inspectors had also urged on the guardians – and the Lancashire marchers showed how on their second day out:

... to Northwich where we had to enter the workhouse, commonly termed 'the spike'. We were determined to break down the instructions of the Tory Ministry of Health and went straight to the job by informing the workhouse master to that effect. We succeeded in our purpose and if Neville Chamberlain had seen us tucking into hot stew for tea, with porridge, fresh butter and jam and marmalade for breakfast, he would surely have taken a blue fit. The workhouse master told us when we entered the spike that we would not be allowed out again that night, but we soon settled that little score also, and in the end not a line of Chamberlain's instructions was observed.

The precedent served them well at Market Drayton two days

later and thereafter they had more or less their own way. At Stratford-on-Avon, 'finally we succeeded in getting our own conditions and good food', and at Chipping Norton:

> We again stayed in the spike and had excellent treatment, and when we left, loaded with bully-beef sandwiches, we gave three hearty cheers for the workhouse master and his staff for the splendid treatment that we had received.

By the time they reached High Wycombe the inspector reported that their first demand was for 'tickets for the picture palaces'.[15]

Refusal to accept inferior status inspired all contingents, notably two others, from opposite ends of the country. The miners from Blyth, Ashington, Blaydon, South Shields and Shiremoor and the shipyard workers from Newcastle, Gateshead, Jarrow and Sunderland had every help in the industrial areas. Coming into agricultural country, they showed they would stand no nonsense:

> At Northallerton we had our first conflict with the local authorities. It was arranged that we stay in the Parish Hall the night and our meals should be provided by the local workhouse. The supper meal was the usual casual diet of bread and margarine, which is only changed by changing the design on the pat of margarine –rose one day to a thistle the next. The marchers were not standing for this. So comrades Elias and Thurlbeck met the workhouse master and demanded better food. This he agreed to on the basis of bread and jam for breakfast. It was here that the marchers learned the virtues of a new slogan. Next morning we taught the master the slogan of 'We Want Bacon'. That spike master was much relieved when we left the town. Also we showed him how 'The Red Flag' and 'The Internationale' can be sung.

Ten days later pushing 'forward to Grantham across desolate moorland country' they demonstrated against the diet and got a good breakfast.

And the next day:

> We marched to Melton Mowbray, the seat of the Prince of Wales' Hunting Box, and evidently the news of our tussle with the Grantham workhouse had preceded us for on arrival at the workhouse we were provided with herrings and cake for tea, bacon for breakfast and sausages to take with us.

Again at Oakham they won roast beef for tea and bacon for breakfast, but their last conflict in the rural area against a tough master was not successful:

In the sleepy, one eyed village of Saffron Walden, beloved of all Shakespeare's admirers, the workhouse master, an ex-quarter-master in the navy, refused to give us other than casuals' diet. In spite of the instructions we forced our way out of the workhouse that evening and marched to the market place with the bread and marg in our hands. A great indignation meeting was held, and that night, when we returned to the workhouse to sleep, we conducted a demonstration inside which outraged all the conceptions of discipline which this spike master had thought to impose upon us. The news spread and a big crowd gathered to see us march out of the spike the next morning.[16]

The news also spread from 'Suffering Walden' to Bishop's Stortford, according to the inspector's report:

Accommodated 84. Tyneside contingent – Casual Wards and the new Wood Shed. The Casual Diet was given but a kindly guardian provided out of his own pocket, boiled bacon, suet pudding and jam, and two local butchers gave sausages for their breakfast. The Master said that this was a good job, as otherwise the men had threatened when they were at Saffron Walden to wreck the Bishop's Stortford Institution if they were treated there as they were at Saffron Walden (where, apparently, they only received the casual diet).

In the master's view 'they were not a nice crowd – their standard was not such as would excite sympathy'.[17]

At the other end of England the Plymouth men also took a stand early on. Honiton had treated them as well as it could, the Chard master had prepared a hot meal in the dining-room used by the inmates. On 13 February at Yeovil, where the roads were still snowbound and extremely difficult to march on, the Labour Party had refused to help. George Tremaine wrote:

Arriving at the workhouse we interviewed the Master who told us that a woodshed had been placed at our disposal, and that we were to be treated as casuals. Then the fun commenced and the Master found that we were an organised body of men and that the treatment usually meted out to casuals would not do for us. He informed us that he had been instructed by Mr Duff, 'Inspector of the Ministry of Health', to 'treat the marchers who were coming to

Yeovil as casuals and that a blanket per man in a woodshed would be good enough for them'. We told him that 'he could cut Duff out, and that he would have to supply us with meat for tea and breakfast, a hot dinner on the following day, a room in which we could eat our meals in comfort and at least three blankets per man'. The Master retorted by saying that the Board of Guardians could not afford it and he would, if there was any trouble, send for the police. After further conversation in which he was given to understand that we were not concerned either about the Board of Guardians or the police, he decided that discretion was the better part of valour and acceded to every one of our demands.

The marchers' reputation preceded them to Sherborne and Shaftesbury, and it was not until Salisbury that they again had to 'sing the Red Flag' to the workhouse master.

The marchers neared London, content in the knowledge that not only had they been able to defy the poor law regulations and assert their status, but that also the rank and file of the labour movement, in spite of discouragement from its leaders, had rallied to them. The Welsh in Maidenhead 'spike' received a visit from Tremaine and Forster, the Plymouth leaders, and arranged to rendezvous: 'On Saturday February 23rd we left Slough with spirits soaring, on our way to Chiswick.' Then:

The Lancs, Midland and Staffs [marchers] were to be seen swinging along the road in splendid fashion. Cheer after cheer resounded through the countryside as they approached, and the cheer that rang from their throats when both contingents met almost split our ear-drums. At the entry to the Great West Road the Plymouth contingent were waiting our arrival. Cheer after cheer rang out as we approached. Marching along without a halt we exchanged our fraternal greetings with these comrades who ultimately fell in behind the Lancs. Down the Great West Road we went in fine style and entered Chiswick singing the Internationale with gusto.[18]

In Trafalgar Square the next day the marchers felt that the big demonstration of welcome was a sufficient answer to the opposition from the London Trades Council and the London Labour Party. The press had to admit that it was 'a most remarkable scene and a striking success for the Reds'.

The week until the return on 4 March was somewhat of an anti-climax. The marchers were active in stirring public opinion and in trying to exert pressure on members of the Government and of Parliament. They marched and counter-marched throughout London, keeping up a continual agitation. Their attempts to reach the Cabinet were frustrated, largely because of the hostility of the TUC and the Labour Party. Baldwin wrote to Emrys Llewellyn, secretary of the Movement: 'The Prime Minister thinks that no good purpose would be served by his receiving a deputation from the marchers as the organisers of the march will have seen the public press. The Prime Minister is receiving a deputation from the Miners' Federation on 5 March on the subject of unemployment in the coal fields.' All the Ministers concerned sent an identical letter. The Minister of Labour had written to the Prime Minister advising him to refuse a deputation, stating that 'the TUC General Council has specifically dissociated themselves from this movement, although this is perhaps not a reason which the Prime Minister could give for refusing to see a deputation, especially as A. J. Cook has given the marchers at least a qualified blessing', and had sent copies to the private secretaries of all the Ministers who had received a request for an interview from Llewellyn.[19]

When two left-wing Members of Parliament, George Buchanan and Campbell Stephen, approached Winston Churchill, he replied that the Government could not spend its time seeing a body of men who were not even recognised by Labour.

All attempts by the Movement to persuade members of parliament that the Parliamentary Labour Party should discuss the marchers' petition and charter in order to put down an official motion in the Commons were met with various excuses. Labour did not wish to harm its chances at the general election only three months ahead. Individual Clydeside members who asked questions in the House were answered with the contents of the Prime Minister's letter. Twice marchers raised their voices in the public gallery of the House. A group of twenty succeeded in singing 'The Internationale' inside the lobby. Others got as far as the main entrance to the Home Office and into Downing Street. In the streets, however, the collections were so large that there was enough money to pay for the marchers to go home by train.[20]

Three days later the Minister of Labour announced that the 'thirty stamps' clause, which had been at the core of the march, would be suspended for another twelve months. The marchers felt they could claim a victory. The face of unemployment had been brought home to thousands of people throughout the country, and on that issue the Labour Government of 1929 came into office.

REFERENCES

1. *Bradford Telegraph*, 8.2.29; *Derby Telegraph*, 13.2.29.
2. Hannington, W., *Story of The National Hunger March*, 1929.
3. Hannington, op. cit.; *Western Times*, 22.2.29.
4. Hannington, op. cit.; *Unemployed Struggles*, pp. 184, 186.
5. Hannington, *Story of the National Hunger March*, 1929; *Cumberland News*, 2.2.29.
6. *Bolton Evening News*, 1, 8, 9.2.29.
7. Hannington, op. cit.; *Doncaster Gazette*, 15.2.29; PRO MH 57/98; Camb CRO G/C/AM44.
8. *Leicester Mail*, 14.2.29; *Nottingham Journal*, 13.2.29.
9. *Leicester Mail*, 15.2.29; *Nottingham Journal*, 14.2.29.
10. PRO MH 57/98; *Staffs Sentinel*, 11.2.29.
11. PRO MH 57/98; GLC BG/B195.
12. Hannington, op. cit.; *Birmingham Mail*, 20.2.29.
13. *Nottingham Journal*, 16.2.29.
14. PRO MH 57/98; Hannington, op. cit.
15. PRO MH 57/98.
16. Hannington, op. cit.
17. PRO MH 57/98; *Hertfordshire Mercury*, 22.2.29.
18. Hannington, op. cit.; *Salisbury & Winchester Journal*, 22.2.29.
19. PRO MH 57/98.
20. Hannington, *Unemployed Struggles*, pp. 197–8.

5

Marching Against a Labour Government, 1930

> It is high time something was done by the Government
> to stop these people. They are just joy riding at the
> expense of the public. The public are not all bl--dy
> fools. All my Local Authorities have played the game
> except Coventry City Council. Of course the Police are
> only too kind to the Marchers; their only idea is to
> avoid a breach of the peace and 'Pass along please' to
> the next town. (One of the general inspectors in the
> poor law division of the Ministry of Health in April
> 1930.[1])

It was only a year since he had been busy in his Midland
district encouraging the boards of guardians and the workhouse masters to apply the regulations to the hunger
marchers, and now the marchers were at it again. For him
all marches were the same nuisance, a wilful creation of
difficulties for the poor law authorities. However, for the
marchers 1930 was very different from 1929.

The third national march was unique in several ways: its
challenge to a Labour Government, the rapidity with which
it followed the 1929 march, the marchers' almost complete
dependence on the poor law institutions for accommodation,
the smallness of the march (a mere three-hundred-and-fifty),
and the existence of a contingent of women which, though
numbering only twenty-five, was seen as a significant departure.

When the Movement decided on 9 February 1930 to
organise, at short notice, a march to start less than two
months later, the Labour Government, pledged to reduce
unemployment, had been in office for nine months. During
that period unemployment had risen by 400,000 to a new
total of 1,520,000, plus many more not on the registers at the
labour exchanges, and it was still increasing. That was the
case for a march so soon after the previous one, though it

would have been a stronger one later when the full impact of two and a half million unemployed had been felt. The case was strong enough for three hundred and fifty men and women to march, though not for a thousand as was intended. Enough people had felt at the polling stations on 30 May 1929 that Labour should be given an opportunity to tackle unemployment for Labour to form a government, if not to govern. At the end of five years of Conservative rule it was time for a change. There was no other major question at the election; among the unemployed the burning issue was still the hated 'not genuinely seeking work' rule. Unemployment was only a million so far and showed no signs as yet of worsening, but still it was felt to be a long-standing evil and an unnecessary one. Something certainly ought to be done about it. For the outgoing Prime Minister, Baldwin, the importance of unemployment had been unduly emphasised, and would diminish. He recommended that little need be done – slum clearance, technical education perhaps. The Conservative slogan, 'Safety First', had a great deal of appeal but it was not likely to bring victory, mainly because the Labour Party had by now also established itself as the party of safety.

A year after the General Strike, the Labour Party had begun to prepare a programme for the general election to be held in 1929. Ernest Bevin reminded it that such a programme must be limited since thousands of trade unionists were not socialists or even Labour supporters. Its programme for dealing with unemployment had been vague. In its view unemployment was a disease of capitalism which could be cured only when capitalism was replaced by socialism, and since a socialist society was likely to be achieved only in the long run, not much could be done about unemployment in the short term. In so far as the Labour Party had an unemployment policy, it did not go beyond reviving the traditional export industries by rationalisation. There was little enthusiasm for public works' schemes. There might be some tinkering with the expansion of credit, but there was no question of a national loan to finance it, or of any steps which might lead to inflation. In 1927 the Labour Party rejected a new policy statement on unemployment from the Independent Labour Party, called *The Living Wage*. This pointed to the need to increase purchasing power, partly through redistribution of the national income by taxation, and partly by printing new money to be used for imposing new wage minima on industry. Ramsay MacDonald called the statement a collection of 'flashy futilities' and it was pigeon-holed by reference to the executive.[2] The Labour Party's manifesto, *Labour and the Nation*, issued in 1928, contained generalities about socialism, industry and society.

The Liberal Party set the pace for unemployment policy with the report *We Can Conquer Unemployment* in March 1929, and the pledge given by Lloyd George to reduce unemployment within a year. The report declared: 'At the moment, individual enterprise alone cannot restore the situation within a time for which we can wait. The State must therefore lend its aid and, by a deliberate policy of national development, help to set going at full speed the great machine of industry', and called for a great construction programme to be financed by loan.

Both the Conservative Government and the Opposition reacted to the challenge. The Conservative rebuttal limited itself to a statement of the difficulties of the Liberal scheme and, for election purposes, pointed to its own steady achievements which were to be continued. Labour's counterblast, entitled *How to Conquer Unemployment, Labour's Reply to Lloyd George*, had to include Labour's own proposals as well as attack the Liberal programme. It claimed that the programme would do nothing to restore industry and that it was based on 'madcap finance'. Labour's own policy included projects similar to the Liberals' – on roads, housing, electricity, drainage – but it was all in general terms; there was none of the Liberal detail on cost, timing and employment. Labour had been more specific and more prompt in its proposals for the unemployed. It had not only claimed that every unemployed person ought to have a right to benefit but, of more immediate importance, perhaps, to the unemployed, it had demanded – in evidence to the Blanesburgh Committee in 1925 – higher rates of benefit, abolition of the 'not genuinely seeking work' clause and reduction of the waiting period from six to three days.

Socialism was put well into the background in Labour's policy. Nationalisation of the mines was, indeed, promised, but only if Labour got a clear majority in Parliament. The result of the general election was indecisive, but if Labour and Liberal votes were combined, repudiation of Conservative policies was implied.

Labour won 287 seats against the Conservatives 261, while the Liberals, with 59, again held the balance of power. The Labour Party had high hopes for it had won more seats than it expected. While the Government formed by Ramsay MacDonald was once more a minority one, on the major question of unemployment the Liberal plans were so similar to those of Labour that effective action ought to be possible. Much was expected and particularly by the unemployed who felt that a Labour Government would at least do something not only to remove injustices but also to provide jobs. The leadership of the Movement, however, was deeply sceptical of much improvement being made.

Such expectations suited the new Government well at first. Unemployment seemed to be still a manageable problem at only a little over a million, and above all it was an uncontroversial one: all parties might be reckoned on not to oppose moderate proposals. The King's Speech of 3 July was indeed a moderate one promising schemes 'for the improvement of the means of transport, for the stimulation of the depressed export trades, for the economic development of "my overseas dependencies", for the improvement of the condition of agriculture, for the encouragement of the fishing industry, and for the improvement of the facilities for the marketing of farm and fishery products'. The cotton, iron and steel industries were to be inquired into, consideration was being given to the reorganisation of the coal industry and a general survey was promised for unemployment insurance. There was nothing, as yet, for the unemployed in spite of Labour promises of higher rates of benefit and easier conditions for it. The NGSW clause was referred to a departmental committee. MacDonald himself asked for cooperation from all parties and wondered whether 'by putting our ideas into a common pool we can bring out – from that common pool – legislation and administration that will be of substantial benefit for the nation as a whole'.[3]

However, an initial emphasis on unemployment was shown by the announcement that J. H. Thomas, Lord Privy Seal, would be Minister for Employment Policy and that he would have the help of George Lansbury, First Commissioner of Works, Thomas Johnstone, Under Secretary for Scotland, and Sir Oswald Mosley, Chancellor of the Duchy of Lancaster.

In the meantime, the Movement was growing. Stimulated by the success of the 1929 march and the rise in unemployment, its membership continued to increase until it reached about twenty thousand. However, the attacks of its Communist leaders on the Labour Party were becoming ever more virulent, and this was reflected at the NUWM National Conference in September 1929 at which the newly elected Labour Government was denounced as 'the most efficient organisation of the capitalist class for the exploitation of the workers' (NUWM Report of Sixth Annual Conference). By the time of its Leeds Congress in November 1929, the Communist Party's condemnation of the Labour Party had been extended to include not just the trade union leaders but the trade unions themselves. These were now defined as social fascist agencies in the service of capitalism and the Minority Movement was called upon to exercise 'independent leadership' in industrial struggles outside the purview of the official trade union movement. At this Congress Wal Hannington was re-elected to the Communist Party's Central Committee despite the fact that he was not on the recommended list of candidates put forward by the Congress Panels Commission.

In the event, the new approach to the trade unions resulted within one year in the Minority Movement's virtual collapse and its disappearance soon afterwards. At the same time the Communist Party's own membership fell to its lowest level ever.

In contrast the NUWM remained very much alive. Immediately the Labour Government was formed, it swung into action to bring pressure to bear for improvements. A charter of what were considered to be elementary points, which a Labour Government should at least consider, was issued containing these demands:

Raise the benefit scales of the unemployed.
Remove the 'not genuinely seeking work' clause.
Restore to benefit all unemployed persons who were disqualified under the previous government's administration.

Make benefit continuous during unemployment; no disqualification unless suitable employment at trade union rates has
been offered and refused.

Abolish the six days' waiting period, the benefit to operate from
first day of signing.

Introduce national plans of work schemes at trade union rates and
conditions.

Abolish all test and task work under the boards of guardians.

Guarantee full trade-union conditions for all unemployed transferred under the industrial transference scheme.

Give the lead for a general shorter working-day without wage
reductions, beginning with the mining industry, and government establishments and government contracting firms.

Introduce a system of adequate pensions for all workers over the
age of sixty, in order that they can retire from industry.

Raise the school-leaving-age to sixteen, with government maintenance grants.

Repeal the Guardians' Default Act, and establish a national
uniform scale of relief not lower than the unemployment
insurance benefit scale.

None of these were new except that relating to transference.
Taken together it was a formidable list for any government, but
one calculated to win the widest support. A shorter working-
day for the miners had already been promised. After a
campaign for this charter during the summer, the time came to
impress on the Government that more was expected of them
than of the Conservatives. The new Ministers, Margaret
Bondfield, Minister of Labour, and the Minister of Health,
Arthur Greenwood, refused to see a deputation. Not accepting
this for an answer, the deputation, consisting of fourteen area
representatives led by Wal Hannington, invaded the Ministry
of Labour and occupied its boardroom, only to be ignored by
the Minister and her parliamentary secretary and eventually
ejected by main force. The Movement had demonstrated that it
was on a collision course with the Government.

Soon after, the Minister announced that the 'not genuinely
seeking work' clause of the Insurance Act would not be
abolished. Instead she introduced local assessors' boards to
examine doubtful claims for benefit arising from allegedly
inadequate efforts to obtain work, a return to an earlier system
when the adjudication of such claims had been transferred to

the more remote agency of the Chief Insurance Officer and his department. The new boards were not to start until November 1929 and in the meantime the full application of the NGSW clause was to continue. Although Miss Bondfield claimed that she 'had greatly softened the impact of a cruel and troublesome method', the new machinery met with instant opposition from the Movement, which would accept nothing short of complete repeal and which started a campaign to persuade the unemployed not to appear before the boards. The Movement obtained a ruling that refusal to appear before the boards did not affect claims for benefit and this weakened their authority.

The Government took some tentative steps to deal with unemployment while it continued for the time being to refuse concessions to the unemployed. In August 1929 J. H. Thomas visited Canada in order to obtain orders for British coal and ships. In the same month the Minister of Health rejected a resolution from the board of guardians at Greenwich to abolish task work and told them that 'a labour test was imperative as a condition for the granting of outdoor relief to all able-bodied persons'.[4] It is impossible to say how many men had to do task work, but probably there were scores of thousands, for this survival from the old poor law lingered on in different forms in different places. Men were compelled to work, usually for a full day – at stone-breaking, wood-chopping, on sewerage, roads or parks – in order to receive, not wages, but relief tickets in some places, or payment partly in cash, partly in kind in others. The Government was expected to discourage guardians from operating task work but during the rest of 1929 it continued to persuade guardians to maintain it. The Romford, Dewsbury and Gateshead guardians were all reminded of the necessity of the labour test and task work.

The Movement actively protested, with its demand for trade union rates for all relief work, and also on the question of relief debts incurred by men, chiefly miners during the 1926 strike, who on receiving poor law relief had had to sign an undertaking that they would repay the sums granted. Boards of guardians had found it difficult to get such repayments from miners whose wages had been cut and therefore asked the Ministry of Health for the remaining debts to be liquidated. The Minister, following her predecessor's policy, refused. The guardians at

Swansea, Whitehaven, Mansfield and Pontefract were dealt with in this way during the latter part of 1929, some being additionally threatened with surcharge if they disobeyed.

In September 1929 the Movement girded up its loins at its sixth national conference. The Labour Government seemed to be doing nothing either to ease the lot of the unemployed or to give them work. Unemployment was already increasing. The registered unemployed had increased by 80,000 to 1,200,000 since the Government took office four months earlier, during the favourable summer months. The Movement was also growing. Eighty-two delegates represented fifty-one branches and committees. The name of the Movement was changed; with the omission of the word 'Committee', it became the National Unemployed Workers' Movement, a simplification as well as a recognition that the immediate post-war era was a thing of the past. At the time the conference met, the economic blizzard had not yet struck Britain. The crash of Wall Street was to come six weeks later. Conference was told that while unemployment was in general caused by the capitalist system, its persistence and growth could be laid at the door of Conservative governments and their Labour successor. As Wal Hannington put it in his report to the conference:

> The scheme of rationalisation which the capitalist class, aided by the official Trade Union and Labour movement, are now applying has already meant a widespread displacement of workers from industry.
>
> As the process of rationalisation is pushed forward more and more workers are rendered redundant and the problem of unemployment becomes increasingly severe. Even the capitalist economists are openly admitting that this process of the displacement of workers from industry is inevitable with the development of rationalisation.
>
> The Mond-Turner Memorandum on industrial peace and rationalisation declares that an increase in unemployment must take place with the process of capitalist reorganisation in industry. The unemployed must therefore prepare themselves for long and bitter struggles against starvation.

The apparent continuation of capitalist policies by the Government served to strengthen the arguments for the Communist Party's 'new line' of hostility to the Labour Party, and the trend towards a decision to march against the Government. The effect appeared at the national conference when it reviewed the record of Labour in office. The Government had rejected all the approaches made by the Movement and had refused so far a whole series of requests. It had made no attempt to abolish the waiting period of six days before receipt of benefit or to stem the rising number of men disqualified from benefit for various reasons. It had, indeed, agreed to raise the school-leaving age to fifteen years, but the Bill (if it should ever become law) would postpone the effective date until April 1931, thus producing no effect on unemployment in the near future. Following this arraignment the conference declared its hostility by resolving that:

> Our Movement must view this Government in no other way than as a Government in the interests of capitalism, more dangerous even than the Baldwin Government because of its ability to deceive the workers. Our Movement must fight this Government in the same way as we have had to fight previous Governments, to wring from them concessions for the unemployed. . . . We can no longer support the Labour Party with its capitalist programme and the Labour Government which is the most efficient instrument of the capitalist class for the suppression of the workers.[5]

Next month the scene began to change for the worse. In America a speculative boom came to an end with the crash on Wall Street on 23 October, and this, combined with the upheaval caused in England by the downfall of the Hatry financial empire in September, soon began to affect trade and investment. While unemployment continued to rise, J. H. Thomas reported to Parliament in November on the extent of government expenditure on public works. Its limited scope was a disappointment to both Liberals and Government supporters. For the ILP James Maxton told him to try socialism instead. In the Unemployment Committee of the Cabinet, the Chancellor of the Exchequer, Philip Snowden, successfully resisted numerous but expensive ideas – large-scale road building, early retirement, pensions at sixty years of age, land reclamation. For its part, the Movement organised district marches and decided to hold local conferences of working-class organisations in December.

Early in 1930 the issue sharpened. The rise in unemployment

began to stir feelings of revolt in the Labour Party. The lead
was taken for a time by Sir Oswald Mosley who, with the
support of Lansbury and Johnstone, drew up his own scheme
for unemployment. Ramsay MacDonald made a gesture by
creating an economic advisory council which included some of
the best brains in the country – Keynes, Tawney, Cole, Bevin –
but little came of its deliberations. The Movement's national
administrative council, responding to pressure from the districts, resolved to 'make the necessary inquiries for arranging
the planning and organisation of a national march to London at
the earliest possible date'. In the meantime the slogan was 'On
the Streets with Mass Demonstrations'; membership was still
rising, with six new branches in London.[6]

In February several things happened together. Mosley
submitted his memorandum on unemployment to the Cabinet,
thus promoting a division of opinion within the Labour Party.
The Government stood firm against Mosley's advocacy of
control of imports, public control of industry and the expansion
of purchasing power by the state. It remained without a policy
for unemployment. At the same time the Labour Party,
although becoming uneasy about the Government's policy, or
lack of it, reacted against the Communist Party's hostility by
issuing a circular which forbade affiliation to it of organisations
alleged to be under Communist control. The Movement was
included in this ban. On the 9th of the month it decided to start
the third national march on London.

The preparations were on quite a different scale from 1929.
The Movement was out on its own. Instead of an appeal to all
trade unionists with notable names from the Minority Movement appended and a foreword by A. J. Cook, there was only a
pamphlet written by Wal Hannington with a call for
working-class solidarity. On the March Committee Tom
Mann was now joint treasurer (with Alex Gossip, general
secretary of the National Furnishing Trades Association)
instead of chairman, a position occupied by Sid Elias, former
contingent leader. The committee immediately had an unfore-
seen problem in organising the march to start on 30 March.
The Red International of Labour Unions, issued a call for an
'International Unemployed Day of Struggle' on 6 March, a call
which the Movement could not ignore. Great efforts were made

to couple the work for the March and for the Day but the former suffered and this no doubt helped to reduce the target figures of one thousand marchers to the actual number of three hundred and fifty. The work of organising had to be done in three weeks and it required the example of Scotland, where the wish to march was always strong, in getting eighty men off to a start, to spur on other districts. Among the rank-and-file, conflict between loyalty to the Government and the wish to march induced many to stay at home. The knowledge that they could not expect any welcome on the road from Labour organisations deterred all but the hardiest and the most devoted to the Movement. The march committee found that even those trades councils which in 1929 had given the marchers unofficial receptions refused to do the same again.

In addition, the Movement had some of its thunder stolen. The hated NGSW was to go. The Government had introduced its second Unemployment Insurance Bill in November. The onus would now be on the authorities to show that a man was not genuinely seeking work, he was now innocent until proved guilty. The Bill was a step forward for the unemployed in other ways – the rate for wives was raised from 7s to 9s per week; for men and women aged 19 to 20 from 12s and 10s to 14s and 12s; for those aged 18 to 19 from 10s and 8s to 14s and 12s; for those aged 17 to 18 from 6s and 5s to 9s and 7s 6d. But for those aged 16 to 17 the rates remained at 6s and 5s and the children's allowances remained at 2s. On this score the Bill did not satisfy critics on the left and James Maxton and the Independent Labour Party Members tried, repeatedly but unsuccessfully, to amend it. As it was, the Government – accused by the Opposition of extravagance – had some difficulty with the House of Lords. The major grievance remained, that the rate for single adults was not raised; the least a Labour Government should do was to restore the cut of 1s in the men's rate which had been made by the Conservatives in 1928, but the rate remained at 17s. Although NGSW had been removed from the march armoury there was still plenty of ammunition. In any case the improvements would not have any effect until April and until then the unemployed would still be harassed by NGSW. It was no problem for the march committee to make a list of ten demands and publish them in the new Hunger

Marchers' Charter. The demands were not much different from the previous year; the only new ones were abolition of test and task work and of relief on loan. The scale of benefits included was the same as in 1929, the rate of 30s demanded for adults being nearly double the actual one.[7]

If the march was prepared hastily, the Ministry of Health was readier than before. This was unfortunate for the marchers since they would have to rely almost wholly on the workhouses for accommodation. Before the Scots reached the border, the Ministry had issued to all general inspectors of the poor law a confidential memorandum, together with copies of letters from the Home Office to Chief Constables, requesting them to give whatever support was required. It laid down that the marchers were to be dealt with as before, i.e. enforcement of the regulations except for detention and task work which had been proved impracticable, though they were not to be deprecated by the inspectors. Where, and only where, the casual wards were inadequate, use might be made of the main workhouse where a better dietary was legal. In the last resort temporary accommodation could be hired provided that the food issued was not better than in the workhouse, or tickets on lodging-houses might be supplied. It was lawful to give relief to the wives and children of marchers, but the marchers themselves could not receive either benefit or outdoor relief while they were away from home.

The Ministry could be more hopeful of getting its way with the marchers this year. Poor relief had been removed from the now defunct boards of guardians into the more remote hands of the public assistance committees of county councils and county boroughs. The Ministry had information about the attitude of trades councils and Labour parties on the march. Thirty-two had refused any help and only four had held out some hope. St Albans Labour Party would not make any preparations in advance but if the marchers passed through it would not refuse accommodation; Coventry Trades Council had appointed a sub-committee to help the local Communist Party to make arrangements; Newcastle Socialist Society would give break-fast; Bristol Trades Council had formed an official reception committee; only Guildford Trades Council had agreed to welcome the marchers officially, in defiance of the TUC.[8]

At all the many towns where in 1929 there had been comfort and good cheer, warmth and good food, there would now only be what could be given by the local Communists, Minority Movement groups, branches of the Movement and the efforts of the Workers' International Relief, and that was bound to be limited.

The marchers were as well aware as the Ministry of their prospects. As before, they were determined not to accept the regulations for the casual wards but this time it would be harder. The North-East contingent, thirty strong, scored early on at Durham. They were not searched, were allowed to keep their collecting-boxes which were, according to the master, 'by no means empty' and had their evening smoke in the workhouse. They ordered newspapers, which arrived with their breakfast of tea and corned-beef sandwiches left over from the evening. At Darlington there was no searching and one wholly irregular slice of fried bacon with breakfast. It was easier to reject the regulations if there was alternative accommodation. At Northallerton the marchers refused to enter the workhouse on being told that they would not be allowed out until the morning and found shelter in the Boy Scouts hall. At Thirsk, where the master, mindful perhaps of events in the previous year, had had floors scrubbed and fires lit in readiness, they refused to accept the regulations and marched straight on to Ripon, as they had done in 1929. At Sheffield, their number doubled by the addition of thirty Yorkshiremen. They also refused the workhouse because the master insisted on the rules for searching and bathing; with help from the Co-op they slept in the Trades Hall. Their leader, George Fletcher, master baker and former guardian of the poor in Sheffield, had already learned of a telegram from the public assistance officer to the master telling him: 'Enforce regulations *stop* treat marchers as casuals.'[9]

They again refused casuals' treatment at Loughborough and slept on the floor in the Adult School building. With them now were several local councillors and the veteran J. T. Murphy, founder member and leader of the Communist Party. Banners proclaimed 'Underfed under a Labour Government. We won't starve at home. We demand full maintenance from the Labour Government and a 7-hour-day.' George Fletcher told the *Leicester Mail* why he was marching:

> The time will come when these marches, as in Germany, will accomplish much. From all over the country, bands of unemployed marchers are making their way to London where they will take part in a great 1 May demonstration.
>
> You ask me how it is possible that I, an employer, can be a Communist. I will tell you. It was impossible for me to get a job as a journeyman. I was always victimised because of my political views. The only alternative was to go into business for myself. But I place my politics before my business. That is why I have left it to accompany these unfortunate men on their march.
>
> I have been in the revolutionary working class movement for 30 years, and have been to Russia. The reason why these marches are not being supported by Labour organisations is because they know these demonstrations are being directed against the Labour Government for their lack of attention to the unemployment problem.

He explained why the marchers refused the workhouse under the casuals' rules also at Market Harborough:

> We did not accept as we are not vagrants. The Jubilee Hall was placed at our disposal and we gratefully accepted it, then we sent a deputation to the workhouse for blankets and 150 were given us. The local Labour Party have given us 15/0 and a supply of cigarettes and we have £80 of bread from the Co-op. The Labour Exchange have refused to allow us to sign on. This is the first time we have not been able to sign on.[10]

The Scots, eighty of them led again by Wal Hannington, stood firm as soon as they reached England. At Carlisle they refused to be searched and after a meeting with the town clerk, the chief constable and the public assistance officer, they were 'put on their honour' to give up their tobacco and matches. They earned a commendation from the inspector – 'very good behaviour'. The South Wales contingent at Chippenham rejected the casual wards and, finding that the town hall was refused them, became, in the words of the inspector, 'very abusive to the mayor and town clerk'. They spent the night on the stones of the market place, making a fire in the street, some lying in the empty fountain trough, others on the masonry, while sentries were posted until dawn.[11]

It was not always necessary to demonstrate against treatment as vagrants in the casual wards or the main workhouse. The Plymouth men found a marked difference between the first week of their journey when they slept in the workhouses and the subsequent nights in the casual wards. The fact that throughout Devon, as far as Sherborne, the casual wards were not offered them may have been because of the exposure of their wretched state by the Bishop of Exeter in the previous year. The benefit was substantial. Twenty-one men, a storeman, two hotel workers, an upholsterer, a gardener, a driver, an army pensioner, and thirteen labourers with George Tremaine, their leader as in 1929, arrived at Crediton. The workhouse master sent in his report:

One man came forward on a bicycle at 2 p.m. to enquire if preparations had been made for their arrival. I informed him what had, that only those destitute would be relieved, and there was to be no demands. The nurseries were clear for re-decoration and these were used for sleeping accommodation, straw mattress, pillow, and three blankets on floor for each. The rooms are heated with hot water, floors are wood, there is lavatory accommodation, and a good supply of towels and soap was available.

A stout rick cover was spread out on stable floor for kits to be placed upon, and access for shaving articles was given next morning. The police had informed the leader they would be admitted without having to go to the police station for a ticket.

On arrival kits were placed with belongings in stables, and men given use of board room, supper was served in the dining hall at 6.30, pea soup and bread, those who did not care for pea soup were given bread, margarine and tea. The Chairman of the House Committee, Rev. C. E. Jewell CC, and the Vicar Rev. Darling (Chaplain) called whilst they were at supper and talked with the men. They readily stated there was no solution to the problem of unemployment, and that their demonstration was futile. Each one had a bath, the organiser dealt with correspondence he had picked up at the post office, and the 'Red Cross Orderly' accompanying the party attended the men's feet with applications of iodine, etc. from his surgical haversack. Breakfast was served in dining-hall after the inmates, bread, margarine, bacon and tea. The leader read Prayers which I was about to do. Being Good Friday and Bread Stations closed I issued to each man 8 oz. bread, 2 oz. cheese, and a piece of bacon in grease-proof paper and paper bag. They left at 9.25 a.m. without complaint. The Master from Exeter called on Thursday night and saw what was being done. I informed him and the Master at Honiton by telephone immediately the men left here.[12]

Later on it was more difficult. At Andover it was the casual wards, but there was no searching and they bought fish and chips to supplement the dietary; but at Basingstoke, where the mayor and the Labour Party had refused to help, the work-house master insisted on the rule of detention and so they marched into the town singing 'The Red Flag'. The police persuaded the master to waive the rule, and the marchers eventually slept on the workhouse floor. Next day the Aldershot master would have enforced all the rules, but they had an alternative and marched on to Guildford, one of the few places where they knew the trades council would welcome them.[13]

In Kent the contingent of eighteen men were also able to circumvent the master at Gravesend. They called at the workhouse for food with the intention of going out to hold the usual meeting. When the master, sticking to the detention rule, insisted that once admitted they must stay in, they ate in the town, held their meeting and returned to the workhouse to enjoy beds with flock mattresses, pillows and three blankets each, without being searched, bathed or detained. The women's contingent followed the same line. Eight had come from Barnsley to join with fourteen Yorkshirewomen in Bradford and, led by Maud Brown, women's organiser in the Movement, had set off for Leeds where they had arrived footsore and weary. When they arrived at Wakefield, a dormitory and a day-room in the workhouse had been made ready, but the matron would not cook a hot meal or allow them to cook their own food. They refused to be searched or give up their belongings but left them in the day-room after being told that the alternative was to leave the place. They paid the penalty of a cold breakfast for staying in bed after seven o'clock. That evening at Sheffield they refused to accept the casuals' conditions, requested, unsuccessfully, intervention by the Labour chairman of the Public Assistance Committee, went out into the streets, held meetings, made collections, marched about until 3 a.m., went into an all-night cafe, continued tramping, and at about 5 a.m. had breakfast in the Communist Party rooms. After that night, they rested in a coach all the way to Luton, and at St Albans the ever kindly Labour Party looked after them. They arrived promptly in Hyde Park on May Day.[14]

The marchers did not intend to submit to the regulations in London. The Ministry of Health thought otherwise. Solicitors' advice was to the effect that if men were in a workhouse because the casual wards under the Metropolitan Asylum Board were insufficient, they might 'for example, lawfully be refused permission to attend unemployment demonstrations if no leave was due to them under the ordinary rules'. If the Ministry had thought of getting rid of the marchers by making them go home, then solicitors' advice was that 'in effect removal was possible only if a man wishes to return to the starting place and has a settlement there'. When the Movement, unable to find accommodation, placed the onus on the poor law authority, the Ministry insisted that if the marchers entered workhouses in London, the casuals' conditions would be imposed. Negotiations between the two sides on the day of the marchers' arrival produced some relaxation of the regulations but there was no assurance that they would be waived.[15]

Action decided the issue. After the May Day demonstration in Hyde Park, the marchers advanced on the City of Westminster workhouse in the Fulham Road and demanded shelter, but without the regulations for casuals. When, and only when, this was conceded, they marched through the main gates, took the place over, and did as they pleased. They took possession of the block for the able-bodied after the regular inmates had been put elsewhere, ran up the red flag, and installed the march control council in the board-room where it could receive visitors, discuss reports, and plan activities. On the first evening there was bread, margarine, corned-beef and tea but thereafter a great improvement. Food was brought in, the marchers' cooks took over the cookhouse and store room and with the help of the workhouse cooks prepared the meals which were served regularly by the staff in the dining hall. There was porridge for breakfast and butter instead of margarine. A demand that the women marchers should be sent over from their quarters in Islington to the Fulham Road was not met, however.[16]

The Movement had asked the Prime Minister to receive a deputation but he was more determined than his predecessor had been not to see them. The march council planned to force the issue. While the main body was to march to Hyde Park, drawing the police that way, three small picked bodies of men were to raid the Ministries of Labour and Health and the House of Commons. In the event the Ministry of Labour was barred by police and at the Ministry of Health the unemployed succeeded only in occupying a room for an hour. At the House they sent in cards for interviews with Members. A dozen men tried to rush into the Chamber but failed after a sharp struggle with police in the inner lobby. One, Dan Gillies was arrested. The women marchers saw Jennie Lee and Marian Phillips who told them that, willing as they were, they had no influence with the Government and could do nothing for them.[17]

Meanwhile the take-over at the Fulham Road workhouse was causing some alarm. The question for the authorities was how long could it be allowed to go on and how soon could the marchers be got rid of. The *Daily Sketch* proclaimed – 'Hunger Marchers in Possession. Extraordinary Situation in London Workhouse. Acting Like Owners.' It reported that not only did the marchers hold mass meetings in the dining-hall, but they were arrogant towards the officials, using the telephone and the entrance-hall just as if they were the staff of an invading army in a captured town hall, and actually did no work except clean their own quarters. The police were increasingly dissatisfied as they had to escort the groups of men who were continually going out to meetings. Worse, the marchers might be stranded in London as enough money had not been collected to pay for fares home, and the men were complaining. Wal Hannington was reported as saying that those who complained of being misled on this score had no right to be in the ranks of the marchers: 'They had not the broad principles which inspired the march at heart.'[18]

The Ministry sent an inspector but he found no serious trouble; on the contrary the behaviour was quite good. It would be necessary, however, to consider what was to be done if the men stayed. They were comfortable enough; the master had given them much more favourable terms than was intended. He considered that strong measures such as searching would not do; they would only lead to a riot. Indirect methods would have to be devised. He advised that the London County Council's plan might be the answer – to give the men notice to quit because they were not destitute; they were collecting £50 a day. If they applied for re-admission they would be let in only if there was proof of destitution and strictly in accordance with the regulations. But the question was when? Certainly the Ministry should do nothing to prevent the Council ejecting the men and if the irregular situation continued it would have to take official notice, which would be awkward.[19]

Deliberating in the workhouse boardroom, the march control council was also anxious to get the men home. George Fletcher, the treasurer, appealed in the *Daily Worker* – 'we must have £350'. Enough came in to pay the reduced fares negotiated with the railway companies. On 8 May all, except one, left from Euston, King's Cross and Paddington. The next day Dan Gillies, 27, labourer of Greenock, came up at Bow Street on a charge of assaulting the police and was bound over to keep the peace for twelve months. He declared in court: 'I am one of the five hundred Hunger Marchers who have come from all parts of Great Britain to protest against the Labour Government's betrayal of the unemployed and its treachery to the working class.'[20]

The protest was over for the time being. Marching had again rebuffed the poor law. A reminder that unemployment was not to be taken lying down had been issued. Later that month Sir Oswald Mosley resigned from the Government after his Memorandum had been rejected. Criticism of the Government arose in the local Labour parties and the trade unions as its lack of policy was debated in Parliament and within the Parliamentary Labour Party. On the last day of the month sixty Labour MPs sent a petition to the Prime Minister calling for the dismissal of J. H. Thomas as Minister for Unemployment. Thomas was given the Dominions to look after and unemployment policy was entrusted to a small Cabinet Committee headed by MacDonald.

REFERENCES

1. PRO MH 57/99.
2. Skidelsky, R., *Politicians and the Slump*, 1967, p. 50.
3. Mowat, C. L., *Britain Between the Wars*, 1968, p. 355.
4. Hannington, *Unemployed Struggles*, 1936, p. 208.
5. NUWM, *Report of Sixth National Conference*, 1929.
6. NUWM, National Administrative Council, 25/26.1.30.
7. Hannington, *Why We Are Marching*, NUWM, 1930.
8. PRO MH 57/99; Hannington, *Unemployed Struggles*, p. 212; Hannington, *Achievements and Lessons of the Hunger March of 1930*, NUWM, 1930.
9. *Darlington & Stockton Times*, 12.4.30; PRO MH 57/99.
10. *Leicester Evening Mail*, 21 & 22.4.30.
11. PRO MH 57/99; *Cumberland News*, 12.4.30; *Wiltshire Times*, 26.4.30.
12. PRO MH 57/99.
13. PRO MH 57/99.
14. PRO MH 57/99; *Nottingham Journal*, 22.4.30; *Luton News*, 1.5.30; *Barnet Press*, 3.5.30; *Hertfordshire Mercury*, 2.5.30.
15. PRO MH 57/99; Hannington, *Unemployed Struggles*, p. 213.
16. Hannington, op. cit., p. 214; *Daily Worker*, 1.5.30; *The Times*, 2.5.30. *The Times*, 2.5.30.
17. *Daily Worker*, 8.5.30; *The Times*, 8 & 9.5.30; Hannington, op. cit., p. 215.
18. *Daily Sketch*, 6.5.30.
19. PRO MH 57/99.
20. *Daily Worker*, 6 & 9.5.30; *Daily Sketch*, 7.5.30; *The Times*, 8 & 9.5.30.

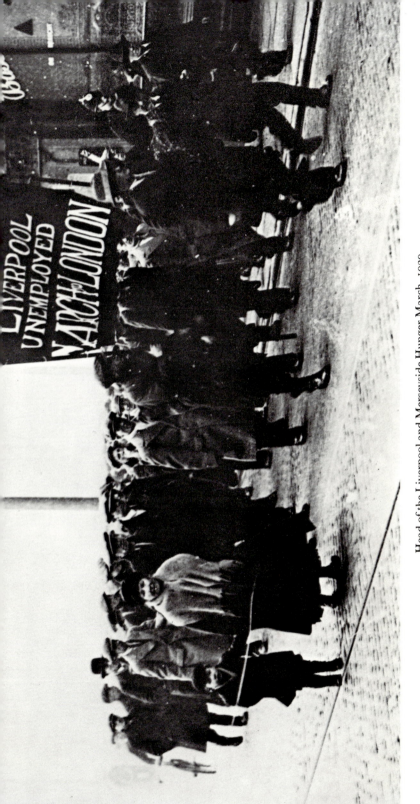

Head of the Liverpool and Merseyside Hunger March, 1929

Women's reception committee for Hunger Marchers, Deptford, mid-1930s

Lancashire contingent of Hunger Marchers, joined by undergraduates, Oxford, October 1932

Wal Hannington (*second from left*) outside Pentonville Prison after serving a three-month jail sentence in 1932 (note package of letters he had not been allowed to receive until his release)

Wal Hannington (*sitting*) with other NUWM leaders, including Pat Devine (*left*), Maud Brown, Harry McShane (*on her left*) and Peter Kerrigan (*above and behind him*)

Women's contingent marching against the means test, date unknown

JUBILEE
CHIMP

HER
BIRTH, FOOD AND DRINK

By One of Her Poor Relations—MAN

PRICE - ONE PENNY

**The National Unemployed Workers Movement
11a White Lion Street, London, E.1**

Vividly drawing public attention to the plight of the unemployed, this penny pamphlet issued by the NUWM in 1935 contrasted the plush living conditions of the London Zoo's highly-publicised chimpanzee, 'Jubilee' (named thus to celebrate twenty five years of the reign of King George V), with the conditions of the unemployed

Head of Scottish women's contingent of Hunger Marchers nearing London, Barnet, February 1934

Harry Pollitt speaking at a Hunger March rally in Trafalgar Square, March 1934 (Maud Brown is behind him)

Welsh Hunger Marchers, with first-aid man attending blistered feet, Severn Tunnel, October 1936

Unemployed demonstrators at the Ritz Hotel in Piccadilly, Christmas 1938

Two unemployed demonstrators being escorted off the pitch at half-time during a match between Arsenal and Charlton Athletic at Highbury, January 1939

6

Climax of Conflict, 1932

'I have worn out two pairs of clogs on this 200 mile march. I have had sore feet and blistered feet but my spirit is not broken. I am going to get to London even if I have to do the rest of the journey on my hands and knees' (Woman marcher from Burnley).

'I am convinced that a lot of these people who are going about committing disturbances are people who don't like work' (Mayor of Nottingham).

'We have got to bluff the marchers pretty hard at the start' (Poor Law inspector).

'They expect you to answer our cry for bread with batons' (NUWM leaflet 1932).[1]

These four statements give the gist of the fourth national march of 1932. They express in turn the determination of the marchers, the myth of voluntary idleness, the hostility of governing circles, and the violence which developed. The unemployed now occupied the centre of the political stage. Their dole became the main financial issue and their acquiescence a major political concern. 'The cost has been so great,' G. D. H. Cole wrote a few years later, 'that there has been a continued hunt for persons who could have their doles taken away or reduced without provoking too intense a social conflict.'[2]

The march of 1932 was no mere repetition of 1930; it was a big battalion of fifteen hundred instead of a company of three hundred and fifty, militant for struggle rather than persevering in demands for improvement. More than a reduction of 1s 9d in the dole was at stake. By 1932 it was a National Government with whose policies the Movement came into conflict.

The year 1930 was a lull before the political storm but working people felt the full blast of the economic blizzard. By

June the registered unemployed rose to 1,912,000 or 15 per cent of those insured, by December the total would be up to the unprecedented total of 2,500,000, or nearly 20 per cent. In August the Movement set itself a membership target of a hundred thousand and aimed to have a women's and youth section in every branch by the end of the year.[3] Its membership did increase, reaching 37,000 by 1931.

The main issue at the Labour Party's annual conference in October was employment policy. A move by the Independent Labour Party to attack the Government directly for its 'timidity and vacillation in refusing to apply Socialist remedies' was heavily defeated but received over 300,000 votes. Conference then accepted without division a resolution from the National Union of General and Municipal Workers calling for a more active policy. A demand for consideration of Sir Oswald Mosley's proposals was narrowly defeated by a million and a quarter votes against a million. Such support for his ideas showed the discontent within the Labour Party and was enough to ensure his election to its executive. Thereafter Mosley's refusal to compromise and his defeat by party solidarity led him to start his New Party and later, in the autumn of 1932, the British Union of Fascists.

When Parliament reopened on 28 October 1930, the King's Speech had little to say about reducing unemployment, beyond intentions to raise the school-leaving age and to introduce a Bill 'for the promotion of increased settlement and improvement on the land'. There was to be a Royal Commission on Unemployment Insurance to counteract the Conservative and Liberal pressure for the rising cost of benefit to be reduced. On the other side of the fence, the Movement decided to campaign for special extra relief during the coming winter, basing itself on the principle recognised in the days when Sir Alfred Mond was Minister of Health in 1923, and also for extra Christmas relief. The demand for Christmas week was 6s for each adult, 3s for each child, one hundredweight of coal and free boots and clothing.

Early in 1931 the Government, with Tory and Liberal pressure threatening its tenure of office, considered cutting insurance benefits, but in February it accepted a Liberal proposal for the appointment of an economic committee, and in

March it appointed Sir George May, secretary of the Pruden-
tial Assurance Company, as Chairman. The May Committee
on National Expenditure, composed of four other leading
business men, and two Labour members, was to 'make
recommendations to the Chancellor of the Exchequer for
effecting forthwith all possible reductions in the National
Expenditure, having regard especially to the present and
prospective position of the Revenue'. In February the Movement held its seventh national conference. The presence of a
hundred and twenty-four delegates including fifteen women
was an encouraging sign of growth. In the lengthy main
resolution on the 'broad immediate tasks of the NUWM',
written and moved by Wal Hannington, delegates heard about
the evidence already given to the Royal Commission, and the
probable outcome. Hannington forecast that the unemployed
to be specially singled out for attack would be part-time
workers, casual labourers, married women and youths, and the
long-term unemployed, at the same time as the case would be
made for cutting benefits for all on the grounds that the existing
scales destroyed the incentive to work.[4]

That forecast was confirmed in June by the interim report, a
majority one, of the Royal Commission. Benefit was to be
limited to twenty-six weeks in the year and to be reduced by two
shillings for each adult, while contributions from workers,
employers and the state were to be increased. A means test
would control the transitional benefit, to which many unemployed would be transferred by the limitation of ordinary
benefit. In addition the conditions under which married
women, casual, seasonal and part-time workers received
benefit were to be made much more stringent. The Government acted against these workers in a Bill to deal with
anomalies, which was to effect a saving of five million pounds.
The Bill became law without any opposition except from the
ILP and Mosley and his followers. The General Council of the
TUC had announced demonstrations against the report and
the Government was not prepared, at that stage, to reduce
benefits generally.

At the end of July 1931 the report of the May Committee, or
rather the majority report, proposed extreme measures for the
unemployed. Its estimate of a budget deficit of a hundred and

twenty million pounds was to be met by twenty-four million from new taxation, and by sixty-six and a half million from Unemployment Insurance, the rest coming mainly from cuts in the pay of teachers, the armed services and the police. It called for a 20 per cent reduction in standard benefits, i.e. cutting the basic rate from 17s to 13s 7d; raising by twopence the contributions, limiting benefit to 26 weeks in any year, and called for a means test for all transitional benefit. Given headlines in the press, the report and the alarming news of the budget deficit had immediate effects. The Cabinet appointed an economic committee to consider how far it would have to go. The Movement organised demonstrations far and wide; on Clydebank, the unemployed, of whom six were arrested, occupied the council chambers.

The downfall of the Labour Government and the formation of a national one took place rapidly during the parliamentary vacation. During July the flight from the pound, occasioned by the Austrian and German financial crisis, had resulted in London obtaining considerable credits from America and France. The May Report, with its emphasis on budgetary deficiency, taken together with the deficit in the balance of payments, created the impression that the pound was in danger, and led to a call for the Government to counteract inflation, reduce incomes, and announce its intention to protect the value of sterling and the gold standard. After warnings to the Government from City bankers that further credits would be required but that they would not be forthcoming unless the budget was balanced, the Cabinet Economy Committee met but reached no decision. In the Cabinet twelve members supported a proposal to effect the economies declared to be necessary if the credits were to be made available in New York, but nine members were against. Immediately after this split, MacDonald, with the agreement of Stanley Baldwin and Sir Herbert Samuel, formed a National Government composed of four Labour, four Conservative and two Liberal members.

The new Cabinet rapidly agreed on the economies to be made and when Parliament assembled on 8 September it approved without difficulty what had been done, and the National Economy Bill to give effect to the cuts. These were to be 10 per cent all round, in unemployment allowances and in the pay of public employees, the armed forces, the police, civil servants and even Members of Parliament, Ministers and judges, except for teachers who were to suffer by 15 per cent. Protests were immediate. The Movement started with a march of Welsh miners to the Trade Union Congress in Bristol on 7 September. Ninety-eight men came down from the Rhondda, Merthyr Vale, Clydach Vale and the Taff, mostly miners and colliers, but also many labourers, a few tin workers from Llanelly, some lads who had never worked, drivers, engineers, a tailor, a steel-erector, a haulier, a teacher of communism; all religious sects were represented – Baptists in the lead, followed by Church of England, then Roman Catholic, Methodist and a dozen with no affiliation, and all ages, from fifteen to fifty-six, most between twenty-five and forty but half under thirty. Only twenty of them were still qualified for unemployment pay, the rest depending on transitional benefit and the poor law. When a deputation led by Wal Hannington was denied a hearing by police and Congress stewards, fighting broke out during which Hannington received a blow on the head which required stitching, and six men were arrested.[5]

In London on the day Parliament reassembled, the un-employed marched to Westminster and fought in Whitehall; eighteen men were arrested of whom several received a month in prison. Ten thousand teachers, aroused by the extra large cut, marched through the streets of London. There was discontent among the police. On 15 September the mutiny in the Royal Navy at Invergordon startled the whole country. Twelve thousand sailors of the Atlantic Fleet refused to put to sea, in a well-organised strike against disproportionate cuts in the pay of ratings. Six days later the Government announced that no reductions would be greater than ten per cent. On the same day, faced with a continuing and uncontrollable run on the pound, stimulated by the mutiny, Britain came off the gold standard.

The cuts for the unemployed, which had caused the downfall of the Labour Government and had been intended to save the gold standard, remained to be put into operation. This was made clear when, at the request of two left-wing members of Parliament, Ramsay MacDonald agreed to see a deputation from the Movement and told them that the financial crisis still

made the cuts imperative. The news provoked massive demonstrations. During September 1931 tens of thousands marched
in Dundee, in Birmingham, in Manchester, and in Glasgow
where a pitched battle with the police followed.[6]

Early in the following month the Government spelt out the
cuts by two Orders in Council. The first on 1 October reduced
the rate of benefit for an adult man from 17s to 15s 3d and that
for his wife from 9s to 8s; for an adult woman from 15s to 13s 6d
and for all young persons similarly, only the 2s rate for children
being left untouched. Thus the income of a man, wife and two
children would be cut from 34s to 31s 3d per week. The second
Order of 8 October, brought in the family means test. It
separated those eligible for benefit as of right from those who
were not. The duration of benefit was limited to twenty-six
weeks per year and every claimant had to prove thirty
contributions in the preceding two years. These restrictions
excluded over half of the registered unemployed men and thus
over a million claimants, including those who had been longest
out of work, were cut off from further benefit. They were to have
a new relief called transitional payment obtained after a means
test at the hands of the local poor law authorities, i.e. the Public
Assistance Committees. Many men who now qualified only for
transitional payments had to submit to the poor law for the first
time in their lives, a humiliation they had never envisaged.
They were frequently, middle-aged skilled men who had paid
contributions for many years and regarded unemployment
benefit as a right. The Orders were to come into effect in
November, in time for the winter. In addition, married working
women became the chief subjects of the Anomalies Regulations
which had been made under the Act passed by the Labour
Government but were now to be strictly administered. By the
end of that year a hundred and thirty-four thousand of them
had been disallowed benefit.

These measures started the long protest which culminated in
the national march of 1932. The political importance of the
cuts, originating in the downfall of the Labour Government,
underlined the necessity of enforcing them, while the Movement was equally determined not to accept them. This dictated
the violence which became common. Throughout October,
November and December 1931, continual marches and de-

monstrations against the means test and to demand extra
winter relief, and to be seen and heard by the Public Assistance
Committees (PACs), in all the big towns and many smaller
ones were met, more often than not, by police baton charges.
The leaders were put out of the way: Hannington and Elias
were put in prison for a month for inciting a breach of the peace;
Harry McShane was arrested but acquitted.

At the general election in October 1931 the great majority of
voters sought the security offered by the National Government.
Many Liberals appeared to have voted Conservative; great
numbers of Labour voters, disillusioned with the Labour Party,
stayed away from the polls. In the landslide, Labour won only
forty-six seats compared with two hundred and eighty-nine in
1929. The Conservatives had a clear overall majority of three
hundred and thirty to govern under the name of a National
Government.

As 1932 opened it seemed that the cuts had been accepted in
the national interest, except for those affecting the unemployed.
The TUC sent a protest against the means test to the Minister
but did nothing more. The Government brought forward its
solution to economic depression, the Conservative policy of
protection. General tariffs on imports were imposed by the
Import Duties Bill but their only effect on the unemployed was
to add to the cost of living. At the same time the Government
intended to gain the large economies expected from the means
test. It did not have it entirely its own way, quite apart from the
agitation by the Movement which, proscribed as it was by the
Labour Party and the TUC, never let up. Labour itself could
and did resist, not in Parliament where it was helpless, but in
the Public Assistance Committees appointed by Labour-
controlled local authorities.

The means test caused bitter resentment. The test was not
one of an individual's means but of the household he lived in.
Any income of any member of the family had to be declared,
including any pensions of any kind, and savings in the Post
Office or the Co-op. The means test officer entered houses to
inspect the furnishings and might interrogate neighbours as to
claimants' means. Total income was deducted from the
standard adopted by the local PAC for its relief payments which
varied according to the custom and politics of the local council.

Often relief was below unemployment benefit, reduced as this had been. The worst effects of the means test came when young workers were expected to live on their parents' earnings or even grandparents' pensions, and parents had to rely on their children's wages. Cases such as the following were reported at that time:

> Daughter living with unemployed father, mother and younger brother under 16 years of age. She earns on an average 35s per week. Father disallowed benefit, as the daughter's earnings are 2s above the relief scale for the whole family.

> Unemployed man living with aged parents who are both in receipt of Old Age Pension of 10s per week each. Father also has a superannuation pension of 10s per week, making a total income of 30s. Son disallowed benefit and has to live on parents' pensions.

> Unemployed son living with parents receives 5s unemployment benefit from his trade union. Father earns 25s for 3 days' work. No benefit allowed.

> Widower, unemployed, living with single daughter, who is working and earning wage of 18s 6d per week. Father has life savings of £80 in bank. Under Means Test, benefit is completely disallowed and he is told he cannot receive benefit until his savings have been reduced to between £5 and £10, and that it should last him six years at 5s 6d per week.

> Unemployed miner, wife and six children. Had £15 saved in the Co-op. Means Test Committee ruled 'not a case for help so long as this sum was on deposit'.[7]

Those PACs who were opposed to the test and either refused to operate it, or did it in such a lenient way that claimants got the maximum possible relief, came into conflict with the Government and were warned of their conduct. They were mostly in areas of heavy unemployment – Glamorgan County, Merthyr Tydfil, Monmouth, Northumberland County, Barrow-in-Furness, Blackburn, Barnsley, Nelson, Oldham, Manchester, West Ham, but also in other parts – Essex County, Southampton, Stoke-on-Trent, Wolverhampton, Lincoln. Most of these, being Labour-controlled, were sympathetic to the unemployed demonstrations at their doors and not unwilling to give way to their demands. The Government, determined on the full rigour of the test, finally appointed commissioners to operate it in place of two obstinate authorities, Rotherham and County Durham. The commissioners succeeded in cutting the cost and the other rebellious PACs had to give way, but not entirely, as West Ham made known:

> We were threatened with supersession, and in face of that threat we prefer to keep our own poor under our own care and do what we can for them rather than hand them over to an arbitrary Commissioner from whom they could expect little humanity.[8]

Profiting from the resentment at the test, the Movement had hopes of winning some recognition from the TUC at the forthcoming Congress in September. It could claim to have shown its growth and influence by the number of PACs which, under pressure of numbers, had modified the means test. It was not perhaps a coincidence that the police, acting under the Metropolitan Police Act of 1839, banned the meetings which had always been held outside labour exchanges in London, the Movement's most effective sources of recruitment.

> The Commissioner directs that, in future, no meetings are to be held by unemployed or other person in close proximity of Labour Exchanges, irrespective of whether or not any actual obstruction is caused, on the ground that such meetings have been found liable to lead to breaches of the peace.

Suspecting the policy behind this, the Movement persisted so successfully that the police temporarily withdrew the ban after two months' conflict in the streets.[9]

In May the Movement organised a two-day conference against the means test which drew six hundred and fifty-seven delegates from trade unions and trades councils all over the country. The conference decided to obtain a million signatures on a petition to Parliament and to organise a national march in the autumn which would present the petition on arrival in London. The petition ran:

> To the House of Commons.
>
> We, the undersigned citizens, in view of the increasing poverty amongst the working class arising from the operation of the present Economy Measures, do hereby speak our demands on the National Government for:
>
> 1 The abolition of the Means Test.
> 2 The abolition of the Anomalies Act.

3 The restoration of the ten per cent benefit cut.
4 The restoration of the cuts which have been made in the social services.

All efforts in the Movement were now directed towards getting the one million signatures on the street corners, outside labour exchanges, in the trade union branches and Co-op Guilds, in the workshops and at public meetings, while the national administrative council concentrated on preparations for the march. The men and women in the council were, as well as Wal Hannington, Emrys Llewellyn (secretary), Sid Elias (chairman), Harry McShane (Scottish Organiser), and the area representatives – Len Youle (Yorkshire), Philip Hicken (Notts and Derby), George Jane (Lancashire), George Staunton (Manchester), Sam Langley (Northumberland and Tyneside), Jack Benjamin (South Wales), Jack Jones (Monmouthshire), Charlie Webber (Bristol and West England), Joe Rawlings (Merseyside), E. Robinson (Teesside), Tom Roberts (Midlands), Fanny Deakin (North Staffs), A. Denn (Kent) and H. Abbot (London). The authorities began to take notice and to gather information. In August the Commissioner of the Metropolitan Police informed all superintendents and districts that the Movement would concentrate on activity at labour exchanges near PAC offices as a prelude to the national march for the opening of Parliament. The national administrative council stopped recording the names of those present, as a precaution against harassment, but the Special Branch at Scotland Yard knew them through its own sources of information.

Early in September 1932 the Movement nearly succeeded in getting a hearing at the TUC in conference at Newcastle-on-Tyne. Its own conference in May had encouraged it to hope that the delegates at the TUC might overcome the leadership's opposition. The ground was well prepared with a march, some thousands strong, led by Wal Hannington, to Congress in the City Hall; the motion to receive a deputation was lost by a million votes to one and a half million. It seemed probable that the vote could have gone the other way if delegates had been consulted on the card vote of the Miners' Federation. The Movement was still on its own; it would have to reply entirely on rank-and-file sympathy, and the authorities could deal with it accordingly. The possibilities of violence were shown during the same month in Birkenhead. In that town the PAC was making transitional payments on a scale more than 3*s* below the permitted level, i.e. 12*s* instead of 15*s* 3*d*. Several thousand workers marched to demand an increase. After the Committee had made some promises, violent battles broke out with the police and raged all day. Many police as well as unemployed were injured and the police seem to have lost self-control, for during the night they broke into tenements, batoning men and women indiscriminately. Forty-five demonstrators were put on trial; Joe Rawlings, the Merseyside leader, was sentenced to two years' imprisonment. The local PAC then raised the relief scale to 15*s* 3*d*.

A week later, on 26 September, the fourth national march got under way when the Scots left Glasgow, the first of one thousand five hundred on the road to London. It was the largest, best-organised march to date. The big questions were: would the marchers get support from Labour rank-and-file, would the authorities try to stop them, would the petition reach Parliament, and, basically, how often would they meet police batons? By Guy Fawkes' Day the answers were clear enough.

If the marchers were stronger than before, the authorities were in a better position to harass them, not only because of the change of government. The reorganisation of the poor law in 1929 meant that police and poor law now came under a single authority in the counties. It was clear to the Home Office and the Ministry of Health that this should make it easier to deal rigorously with the marchers if they entered the workhouses or casual wards. Resulting from discussions between the two ministries, the memorandum of instructions sent out by the Ministry of Health to the general inspectors of the poor law on the day the Scots set out was a good deal tougher than in 1930; copies went to the Home Office for Chief Constables.

The treatment of the marchers was to be the same as before but 'in view of the changes in the poor law administration it is hoped that the poor law authorities will be less inclined to weakness in action. Their close connection with the police may help. Previous Hunger Marches have inquired in advance for accommodation and assistance and have taken advantage of any sign of weakness.' Further, there was nothing to justify the discharge of marchers from workhouses on the day after admission and they should be detained for two nights unless it was administratively impossible, and the poor law officers must be protected against intimidation. The inspectors were 'to use every effort to prevent any action likely to encourage the march or repetitions of it'.[10] Such effort was soon shown by the inspector who, fearful that Coventry Council would repeat its 'weakness' in a previous year when it accommodated the marchers in a school and paid for food supplied by the Co-op, requested a telegram from the Ministry to confirm that the Council would be surcharged if it repeated that action.

At Warwick there was promise of new cooperation between poor law authorities and the police; the NUWM wrote to the Public Assistance Officer: 'It is expected that your committee will provide food and shelter for these men, also that they will not be treated as Casuals or be put under the same restrictions', and received the reply that the Public Assistance (Casual Poor) Order of 1931 would be enforced, the chief constable having assured the assistance officer that 'the police will give all necessary assistance to your committee in dealing with them'.[11] This was in line with police instructions from the Home Office that 'strict insistence on the conditions attached to the grant of relief may give rise to disorder. Therefore the police must prevent breaking of the peace specially near Casual Wards en route.'

The Metropolitan Police were also making careful preparations. 'In the meantime,' according to a later report, 'endeavours were made to ascertain the names, addresses and other particulars of local leaders of the movement; subsequently particulars of the more notorious of the leaders, together with photographs and previous convictions, were forwarded to Divisions.'[12]

Special Branch reports poured in, from informants, more or less highly coloured. It appeared that the marshals would not lead the march but would be among the rank-and-file; dummy leaders would take their place. The march was 'to be as spectacular as possible [with] as many clashes with the police as possible'. The intention was 'to concentrate on local demonstrations to keep the police busy in the suburbs while the main demonstration forces its way to the Houses of Parliament'. There were to be 'demonstrations at Public Assistance Committees, the houses of Members of Parliament, embassies, entry into workhouses to create disturbances therein, and as much trouble as possible for the police'. One informant gave details of an NUWM conference called on 25 September to elect a reception committee. His report included the names and affiliations of the committee, which included seven trade unionists and one 'elderly woman'; the alleged remarks of Emrhys Llewellyn to the effect that all efforts of the authorities to prevent the marchers reaching the House of Commons would have to be countered (new methods would be used against the police, and new demonstrations would take place, for example, at the Stock Exchange and the West End hotels, restaurants and theatres); the contribution of chairman Fred Thompson that it was hoped to mobilise thousands of dockers who would travel to Parliament by water and demonstrate inside the Port of London; and the reply to a delegate, who asked if police permission for the march had been obtained, that it was a matter of 'direct action' not permission. All agreed, it was reported, to be prepared to resist police opposition which was certain. Special Branch also received information about the National Minority Movement, now in fact a spent force – in particular of a meeting of its executive committee, with a list of those present, at which the part to be played in the march by trade unions was emphasised – 'trade union banners to be used at demonstrations and then used in open conflict with the police'. It was reported that 'Moscow was very anxious for successful demonstrations in England as they would synchronise with troubles in Germany'.[13]

The marchers were in eighteen contingents, some small, some large, like the two hundred and fifty men from Scotland in a highly-disciplined and well-organised body, with its own first aid, cooks and field kitchens, barber and cobbler. Accommodation had to be organised in a hundred and eighty-eight main towns, and the routes, though basically the same as before, were modified to ensure as far as possible that the marchers stopped overnight in towns where there was known or potential support. Strenuous efforts had been made to form reception committees along the routes, and with considerable success. Based where possible on the NUWM branch, the committees

often included councillors, Co-op activists, disillusioned
Labour Party members, trade unionists, members of the
Independent Labour Party, and of the churches, and Communists. They raised money, organised provisions and accommodation and entertainment whenever possible, met the
marchers in procession when they entered the town, gave them
a send-off in the morning, and could turn out a crowd of
supporters for meetings or as allies if there was friction with the
poor law authorities and police. They embodied the Movement's policy of a united front of unemployed and employed,
which was intended to counter the aim of the Labour leadership to isolate it.

Of all the many reception committees, St Albans's was an
outstanding example.

A fortnight before the women's contingent assembled at
Burnley on 9 October, Maud Brown of the women's department of the National March Council wrote to W. H. Gardner,
secretary of St Albans Trades Council, reminding him that the
town had given hospitality in 1930 and asking for it again.
About fifty women were due to arrive from Luton on Monday,
24 October. The Trades Council agreed and in return received
from Maud Brown a few days later the pamphlet *Why We Are
Marching* and other material. She promised to give the number
of women as soon as the contingent arrived at Northampton on
21 October. At the same time the march treasurer, Alex Gossip,
sent St Albans ten collecting cards for fund-raising with
permission to retain all the money collected, unless there was a
surplus, contrary to the usual practice of sending half to the
national march fund.

Gardner had already begun to organise the local reception
committee of two women and four men, with himself as
secretary. At the first meeting on 6 October it was agreed to
write for help to various local organisations and sympathisers –
the St Albans Co-operative Society, the Women's Co-operative
Guild, the local Labour Party and its women's section, the
Trade Union and Labour Club. Two members were to see the
directors of the Co-op; the Friends of the Soviet Union (FSU)
were to be asked to run a dance; and collecting cards were to be
ruled up and sent round. The police were to be informed. At the

second meeting on 11 October the committee decided to have 2,000 leaflets printed and drew up a list of twelve supporters to whom they would be distributed. Maud Brown's suggestion of an outdoor or indoor meeting was put in hand. The item of food supplies was deferred for final arrangements to the next meeting on 17 October. By that time the reception committee had done its work thoroughly. The Labour Party had agreed to give the use of its rooms and to send a delegate to the committee; several Labour Party members had signed the national petition which was now displayed for more signatures; and the Labour Party had collected 2s 6d.

The Club would give its concert room for an entertainment. The Women's Co-op Guild had given 10s on the authority of its committee. The Co-op Society would not only supply bread, groceries and meat at cost price but would deduct £1 from their bill, as they had done two years before. There was still much to be done. Two comrades were to buy food, two were to see that the vegetables were delivered on the right day, and two others to prepare the vegetables. Beds were the responsibility of another comrade. Spare clothing was to be looked after by another, and the cobbler in the London Road was to be asked to be available for any boot repairs which might be required. Four other comrades would undertake any washing and supply soap, and the Club was to be asked to provide baths. Another comrade would go along the road to meet the marchers and everyone was to meet at six o'clock for their reception.

On the day the marchers were met on the outskirts of the city and were led to the market square for a short meeting. There were thirty-eight women; only two had dropped out since Burnley. The youngest of these cotton-mill workers was sixteen, the oldest sixty-three. After a hot meal at the Trade Union Club where they were to sleep the night, they returned to a second meeting in market square. 'We are out to smash the means test', cried Lily Webb. 'We are fighting for the abolition of the Anomalies Act. We are out to smash the National Government which is operating the means test and which is bringing poverty and misery to the unemployed workers. We are out to smash the present capitalist system and set up in its place socialism as our comrades in Russia did.' Mrs Paisley of Burnley, a woman of sixty-three, with sixteen children, twenty-three grandchildren and one great-grandchild, climbed the rostrum and told of her privations under the means test – 'I have had that much good food on the march that I don't want to go home.' They sang marching songs and 'The Internationale' and returned to the Club for supper and a warm social evening. In the morning, after a good breakfast and each marcher had received a packet of sandwiches, they held a third meeting in the market square before leaving for Barnet. As they marched out they called on the citizens of St Albans: 'Unite with us to smash the National Government.'

The money had come in to the reception committee readily, and in time. The collecting cards brought in £1. 10s 7d, mostly in threepenny donations; the women's adult school gave 11s 2d, the printing trade 10s, the FSU dance contributed 10s 3d; altogether £6. 12s 5d was received. Out of this they paid 18s 6d for printing, £1. 14s 2d for the Co-op bill, 2s for coal and other items, not forgetting 5s each to the Labour Party and the Trades Club for the use of their premises, totalling £3. 12s 1d. On behalf of the reception committee, Gardner was able to send a balance of £3 to the national march fund. Maud Brown wrote to him in November: 'The women have now returned from London to their various areas, though the majority of them were anxious to stop to carry on agitation against the National Government. The women will not forget the comrades who made the march very much easier by the reception that was given to them.'[14]

Largely because of that kind of support there were few serious conflicts on the road. The authorities often received, as well as a realisation of local opinion, the impact of demonstrations immediately before the arrival of the marchers. At Bolton, the day before the Scots arrived, the local NUWM marched to the PAC offices and sent in a deputation to demand an increase in the scales of transitional payments. Thousands gathered round the hundred who marched and there were cries of 'another Birkenhead' in Bolton. The local paper gave a dismal picture of the Scots' arrival; how could 'such a wet and bedraggled army reach London. Some of the marchers had old army haversacks slung on their shoulders; others not so fortunate had wrapped their possessions in sacking. I saw men who had made bits of string serve the purpose of shoulder straps and I wondered how many miles they could march before it started cutting into the flesh. A good many marchers wore open-necked khaki shirts which were sodden with rain. As the men passed a fife band played a dismal tune and there were hoarse Scottish cries of "Down with the Means Test" and "Fight for Liberty". It was a depressed and depressing procession.' The marchers were, in fact, far from downhearted. The reception committee fed all two hundred and fifty with hot potato pie, rice-pudding and tea; they had baths and a hot breakfast and declared that the hospitality was the best since leaving Scotland.[15]

When the reception committee was unable to provide sleeping accommodation because of the weight of numbers, the marchers had to fall back on the workhouse, now called 'the institution'. The main point of conflict, the casuals' diet, could be avoided if the committee gave food to supplement the diet or if the marchers collected enough money to buy it. A hundred and fifty men of the North-East contingent had 4*s* each from a collection at Ripon, and the food they bought meant that there was no need to make demands on the workhouse master for adequate nourishment. The Scots, arriving at Carlisle, took a collection, supplemented the casuals' diet with the food bought to make acceptable meals which they prepared and ate in the covered market, using the workhouse only for sleeping. This arrangement was deplored by the poor law inspector who regretted that the town council had not taken a firmer line, particularly as it would have had police support, and saw the incident as an encouraging success for the marchers in 'intimidating their first English authority'. When the Scots got to Warwick they were given only the casuals' diet but, the inspector reported, they had four hams of their own for tea, and porridge and sausages for breakfast, all excellently cooked. They had 'collected plenty of money for provisions'. Beyond a little 'lip', they were 'no trouble at all'. It was not always so. A hundred and sixty Yorkshiremen found no reception committee at Loughborough, nor help from trades council or Labour Party. Put into the Churchgate Schools, they were told to sit down to the standard supper of bread, margarine and tea. To this was added, as a concession, the cheese for the following day, so that the lunch to be taken away was just bread. They stuck this on the school railings, where it was later collected by 'certain poor townspeople who were able to put it to proper use', and they left the following message on the blackboard: 15 MILES ON FRESH AIR, WE WANT FOOD NOT DRY BREAD. They had collected £17 in the town, but had not been able to spend it.[16]

The men from Plymouth dealt with the food issue in different ways. The poor law inspector reported how this worked out at Andover when they had been on the road eleven days.

> The Advanced Guard saw the Master who stated that the Hunger Marchers would have to conform with the Casual Regulations. It included an exceedingly cheeky youth whose first remark to the Master was 'Well! Here we are. If you want trouble you can have it the same as at Shaftesbury.' This apparently referred to their stay in the Institution there, when they raided the stores and the kitchen.
>
> The main body arrived wet through at 8.0. The ring-leader said to his followers, 'Boys, we are up against it here.'
>
> They refused to be admitted on Casuals conditions and marched down to the police who asked the Salvation Army to accommodate them. They spent the night in the Salvation Army hall where they were given food and fires were lit to dry clothes. The Master lent blankets at the police request. Three police were secreted in the Institution but were not required. Two police were at the Salvation Army with orders to prevent men going out and wandering about the town at night. In the morning the police shepherded the men out as they did not want a meeting on market day. The local Labour Party gave no support to the marchers who were unable to collect a halfpenny. There was no trouble because a firm line was taken.[17]

The advance on London did not pass off so peacefully for the Lancashire and the women's contingents. The women, forty strong led by Maud Brown and Lily Webb, were on their mettle in view of criticism in the Movement of the backwardness of the women's organisation. They had avoided conflict for several days after setting out from Burnley, as reception committees were ready for them. At Rotherham where a government commissioner had been appointed to supersede the PAC, they refused to give names and addresses or be searched in the workhouse, marched out in the pouring rain and eventually re-entered on their own terms, to be rewarded in the morning with breakfast in the town hall, by courtesy of the mayor. Later at Burton-on-Trent there was nearly violence. When the women were told they must be in the workhouse by 8.0 p.m. they refused and held meetings in the market place until 9.30 p.m. while the PAC deliberated. As a large crowd gathered at the workhouse, the women were informed that they could enter if only they would give their names. Searching and bathing would be waived. However, their leader told the crowd: 'We refuse to give our names. We refuse to be treated like tramps. We are marching to London on an important mission. The workhouse authorities at Rotherham and Derby allowed us in without any restrictions whatever. They only want our names so they can victimise us.' There was a move to rush the gates and shouts of 'Don't give in', 'We'll help you'. Eventually the women went in at 11.45 p.m. on their own terms. 'We have to thank you outside for this,' they said. A 'simple meal of bread, margarine, etc.' was provided.[18]

The Lancashire contingent met violence. It had been strengthened at Northwich by a separate group from Merseyside where the recent battles in Birkenhead and Liverpool had made a deep impression. This small group of twenty-six had already shown its mettle at the Warrington workhouse. They had gone to the drying room and taken off their sodden clothes but on being told that they would be searched and would have to give up their belongings, they had dressed and left, refusing to return in spite of advice from the reception committee, and at midnight had found rest on the floor of the Independent Labour Party club. The whole contingent, two hundred and eleven strong, became the subject of particular attention by the police and the poor law inspector by the time they arrived at Market Drayton workhouse. They were reported to be 'more difficult to deal with than the Scottish' and 'to contain rough elements and resolutely refuse to be split up, the most troublesome group'. At Market Drayton they enjoyed stew for supper and porridge for breakfast. And again at Birmingham workhouse there was ham for supper as a gift from the chairman of the PAC, though the inspector did his best 'to discourage the Chairman's ill-advised action ... 50 per cent of the marchers were of a very low mentality'.

At Bromsgrove next day, the inspector reported, 'When they heard they were to have nothing but casual dietary they demonstrated in front of the Institution, shouting "We want hot-pot".' As the demonstration continued, the public assistance officer, having consulted with the chief constable, thought it wisest to have some hot-pot made, on condition that the marchers did no damage and left the drill hall clean, since the police force was inadequate. The marchers also had bully-beef for breakfast. 'This sort of thing could not be allowed to continue', the chief constable, the public assistance officer of Warwickshire and the poor law inspector all agreed. The chief constable sent a strong body of police to Stratford-on-Avon, the next stopping-place, where there was no reception committee or Labour support. Eighty-seven police were billeted in the workhouse when the marchers arrived and demanded a hot supper and bully-beef for breakfast. The public assistance officer agreed to hot-pot and when the police superintendent informed the marchers their leader said, 'We accept these conditions. We know we shall have the meat if the Superintendent tries to get it.' When the marchers wanted tea with their supper the superintendent advised the public assistance officer to allow it, but not the meat for breakfast. In the morning there was only bread, margarine and tea in buckets to be had in the timber yard. The leader told the master and the superintendent, 'There is bound to be trouble. The marchers must have meat to sustain them.' Tables and benches were broken up in protest, the police turned out. There was a fierce battle in the yard but walking sticks were no defence against truncheons and the police 'rounded them up and herded them on their way', in the inspector's words. As the marchers limped out of the town, unknown to its citizens, many had bleeding and bruised heads and limbs. The lunch they left behind was given to the deserving poor in Stratford; about a hundred and fifty school children paraded at the workhouse and each received a bag containing eight ounces of bread and two ounces of cheese. The damage to furniture amounted to the sum of twenty shillings. When the Lancashire men reached the Corn Exchange at Oxford where they were billeted two days later, a dozen doctors were in attendance to dress the head injuries of some fifty men, while the undergraduates worked to make their weekend a comfortable one. The poor law inspector reported that 'the whole affair was most satisfactory. It anyhow successfully stopped a bad "riot", and in all probability prevented much more serious trouble later on. There is nothing like being prepared for the worst.'[19]

It was a foretaste of the violence to come.

As the march drew nearer London the police were concerned whether the marchers had weapons. Public assistance officers undertook to keep them informed; workhouse masters were instructed that walking-sticks should be collected from the marchers 'as pleasantly as possible' and be re-issued in the morning. Reports came in: the Yorkshiremen had 'strong sticks'; the Scots had walking-sticks at one place, they had cudgels at another; the Tynesiders were armed with 'broomsticks which seemed to be designed for something more than walking being fitted with thongs to attach to the wrists', but the sticks turned out to be harmless; the Plymouth men, 'a weedy miserable lot, all that they seem to have in the way of weapons is ordinary walking-sticks'; a woman pushing a cart apparently loaded with blankets was a proper object of suspicion. The police had been able to produce some weapons captured at Stratford in support of their inquiry. The Metropolitan police banned the carrying of sticks by demonstrators in London. As the marchers came to the outskirts of London they countered this by concealing their walking sticks on their person, but the women, finding this difficult, had their sticks confiscated. The obsession with weapons was fed by reports of conversations overheard in public houses about demonstrators' intentions to throw vitriol and feathered darts at the police and pepper in the eyes of their horses.[20]

Scotland Yard believed that the best way to disarm the marchers was to watch their leaders and arrest them when necessary. It now had the names and records not only of the well-known men like Hannington and McShane but, by dint of passing photographs along the routes, also of marchers who had any kind of police record. The Government use of such information to discredit the marchers in 1922 was still on the files. The men now described would be easy to pick up. There were twelve from the North East, eleven from Scotland, three from Norfolk – half of them recorded for offences such as rioting and assault. The chief menace to law and order seemed to be in the South Wales contingent. Out of a hundred and ten men –

colliers, labourers, seamen, foundry men, tin workers – fifteen were described as men to be watched: 'professional agitator under recognisances to keep the peace', 'dangerous man and should be well noted, convicted of rioting', 'dangerous man – against all law and order, convicted of rioting', 'violent revolutionary tendencies, convicted of riot', 'distinct menace, convicted of riot'. A report from the workhouse master at Leicester, was consistent with this information:

> From my personal conversation with various small groups of men accommodated at this Institution I am convinced that the protest against the Means Test occupied only a small place in the minds of the men. The only aim strongly expressed by them was that the solution to all our present Economic difficulties was to be found in the adoption of a Soviet State for this country.[21]

It was a small step to a search for the Moscow connection.

During the weeks prior to the arrival of the marchers, detectives and informers swarmed all over the haunts of the Movement and the Communist Party in London. Reports poured in daily from the working-class districts, reports of public meetings in the streets and on the greens, of private meetings of the reception committees, of local activists of the Movement and even of its council, and of the Communist Party. Long lists of activists were compiled, and the names of all who opened their mouths, with revolutionary or counter-revolutionary sentiments. The numbers present at meetings, and sums collected, were noted in detail.

The meetings of the All-London Reception Committee at 35 Great Russell Street were infiltrated, and the membership of its sub-committees for organisation, accommodation, catering and for presentation of the petition were reported. Inflammatory remarks alleged to have been made were duly noted: nothing would stop the marchers getting to the House of Commons, no interference would be tolerated, men were entitled to take whatever means they liked against an onslaught, heads would get broken but the police would be overcome by force of numbers, ex-soldiers must give instructions in methods of defence, guerrilla tactics would be required, special groups must be formed to dismount the police and ride into the foot police, trip ropes would stop the mounted, street committees must be established to eliminate informers. The stream of information continued: in Hyde Park on 27 October many would march well armed, men would be detailed to saw through the railings and carry the short iron bars up their sleeves; the committee of young pioneers would bring children so as to hamper the police; missiles would be accumulated.

> Six young men left the meeting and were followed by me. They took a devious route to the edge of the Thames at Limehouse opposite Stepney Power Station. They ran down a cut to the river's edge, the tide was out, where they dug up large stones, placed them in a sack and carried the sack back where they entered with the stones. Observation continued.

The reports poured into Scotland Yard from all quarters, from Croydon, Fulham, West Ham, Canning Town, Stratford, Bethnal Green, Limehouse, Barking, Hammersmith, Chiswick, Brentford, Hayes, Greenford, Uxbridge, Acton, Southall, Walthamstow, Tottenham, Hackney, Camden Town, Edmonton, Battersea, Southwark, Willesden, Deptford, Westminster, Brixton. As yet no Moscow connection could be uncovered.[22]

The London District of the Movement was in a ferment of activity with the organisation of reception committees, the collection of signatures, intensification of propaganda in the streets, open-air meetings daily and demonstrations by the score, setting up local cadres of leadership in order to secure maximum support on 27 October and the days following. The national administrative council was settling on a course of action for presenting the petition. Rejecting the services of any Member of Parliament, it resolved to call on the ancient right of citizens to be heard at the Bar of the House of Commons; the petition must be presented by a deputation of the marchers themselves, whatever the opposition. Conservative members of Parliament alleged in the Commons that the march was organised in Moscow and demanded that it should be stopped from reaching London. A preliminary conflict between the unemployed and the police gave rise to debate in Parliament. On 18 October, while a deputation from the Movement met the leaders of the London County Council in County Hall with demands for more relief, there were demonstrations outside. When the unemployed began to assemble in St George's

Circus, mounted and foot police attacked in force. They fought back with bricks and stones throughout the evening but were eventually driven off. Over forty were arrested, many were injured, as were some thirty police. When a second deputation visited the London County Council, County Hall was packed with an overwhelming force of a thousand police.[23]

In the House of Commons next day Labour spokesmen drew attention to the police action and obtained time for a debate. George Lansbury, leader of the Parliamentary Labour Party, said that these disturbances throughout the country were due to unemployment. In the past the authorities had carried out their duty of allowing demonstrations of the unemployed. The tendency now was to get another kind of police in the metropolis and, as he read, in Birkenhead, where half a dozen police on motor cycles had charged at people as if they were an armed crowd. In London there were the new horse patrols who carried long staves and used them very effectively. Now these heavily armed police could take action and charge without the Riot Act being read or any magistrate being present. On the previous evening in Lambeth, in Wackwood Terrace and Russell Gardens, the police had charged from the two ends of the street to the centre and many people going about their business were hurt. People had opened their houses to shelter others and pelted the police who were battering on their doors. Before armed mounted police charged there should be a warning. As for the conditions of the unemployed they were worse than ever. It was these conditions, not the Communist Party or the NUWM, which was stirring people up. The Government should organise hospitality for the marchers and send them back with a promise to revoke the 'damnable means test'. George Buchanan, member for Gorbals, followed: the demonstration was making those same demands for work and increased relief which the Prime Minister had once made; men fought back against what they saw as police aggression because of fear of starvation and of the police; what instructions to deal with them severely had the Home Secretary given? The Home Secretary denied any wish for conflict. He felt he need only refer to the connection between Moscow and the NUWM, the Communist calls for mass struggle in the streets to compel the Government to abandon the means test, the quantity of missiles used, and the number of police injured. George Hicks, veteran trade unionist followed:

> The unemployed try to call the attention of the authorities to their plight. The authorities issue instructions to their forces, forces that have been generally regarded as being guardians, not as persons employed for the special purpose of bludgeoning and batoning people who have just grievances and desire to ventilate them. If this present policy is to be pursued with mounted police charging into crowds and if this batoning of people goes on there is bound to be resentment aroused. The authorities give instructions to our police forces, either mounted or on foot, but particularly to the mounted police to charge into crowds in the way they do. The Home Secretary said the people should not be there. Our place is with the people who are suffering, it is no desire of theirs that they are unemployed or poor. We ask you to recognise the right of these people to assemble and present their grievances. We ask you to instruct your forces to withhold from savage and brutal attacks on them and we ask that substantial relief shall be given to them in their misery and suffering until changed conditions lead to general employment.

Finally Sir Stafford Cripps, former Solicitor-General, tried a different approach. It was known that the Government had in mind some alleviation of the means test. Why did it not make its intention clear now so as to reduce the threat of more disorder? Were the unemployed to believe that rioting was the only way to win concessions, as the battles in Birkenhead and Belfast had shown? He himself had refused to lead unemployed demonstrations in Bristol because they could produce disorder but he could not continue to refuse if rioting was needed for results. In reply, Ramsay MacDonald promised to make a statement. Two days later, this revealed that the Government would, when it was ready, introduce a Bill on the means test, without saying anything as to its contents.[24]

The Government again defined its attitude three days before the marchers were due when Major Attlee, vice-chairman of the Parliamentary Labour Party, asked: 'Will the Minister of Health tell the London Public Assistance Authorities to say that the usual facilities for persons in need are available for the Hunger Marchers and to specify accommodation and areas where available in order to avoid confusion and disorder?' The answer was that they had to deal with a Communist organisation and it was not the duty of the authorities to help political demonstrations by making exceptional arrangements. The Minister denied, however, in reply to James Maxton, that the fact of Communist organisation made any difference to the treatment given. A Conservative Member thought that the marchers should pay for themselves with the large sum of £37 which they had collected and banked. Well before this in fact the London County Council had already given Scotland Yard the information Major Attlee asked for but on the understanding that it did not leak in case it gave comfort to the Movement.[25]

On Thursday, 27 October, at 2.30 p.m. the disciplined columns of marchers rounded the Marble Arch and entered Hyde Park to take up their positions at the seven carts drawn up as platforms. A crowd of a hundred thousand which had converged from all parts of London, covering the whole area and the neighbouring roads, waited. The police had had all contractors' and road repair material removed from the sites near Marble Arch and Grosvenor Square. Two thousand six hundred police including a hundred and thirty-six mounted were on parade. This total included seven hundred and fifty-eight special constables. It was with them that the violence started.

These part-time policemen, always intensely disliked by working men, vilified in the *Daily Worker*, were drawn up along the pavement from the gates into the Park, as their inspector put it, 'receiving for the first time their first dose of real trouble'. Resentful of 'the general attitude of the rabble', they became restive under the pressure and abuse of the crowd, drew their batons and struck out, in their confusion felling a plain-clothes detective to the ground, but were unable to hold their ground and had to be rescued by mounted police. These charged repeatedly and vigorously into the crowds massed in the Park and around the platforms. Bitter fighting continued throughout the afternoon, men tearing up iron railings and stripping branches from the trees to defend themselves. Two observers, Reginald Reynolds, general secretary of the 'No More War Movement', and his friend James Grant were there to see for themselves 'how much truth there was in the statements that the police treated the unemployed demonstrations as an occasion for beating up people'.

They wrote:

> There was a lot of booing going on from the unemployed towards the police gathered there, but otherwise no sign of any kind of disorder or disturbance being created by the unemployed. Suddenly, for no apparent reason, the mounted police accompanied by foot police began to charge the crowd right and left, the mounted police produced long wooden staves with which they began to belabour anybody who happened to fall foul of them, both unemployed and innocent spectators and passers-by. Next, the mounted police made a charge into Hyde Park at the Marble Arch end, and proceeded to lay about innocent citizens and unemployed alike with their staves.
>
> Turning round we were faced with a body of mounted police bearing down upon us, one of whom made a rush for Mr Reynolds with his stave, at the same time calling out 'Get out of the b—— road or ——'. The next performance of these riders was to charge into the peaceful groups standing around the meetings. People were forced to run for their lives in order to escape being trampled upon by the police horses or beaten by staves. There was no kind of disorder at any of these meetings, and no reason at all for the police to charge into them in the wanton way they did ... It would be of some importance to know just what kind of instructions are issued to the police on occasions of this kind.[26]

As dusk fell, the speeches from the carts ended, bugles recalled the marchers to their places, and the contingents, still disciplined and steady, marched off without interference to their workhouse accommodation.

The official figures of casualties were nineteen police and fifty-eight demonstrators, while fourteen were arrested in what the Home Secretary called a 'general mêlée'. Scotland Yard received protests from trade union branches against savage attacks on men, women and children, and unsolicited testimonials from ladies and their maids living in Great Cumberland Place and clerks of works and foremen at Cumberland Hotel who had witnessed workmen pelting the police. The Yard, still hunting for weapons and any other evidence of revolutionary intent, searched a marchers' van, found suspicious contents and arrested 'P' for trying to remove them. Instructions were issued: 'P is a well known Communist agitator and was in possession of £40. Get somebody good on to this and see if possible to connect P with this van.' The contents proved to be walking-sticks and collecting-boxes and 'P' could only be fined £5 for obstruction. Out of a hundred persons searched for weapons three were arrested and charged.[27]

In Parliament McGovern and Maxton raised the question of presentation of the national petition only to be told that they must be in possession of the petition from those persons who wished to appear at the Bar of the House. They then tried to move the adjournment on a matter of public importance, i.e. to discuss the question that:

> In view of the fact that thousands of unemployed Hunger Marchers have arrived in London from all parts of Britain to bring to the notice of the Government the evil effects of unemployment and recent legislation, namely the means test, health and social service cuts, the Anomalies Act, the taking away of maternity grants from the wives of unemployed men, and also the large number of evictions due to inability to pay high rents, we desire to know forthwith the intentions of the Government with regard to this serious and tragic state of affairs in relation to millions of working-class homes.

The Speaker refused permission on the grounds that the Government had promised a Bill to deal with unemployment.[28]

On the following Sunday, the 30th, there were similar scenes of violence in Trafalgar Square where the crowd overflowed into Charing Cross Road, Northumberland Avenue, the Strand and the north end of Whitehall. Appeals to keep away by the BBC had had little effect.[29] The newspapers called for the arrest of Wal Hannington and his fellow plotters of revolution. They claimed that every disorder so far was merely a preliminary to the attempt to be made on 1 November to present the petition at the Bar of the House, but that provided the police stood firm, all would be well. Stickers had appeared: 'Policemen! Defeat your own pay cuts by supporting Tuesday's demonstration against the Economies!' Leaflets called on the police for sympathy.

In Trafalgar Square Hannington had appealed to the police not to use their truncheons against the unemployed and employed who were acting together: 'Let the working class in

AN APPEAL TO THE POLICE

We, the unemployed workers, are fighting for Bread, for Work, Against the Means Test, for No More Economies.

You London Police know what the Governments' Economies have meant for us. As you walk the streets you see on every side of you the hunger, the misery, the bitter suffering forced on us and our families.

You, also, do not escape. To-day you are faced with another pay cut. Despite promise made you, despite your Albert Hall protest, the Government bluntly tells you that "there is no alternative but to insist on the full police economies decided, ou last year."

Yet these same people rely on you to smash our fight against starvation.

They use you repeatedly to break up our Demonstrations. At Hyde Park, on Thursday, they ordered you to attack us. And they expect you to do the same again at Tuesday's Demonstration; To answer our cry for bread with batons.

Why do it? Why act as thugs against hungry men and women? Why fight for the parasites who wallow in luxury while we, the masses, starve?

We call on you. Help us in the fight to end the economies. Keep out of the way on Tuesday. Your own relatives are among our number. And only by support our fight against the economies can you defeat the cut in your own pay.

This is our call to you. But we also warn you. If you attack us, we shall know how to defend ourselves, how to fight back.

REMEMBER BIRKENHEAD!
REMEMBER BELFAST!
(The London Unemployed.)

NUWM leaflet addressed to the police, 1932.

uniform and out of uniform stand together in defence of their conditions.'

On Monday morning the Prime Minister told the Cabinet how he would deal with the petition. He had received a letter from the so-called hunger marchers asking to be received at the Bar of the House and his reply would be to send a copy of *Hansard* reporting the debate on the previous Thursday. If Mr McGovern (ILP member for Glasgow, Shettleston) presented the petition that day the Prime Minister would say very little but if necessary he would reply that he would carefully examine the proposed Resolution and announce a decision the following day. If Mr McGovern still pressed for procedure he would say that two-and-a-half days had already been assigned to a debate on unemployment and that legislation was to be introduced shortly. The Home Secretary, the Conservative Lt.-Col. Sir John Gilmour, who had just replaced the Liberal Herbert Samuel, pressed for steps to be taken to remove the marchers out of London where they were a heavy burden on the police. The Cabinet meeting dealt with this by requesting a memorandum from the Minister of Health, in consultation with the Minister of Labour, on 'the question of getting rid of the Hunger Marchers from London'. The Movement had, however, already repudiated McGovern's claim to be its spokesman in the House as he was obliged to admit that afternoon, when he also named Wal Hannington and Harry McShane as the advocates of direct action. The House received his explanation sympathetically, and *Punch* marked the welcome disclosure with a cartoon showing McGovern eating a piece of humble-pie labelled as a present from the hunger marchers.[30] The intention of the Movement was clearly announced in its leaflets.

The same evening, while the marchers' control council was meeting, an agent provocateur left a letter for Hannington which implicated him and McShane in plans for violence against the Cabinet Ministers and for setting fire to Government buildings. The council burnt it. Next morning the authorities arrested Hannington and charged him with the lesser though serious crime of 'attempting to cause disaffection among members of the Metropolitan Police contrary to the Public Act 1919'. The Court, by remanding him in custody for a week, effectively removed him from the centre of agitation at a critical point.

The demonstration to support the national petition went ahead. The plan was that the petition would be deposited in large bundles in the cloakroom of Charing Cross Station where it would be collected by the fifty-man deputation who were to carry it down Whitehall to Parliament. By that time thousands of men were to march from all quarters to within a mile of Parliament, break up into small groups and reassemble in force in Parliament Square to carry the deputation forward into the House of Commons.

Scotland Yard had an unprecedented concentration of three thousand one hundred and seventy-four police, including two hundred mounted, ready to defend Parliament from assault. Horses had been borrowed from the army and hired from riding-schools. Eight hundred special constables were on parade but, this time, only to relieve the police of their regular duties. The press had called for strong measures. 'Peremptory warning should be given that the rule against processions of any sort coming near the approaches of Parliament will be enforced to the letter. Sentimental weakness in handling the situation will only ensue in more disturbances and a longer list of casualties. These marches are a public nuisance and a public danger,' cried the *Daily Telegraph*. The plan miscarried. As the deputation, led by Sid Elias and Emrhys Llewellyn, collected the bundles of petition at Charing Cross, the police closed the gates of the station yard, overpowered the deputation and confiscated the petition. The news did not reduce the demonstrators' determination to reach Parliament Square. They pushed forward from all directions, northwards up Victoria Street, south from Trafalgar Square and west over Westminster Bridge, and there was heavy fighting. The battle for those areas continued until midnight, spreading out north to the Edgware Road and south over the river to the Westminster Bridge Road and beyond. Forty-two arrests were made including only two marchers, but one of them 'a pronounced revolutionist with previous convictions'. The official number of injured was twelve police, thirty-two demonstrators.[31]

Next day in the House of Commons James Maxton and David Kirkwood pleaded with the Government to send the marchers home, without effect. The police, having handed back the now innocuous bundles of the petition, arrested Sid Elias and charged him with 'attempting to cause discontent and disaffection and ill-will between different classes of His Majesty's subject and to create public disturbances against the police'. This charge was based on a letter, sent by Elias to the Movement in London when he was in Moscow, which had been seized with all other records at the time of Hannington's arrest two days earlier. At last something had been found to establish the Moscow connection. The *Sunday Despatch* announced on the front page: HUNGER MARCH BACKED BY RED GOLD. FIVE THOUSAND POUNDS IN HARD CASH SMUGGLED FROM MOSCOW INTO BRITAIN. FOMENT HATE, COMMAND. BOL- SHEVIST AGENTS WHO PLOT TO COERCE UNEMPLOYED. SECRET PAYROLL. It stated that the source of this inside information was a 'London Communist Official' who had told how the cash had been brought in by courier and how he himself had been given a £100 Bank of England note by the wife of a Russian diplomat with which to carry on propaganda.[32]

While Hannington and Elias were in custody the Movement had to decide the next steps; whether to return home or stay on, perhaps bring in reinforcements and renew the struggle for the petition. The London County Council helped towards a decision by announcing that casual ward conditions would be applied at the workhouses, and in exchange obtained an assurance that the marchers would leave within three days at their own expense. Many marchers had had enough; the small South Coast contingent broke away on its own. The return of all the rest took place as an organised body on 5 November, sufficient money for railway fares at reduced rates having been collected. The national petition was not to be filed away. The plan was that the marchers were to continue the campaign in their home towns, particularly for extra winter relief, and that there would be another attempt to present the petition on 19 December which would be a day of national demonstration.[33]

The imprisoned leaders remained to be dealt with. A *Punch* cartoon entitled 'Master of the Situation' set the tone; in the background an orderly march of respectable unemployed, in the foreground a villainous character holding an ugly cosh being arrested by a stalwart policeman saying, 'We've nothing against the genuine article but we've had enough of you'. Hannington's defence at Bow Street Court was that he did not cause disaffection in the police force since there was evidence in the *Police Review* that it already existed. The magistrate assured him that he had not damaged his case by conducting it himself, but sentenced him to three months' imprisonment. That was Hannington's fifth term in prison within ten years.

The trial of Sid Elias at the Old Bailey was a more serious affair. It was alleged that Elias, in a letter he sent from Moscow, incited Hannington and Llewellyn to stir up the hunger marchers to acts of disorder. There was no doubt about the existence of the letter, although neither Hannington nor Llewellyn ever received it, but it contained nothing which could not be read in the *Daily Worker*, referring, for example, to the need for strike action in support of the marchers. It was clear that Elias had relations with the Communist International and this, reinforced by the judge's summing up, was enough to convince the jury of his guilt. In passing sentence Mr Justice Charles commented: 'One knows from the evidence and from one's own knowledge to an extent that the activities of this National Unemployed Workers' Movement are as inimical to the interests of the working man as anything one can well imagine. The result of your efforts has been disorder, riot and damage in various parts of this land. The maximum sentence I can pass upon you is in my judgement far, far too short. You will go to prison for two years.' A woman shouted, 'How dare you arrogate to yourself the right to speak on behalf of the workers and to perpetrate this frame-up', and as she was removed cried, 'To hell with capitalist justice.' In the *New Statesman*, Lord Allen of Hurtwood, uttered a word of protest: 'The use of the words "discontent and dissatisfaction" in the indictment are a serious menace to our legitimate civil liberties; it challenges the right to arouse dissatisfaction against the established order. Is not common action desirable to watch this question?' It was probably the first step towards the formation of a council for civil liberties.[34]

Five days after Elias's trial the Government made a clean sweep by arresting the Movement's secretary, Emrhys Llewellyn, and its treasurer, the veteran Tom Mann, seventy-six-year-old pioneer of trade unionism. While Elias was awaiting trial the Cabinet had appointed a committee on the hunger marchers, consisting of the Home Secretary, the Minister of Health, the Secretary of State for Scotland, the Attorney-General and the Lord Advocate, and shortly adopted its recommendations, attaching particular importance to the third of them. They were:

1 That before resorting to new legislation further trial should be given to the procedure by which a Court of Summary Jurisdiction may, upon complaint, order any person to enter into a recognisance and find sureties to keep the peace or be of good behaviour.
2 That if this experiment proves unsuccessful the question of strengthening the existing law should be again considered.
3 That the present Committee should be authorised to proceed with the examination of the existing powers relating to matters such as the importation of funds destined for seditious purposes, and communist propaganda in the Services.

In view of the prospect of renewed agitation to present the petition, the Committee had drawn attention to the Court of Summary Jurisdiction, authorised by an Act of Edward III, and had minuted that 'in view of the very serious disturbances which accompanied the recent Hunger March in London the procedure should be more widely used'. It had made the third recommendation because in its view existing powers had been found inadequate, as the judge remarked when sentencing Elias.[35]

Under the Act of Edward III as well as the Seditious Meetings Act of 1817, Mann and Llewellyn went to prison on 17 December, two days before a demonstration in London was again to demand that the petition be received by Parliament. At Bow Street Court they were ordered to be bound over to keep the peace in the sum of £200 in their own recognisances and each to find two sureties of £100, or else go to prison for two months. Both chose prison. Tom Mann spoke out in court:

If I am to be tied, if my mouth is to be closed, if I am not to participate in voicing the grievances of those who are suffering, while the incompetency of those responsible cannot find work for them, and is knocking down their miserable standards still lower, then whatever the consequences may be – if I am to be shot in the next five minutes – I would not consent to any undertaking. Regardless of my age or anything else I will not give an undertaking not to be identified with the further organisation of mass demonstrations and the ventilation of the troubles of the unemployed and of the workers generally. What am I here for? What offence have I committed to give anyone the right even to call me a 'disturber of the peace'? I believe that it is entirely unwarranted.

Protests poured into the Home Office, notably from the National Council of Labour. George Lansbury asked in Parliament whether it was to be taken for granted now that the holding of demonstrations of the unemployed would be forbidden; did the Home Secretary think that the unemployed demonstrated for the fun of the thing or perhaps to draw attention to their many grievous ills?[36] But it was without effect. All four leaders of the Movement remained in jail until February 1933.

What had resulted from the violent conflict of 1932? There was a wider realisation of the resentment against the means test and that, however active the Communist leaders of the Movement were, marchers and unemployed would not willingly face police truncheons without good cause. The allegations concerning Moscow gold did not carry much conviction. In Parliament some impression had been made. The conflict had contributed to a three-day debate on unemployment and the Government had made a concession with meaning for many unemployed. This was the legislation promised while the marchers were approaching London, the Transitional Payments (Determination of Needs) Act. Under it, half of a disability pension or workman's compensation or savings up to £25 were not to be counted when the means of a claimant were assessed. So much could be claimed as a victory. The morale of the Movement remained high, higher if anything, because of the severity of the conflict and the imprisonment of its leaders; that was taken to be proof of the Government's alarm. The marchers had developed greater discipline and courage and had given a strong lead to the unemployed, while the rank-and-file of the labour movement had rallied to them in spite of discouragement from the leadership. There had been public expression of disquiet over the provocative use of the police.

The trials had begun to arouse middle-class Labour sympathisers in the cause of civil liberty. Strong criticism appeared in the weekly journals at the end of 1932 of the use of the 1817 Gagging Act as much for the infringement of liberty as for the bonus of propaganda it offered to the Communists. 'This is precisely what bourgeois democracy means in actual practice', said the *Daily Worker*. In *Time and Tide* Amabel Williams-Ellis, Storm Jameson and Vera Brittain conveyed the growing sympathy for the unemployed:

> The arrest of Mann and Llewellyn was only one in a list of imprisonments and fines of unemployed leaders. The most important point about the recent demonstrations and hunger marches is this. Other minorities have channels for airing grievances. The unemployed who have the most serious complaint are the least articulate. Their way of saying what they want to say is taken from them if it is made impossible for them to demonstrate or to hold meetings or to state their case directly, whether it be to Parliament or to the local Public Assistance Committee. Can it be that the Government are so anxious to silence them because it would rather not hear too much of what it feels like to try to feed a child on two shillings a week? It is with considerable disquiet that we see a National Government attempting to suppress the views of any body of its subjects and especially that section which has the fewest opportunities of making itself heard. The unemployed are muzzled as they have no other means of publicity for their grievances.

Similar sentiments appeared in the *Week End Review*. That journal attacked the Bishop of Durham for his 'pharisaical letter' rejecting George Lansbury's appeal for a Christian crusade which, whatever its weaknesses, was 'backed by a depth of feeling which was coming to be shared by evergrowing numbers of the public'. The Cabinet should not try to dispose of the Hunger Marchers through rough treatment, men whose main crime was that they reminded the Government of its incompetence. The arrest of Hannington would do no more than soothe certain newspapers which had been crying for his blood. He and the Hunger Marchers had 'put unemployment on the map, and this was a genuine gain'.[37]

The 1932 march was the last one to take place during the period of the Communist Party's 'Class-against-Class' line. Not that the line had continued with undiminished purity since 1929 – it had in fact been considerably modified. The idea that the National Minority Movement should lead industrial struggles independently of the trade unions had been discarded towards the end of 1931 in favour of building up rank-and-file movements within the existing unions. The joint activity between Communist and non-Communist trade union activists had a growing impact. The support given to the 1932 march by local trade unionists and by trades councils, despite the disapproval at TUC headquarters, was one symptom of a change in climate.

On the other hand, the attitude of the Communist Party to the Labour Party had not changed since the latter had been denounced as a capitalist party in 1929. This was no doubt responsible for the decision of the NUWM leadership to refuse to allow either McGovern or any other MP to present the Movement's petition to the House of Commons, and to insist on the attempt to deliver the petition by a deputation of fifty direct to the House of Commons, regardless of opposition. The fact that the Labour Party had in 1930 listed the NUWM as a proscribed organisation, and the Movement's refusal to allow any MP to act as a sponsor, made it much easier for the Government to respond to the march with unusually repressive measures.

REFERENCES

1. *Hertfordshire Advertiser*, 28.10.32; *Nottingham Journal*, 18.10.32; PRO MH 57/101; NUWM archive leaflet, 1932.
2. G. D. H. Cole, *The Condition of Britain*, 1937, p. 205.
3. NUWM National Administrative Council, August 1930.
4. NUWM, *Report to Seventh National Conference*, 21–23.2.31.
5. PRO MH 57/100; NUWM NAC, 3–4.10.31.
6. NUWM NAC, 3–4.10.31.
7. Hannington, *Ten Lean Years*, 1940, pp. 40–3.
8. *Daily Herald*, 1.11.32, quoted in N. Branson & M. Heinemann, *Britain in the 1930s*, 1971, p. 38.
9. PRO Mepol 2/3064.
10. PRO MH 57/101.
11. Warwick CRO 1238/9.
12. PRO Mepol 2/3071.
13. PRO Mepol 2/3064.
14. *Hertfordshire Advertiser*, 28.10.32; Private communication.
15. *Bolton Evening News*, 11.10.32; PRO MH 57/101.

16. PRO MH 57/101; *Cumberland News*, 6.10.32; *Nottingham Guardian*, 20–21.10.32.
17. PRO MH 57/101.
18. PRO MH 57/101; *Derby Evening Telegraph*, 18.10.32; *Yorkshire Evening News*, 14.10.32; Hannington, *Unemployed Struggles*, p. 245.
19. PRO MH 57/101; Warwick CRO 1238/9; *Birmingham Mail*, 24.10.32; Hannington, op. cit., pp. 243–4.
20. PRO MH 57/101.
21. PRO Mepol 2/3064; MH 57/101.
22. PRO Mepol 2/3064.
23. PRO Mepol 2/3071, 2/3064; *New Statesman & Nation*, 29.10.32; Hannington, op. cit., pp. 245–6.
24. *Parliamentary Debates*, vol. 269, 19.10.32.
25. PRO MH 57/101; Mepol 2/3071.
26. PRO Mepol 2/2518, 2/3065; *New Statesman & Nation*, 5.11.32.
27. PRO Mepol 2/2518, 2/3065, 2/3071; *Parliamentary Debates*, vol. 269, 28.10.32.
28. *Parliamentary Debates*, vol. 269, 27.10.32.
29. PRO Mepol 2/3071.
30. PRO CAB 23/72; *Punch*, 9.11.32.
31. Hannington, op. cit., pp. 254–5; McShane, op. cit., p. 192; PRO Mepol 2/3066, 2/3071.
32. McShane, op. cit., p. 193; *Sunday Despatch*, 6.11.32.
33. PRO MH 57/102; *Daily Telegraph*, 5.11.32.
34. *Punch*, 9.11.32; *The Times*, 13.12.32; *New Statesman*, 24.12.32.
35. PRO CAB 23/73, CP 434/32.
36. *Time and Tide*, 3.12.32; Hannington, op. cit., pp. 266–7.
37. *Week End Review*, 22.10.32; *New Statesman*, 24 & 31.12.32; *Time and Tide*, 31.12.32.

7

Friends and Comrades, 1934

On 6 March 1934 a superintendent of the Metropolitan Police reported:

> It is remarkable that there was no disorder, no arrests, no personal injury or damage to property, not a truncheon drawn and no complaints against the Police during the whole period of contact with the Hunger Marchers. The morale of all ranks was splendid and their duty performed in a happy spirit.[1]

When the fifth national march started in January 1934 it was only a year and three months since the fourth march had returned home, but there was a marked difference between the two. The chief contrast for the marchers was the absence of violent conflict with the authorities. If the above report had referred to the whole march it would not have been misleading. Only at Birmingham and Cambridge was there almost an outbreak of violence but it was averted. In London, as the Home Secretary explained, 'the position was different from the last time; the marchers were now supported by four Members of Parliament'.[2] This year the situation had changed and peaceful demonstration was now possible.

The background to this change was the coming to power of Hitler. Over the next few years, socialists and communists in many countries came to regard the threat of fascism as an issue overriding all others. When Hitler became Chancellor of Germany on 30 January 1933, both the Socialist and Communist Internationals issued calls for united working-class resistance to fascism. Although nothing came of it so far as those two bodies were concerned, the Communist Party of Great Britain appealed to the Labour Party, the TUC, the Cooperative Party and the Independent Labour Party to form a united front. So began the change in Communist policy from 'Class against Class' to 'People's Front'.

Only the ILP, which had recently disaffiliated from the Labour Party, responded to the invitation; in fact it had already issued its own call for united action. In the ensuing months joint demonstrations were called by the Communist Party and the ILP, and a working agreement for resistance to fascism and activity on other issues was reached.

Predictably, the Labour Party rejected the Communist Party's approach for united action, but, faced with the growth of anti-fascist sentiment in its own ranks, it decided to do more than merely dismiss the offer of association with the Communist Party and in June 1933 issued a warning in the pamphlet, *The Communist Solar System*, against what it called 'Communist auxiliary organisations'. The NUWM was amongst them, classed as 'a mere instrument of the British Communist Party'. In this continued drive to isolate the NUWM, the Labour Party was joined by the TUC which had made its own attempts to provide for the unemployed by means of local Unemployed Associations organised by the trades councils. They were intended to be 'organising auxiliaries of the Trade Union Movement', not bodies for protest.[3] Their failure to make headway against the NUWM could hardly have improved the relationship between the two organisations.

Despite these efforts the Labour ban on the 1934 march was much less effective than before in discouraging trades councils and local Labour Parties. The call from the NUWM to support official Labour became stronger as the Communist Party line of the united front quickly permeated the Movement. Anti-fascists in the localities were drawn to support the march when they saw the NUWM and the Communist Party as active leaders against the twin evils of unemployment and fascism. They were not the only ones to change their attitude. Sir Herbert Samuel, who as Home Secretary had condemned the NUWM, in 1934 demanded that the House of Commons should hear the marchers.

For the unemployed conditions of living worsened, if anything, during 1933. Their number was slowly falling from the peak of almost three million, registered in January, to two and a quarter million in December. There were probably another half million living under the poor law. One in three had been out of work for six months or longer, many for much longer. More jobs in the prosperous parts of Britain towards the end of the year meant little to the men in South Wales, Scotland and the North East, except the relatively few who were able and willing to migrate. Nor could a small fall in the cost of living do much to enrich the lives of a family existing on 27s 3d a week, the result of the cuts in benefit in 1931. Men, women and children had now been bearing the full brunt of the household means test for more than a year. Because more men were out of work for longer periods, more were undergoing the means test for transitional payments. By the end of 1933 there were more men on the means test than were drawing insurance benefit. The improvement hoped for from the Transitional Payments (Determination of Needs) Act had turned out to be little more than standardisation of the deductions made by local authorities. The whole of a disability pension was not allowed for, and the exemption of £25 worth of savings came to have less and less meaning as periods of unemployment lengthened. The misery of the means test continued. Sometimes it led to suicide. The Government's plans for the unemployed began to unfold. To the Movement they appeared to combine the stick and the carrot. As the marchers returned home in November 1932 they learned from the newspapers that the Royal Commission on Unemployment Insurance had issued its final report. Its recommendations were bound to shape the reforms which the Government was planning. The Movement saw them as a threat to the lives of the unemployed because of the changes proposed.

First, the insurance scheme was to be made actuarially sound and self-supporting by contributions, as before, from workers, employers and the state. Second, all those unemployed who had exhausted their benefit and were drawing transitional payments under the means test were to be placed under new bodies, local unemployment assistance committees, which would be closely supervised by the Ministry of Labour. The more immediate danger was the implications of making the insurance scheme self-supporting. The proposals included reductions of benefit for all males and all independent females over the age of seventeen; a return to the old and hated 'not genuinely seeking work' rule; restriction on the rights of a claimant to appeal against a decision on his benefit; and the use of compulsion, if necessary, to make the unemployed labour on public works schemes while receiving appropriate allowances.

At a time when pressure to restore the cuts made in 1931 was building up, these recommendations were condemned not only by the Movement but also by the TUC and by a minority of two on the Royal Commission. The minority report urged that benefits should be increased rather than reduced, because the existing ones were below the poverty line; it also recommended abolition of the means test. The TUC further proposed that the unemployed man should have benefit so long as he was unemployed and that the whole cost should be borne by taxation instead of by tripartite contributions. In this respect the TUC and the Movement had drawn closer together.

All that was seen as a threat to prepare for, while the carrot was available immediately. This took the form of recreational and occupational centres for the unemployed, to be set up by a charitable organisation which had been in existence since 1919, the National Council for Social Service, helped by government grants. The grants were inconsiderable, £25,000 in 1933, £53,000 in 1934, but the patronage was influential. The Prince of Wales and the Prime Minister broadcast appeals for help; in December 1932, while Hannington and Elias were in jail, Ramsay MacDonald called for volunteers to keep the unemployed busy, 'teaching men how they may be able to furnish their homes, to make mats out of bits of old rope, purchased for a few pence'. This response to the growing public feeling that something ought to be done for the unemployed, was rejected by the TUC because the Government was trying to hand over its responsibility to a voluntary body. The Movement condemned it out of hand. Finding that nine government departments were represented on the National Council of Social Service, it could not believe that a Ministry of Labour which operated the means test, a Ministry of Health which had suspended too generous local authorities, and a Home Office which had repressed demonstrations 'had suddenly become philanthropic towards the unemployed by their association with the Council'.[4] Its view was that social service was merely intended to keep the unemployed quiet and divert them from their proper struggle for work at trade union rates or full maintenance, and that it would satisfy the conscience of the middle class without bringing them into the struggle. There was another danger too, according to the Movement. The occupational centres where men worked voluntarily would lead to compulsory training for work on public schemes without wages, as proposed by the Royal Commission. All sides, however, agreed that the social services scheme was cheap, it was bound to have some quietening effect, and it would cost a tiny fraction of the expense of increasing the incomes of the unemployed.

Those incomes came up for review in 1933. The Emergency Measures of 1931, under which benefits had been cut, were due to expire in June. In Parliament Labour and Liberal Members pressed for the cuts to be restored and for the means test to be abolished but they were told by the Chancellor of the Exchequer, Neville Chamberlain, that it was essential for the cuts to remain for another year and there was no question but that the means test must stay.

The Government's refusal to move was a signal for a fresh burst of activity by the Movement. It was decided to organise county and local marches. Scotland, always to the fore, was the first to move. A thousand from Fife, Ayrshire and Lanarkshire, from Renfrewshire, Dumbarton and Glasgow, and from as far as Aberdeen and Dundee, marched on Edinburgh, arriving on 11 June. Each man had signed a pledge:

> I promise that while on the march I will observe strict discipline, as I realise that unless discipline is observed the greatest dangers will arise for the marchers.
>
> I also undertake to stay in Edinburgh until the main body of marchers leave. I have been informed that there are no guarantees about returning on any particular day. I come on the march with that understanding, and will observe the agreement.
>
> I understand the significance of this march and fully support the demands to the Government.

On the second night, there was nowhere to sleep because the authorities wanted the marchers to go home, and so they stretched out on the pavements and roadway of Princes Street, under the floodlit Castle, for a hard night's rest, washing, shaving, having breakfast and dinner on the same spot. The shock to the dignity of the City was such that accommodation for the third night was soon found. Going home, the marchers felt that they had achieved as much as they could expect: promises to consider their demands, free transport home in spite of their refusal to promise never to return to Edinburgh, and recognition by the capital city of the unemployed. They had, however, not won the support of the trades council and Labour Party.[5]

On the following day a thousand Lancashire men marched on Preston. They were, in the view of the poor law inspector, 'the only people who were found really difficult last year' and as such would need special attention from the police to ensure that the casual ward regulations were applied strictly on the way; the Chief Constable had been 'rather weak with them then and it was hoped that the Home Office would improve on that this year'. They succeeded in persuading the PAC to appoint a special committee to inquire into their grievances.[6]

In September there was a third march in the Nottingham and Derby district, well organised, with its own printed six-page programme containing the demands made, a map and details of stopping-places, descriptions of task-work which had been imposed, an exposé of the social service, details of the threat from the Royal Commission, slogans to be used, and songs to be sung. Two hundred of these men converged on Derby by three routes, from Dinnington, from Dronfield, Eckington, Staveley (which had its own newsletter, *The Spark*) and Whittington, and from Hucknall. After two days in the city they won the concession of free school meals for their children. In Yorkshire eight hundred marched to Wakefield and exacted a promise from the county council to look into their grievances.[7]

The local march turned out differently in South Wales. The central marchers' council for South Wales informed the authorities at Bridgend that a thousand men from Maesteg, Ogmore Vale and Blaengarw, with a petition from the residents, would require accommodation and food at Aberkenfig on their way to put their demands in Bridgend. The council was told that a march would be futile as the PAC had no power and had already refused to see a deputation, but it replied that they would march to show that it was determined to get its demands. These included, in particular, coal allowances of two hundredweight per week and boots for the children. The marchers received their instructions and set out.

To ALL MARCHERS.

Points To Bear In Mind
THE MARCH IS A SERIOUS EFFORT TO BEAT BACK
THE ATTACKS OF THE GOVERNMENT
"NOT A JOY-RIDE."

THEREFORE :- EVERY MARCHER MUST OBSERVE
STRICT DISCIPLINE AND OBEY INSTRUCTIONS
ISSUED BY PERSONS IN CONTROL OF VARIOUS
CONTINGENTS.
ALSO CARRY THE FOLLOWING EQUIPMENT.
BLANKET OR OVERCOAT
BASIN AND PLATE
SPOON " KNIFE
TOWEL " SOAP.
STARTING POINT OF MARCH :- COURT COLMAN.
3. P.M.

WORKERS :—
"EMPLOYED & UNEMPLOYED"
YOUR DUTY TO YOURSELVES, YOUR
WIVES, AND CHILDREN, IS TO
"MARCH."

Instruction to marchers on the abortive local South Wales march to Bridgend
in 1933.

The Glamorgan police were too quick for them. Equipped with an aeroplane to watch progress, the police stopped up each of the three valleys down which the men were marching and turned them back before they reached Aberkenfig. The Ministry of Health sent its congratulations to the Home Office: 'The police put an end to the affair with admirable promptitude. One rather hopes this may give the movement a wholesome check, for marches long and short are becoming all too common. I hope that this will encourage the police to pursue the same tactics elsewhere.'[8]

The Movement considered that the county marches were, on the whole, successful in terms of morale, but there was one serious shortcoming. They had not succeeded in getting as much working-class support with food and shelter as had been hoped for. These hopes were linked with a feature of the Edinburgh march, the presence of an Independent Labour Party Member of Parliament, the same John McGovern who had been rejected by the Movement in 1932. His presence was also linked with the new policy of the Communist Party for a united front against fascism.

Although the county marches had not yet won enough support from working-class organisations, there were stirrings of middle-class sympathy for the unemployed. They came from various sources. Perhaps more important than the reaction against the violence of 1932 were the first of a series of medical reports on health and nutrition. They were only a trickle compared with what was to follow, but already in 1933 doctors and medical officers of health were indicating malnutrition among the unemployed. In November the British Medical Association published a minimum diet and its cost, which for a man, wife and two children aged six and ten came to 18s 5d. This expenditure was virtually impossible on the standard unemployment pay of 27s 3d, and the discovery prompted the Ministry of Health to work out a less expensive diet.[9]

Another influence was the involvement of middle-class people in the social service schemes which brought them in contact with hardship. More powerful in the same direction, was the rise of fascism, if only because the Movement was anti-fascist. The shock of Hitler's progress induced many to turn to the left. John Strachey's Marxist analysis, *The Coming Struggle for Power*, sold in great numbers. In the universities students began to turn to the Communist Party; Oxford's October Club had three hundred members. Scientists and writers began to take a Marxist standpoint. The aggressiveness and violence of fascism also produced an anti-war sentiment which favoured the policy of collective security, as was indicated in Labour's victory at the East Fulham by-election in October 1933 over a Conservative candidate who stood for increasing armaments. The anti-war sentiment was now to be seen in the new slogan of 'Against Hunger and War' on the marchers' banners.

Middle-class sentiment was hardly enough to encourage those in the Movement who advocated another national march, but their case was strengthened by the Unemployment Bill. The Bill reproduced the main recommendations of the Royal Commission. Its main features were: the administration of transitional payments to be transferred to a new body remote from local influence, the grounds for disqualification from payment to be enlarged, payments to be conditional on attending training centres, and the means test to be perpetuated. The grim future promised by the Bill and the Government's refusal to restore the cuts in benefit decided the Movement in October 1933 to organise a fifth national march. It was not an easy decision to make and only pressure from the advocates of the united front policy tipped the balance in favour. The Communist Party and the Independent Labour Party had already decided to hold a 'United Front Congress' in London in February 1934 and their view was that a national march should culminate in the congress. There was some dissension, according to the Special Branch at Scotland Yard which, giving details of the National Administrative Council's proceedings, reported that Hannington and McShane considered a march to be premature, that it should be delayed until support from the trade unions had been obtained, and that it was left to William Gallacher to argue the overriding claims of the united front. The following day at a joint meeting of the Movement, the Communist Party and the Independent Labour Party, Hannington and McShane still maintained some opposition but agreed to the march 'because it was the wish of the united front'.[10]

The Movement's directive reflected this situation: 'Before any march was started an intensive campaign was necessary to get sufficient working-class response to overcome the opposition of the authorities; the marchers must not go to the poor law for food and shelter on the road or in London but must develop in every town a United Front Committee for feeding the marchers and for mass demonstrations. This was a prerequisite for the march.' If this was done, it continued, then every effort would be made to get the marchers to London in time for the united front congress to be held in Bermondsey town hall.[11] There were still some differences of opinion. Unity, for the Communist Party, meant working with the Independent Labour Party and any other labour organisations that could be persuaded to join in. For the Movement, it meant primarily solidarity between employed and unemployed. The *Manifesto of the National Hunger March and Congress* (price one penny) showed the degree of trade union support. The signatories included four Members of Parliament, ILP leaders, and eight or nine prominent trade unionists from the railways, and the printing, engineering, distribution and furniture industries. This was a marked change from 1932. The manifesto proclaimed the basis for unity as the fight against the Unemployment Bill and the means test, restoration of the cuts, work schemes for the unemployed, reduced hours and increased wages for the employed.

On 7 December 1933 instructions for the march due to start from Glasgow on 22 January went out to all district councils. The emphasis was on discipline and good organisation in order to counter the well-known intention of the Government to brook no opposition to its reforms. Discipline depended partly on leadership; the instructions read:

> The vital question of leadership of the contingents must be decided upon now. The most reliable comrades in the locality must be selected for the leadership – the comrades with the greatest political and mass experience who can keep a clear head in the most difficult situations. The question is one of the utmost importance, because of the undoubted attempts which will be made by the authorities to stop the progress of the marchers.

Discipline also depended on food, clothes and boots; the instructions continued:

As this march will be taking place in the dead of winter, it is essential that proper provision be made for every marcher having stout clothes, good boots and coat, as well as a real Army pack. No marcher can be sent away without those essentials. We must have shoe-makers with each contingent, or men who can repair boots, provided with proper tools for the job.

It will be necessary to provide hot meals during the day to the marchers, so in the main contingents such as Scotland, North-East Coast, Lancashire and Yorkshire, where the men are more than ten days on the road, we must carry a field-kitchen. This means the procuring of boilers now. Such boilers can be obtained from the big Army and Navy Stores or other Government contractors for about £12 each. The name of these boilers are Sawyers Stoves. It is an enclosed boiler with fire underneath and chimney attached with a capacity of 12 gallons each. Last year the Scottish Contingent had three of such boilers for 220 men, so that gives you a rough idea what will be required for your contingent. This will mean of course getting two or three cooks, with about four assistants for cleaning, etc.

In order to transport these boilers, the cooking staff and other stores, it will be necessary to have motor vans. These should be 1-ton or 2-ton lorries and can be had now in markets, etc., for £8 and £10 each, and in addition, of course, drivers must be procured.

We are convinced, comrades, that these things are essential on this march, so you will realise that the job must be tackled in earnest now. Detail one or two comrades immediately, even though they are not members of the DC to carry through these tasks.

Discipline required that everyone must know why he was marching and to this end each was to be supplied with a copy of the march pamphlet, of the pamphlet on the new Unemployment Bill and of the *Manifesto*, itself a twelve-page document.[12] The distinguishing features of 1934 turned out to be stronger discipline and better organisation.

Perhaps this factor contributed to the change from the authorities' initial hard line against the marchers to the outcome of peaceful demonstration in London. In reply to a question in the House on 21 December, the Home Secretary stated that it was the intention of the Communist Party to represent the march as a 'mass struggle of the unemployed', therefore 'any persons undertaking to furnish means which enable such concentrations to take place incur a very grave responsibility'.[13]

A policy of deterrence had already been worked out by the Ministry of Health and the Home Office acting together. The hard line was to be harder this time, though as it turned out that was to be largely irrelevant. On 9 December the Ministry of Health sent a memorandum to the poor law inspectors:

> Any success of the March in 1932 was due to some extent to the weakness shown by certain Local Authorities and their officers who in their anxiety to avoid possible civil commotion, made concessions by loans of blankets and by issue of rations to the demonstrators who thus conserved for more mischievous purposes funds which they had raised by street collections.

The Home Office followed by sending the document to all chief constables with instructions that the police must deal with any disorder that might arise from strict insistence on the conditions of relief. In discussions at the Ministry the hard line was expressed by the inspector for Gloucestershire:

> It would make it easier for the officials to restrain soft-hearted and foolish councillors. At Stratford last time the marchers tried to do as they liked, demanding extra rations, etc. The police were in ambush and gave them a jolly good hiding and captured all their dangerous weapons. Hence the marchers were avoiding Stratford this year but two contingents were going to Birmingham because the Chairman was idiot enough to give them extra food, not out of the rates but from private sources. If the marchers were dealt with firmly at their first points of call it ought to be possible to stop the whole thing.

The inspectors then received stronger instructions to the effect that the nuisance to the poor law administration must be minimised by refusing any extra-legal help or any departure from the Casual Poor Orders. Supporting this was the promise, more definite than before, of help from the chief constables who would be stiffened by the Home Office if necessary. Finally, on 22 January 1934, the Home Office again instructed chief constables that the police were to meet any eventuality, especially at casual wards.[14]

The hard line having been agreed, it became necessary to correct any local councils which showed signs of weakness. Wigan and Oldham councils were told they would be surcharged if they gave boots and loaned blankets to their marchers. Stoke-on-Trent received a 'stiffening letter' from the Ministry at the town clerk's request. Carlisle, the first point of call of the Scottish contingent on 30 January, also had to be instructed. Its clerk, apprehensive that the 150 marchers who could not be got into the workhouse would suffer severely from the cold weather, asked if he could hire extra accommodation, but was told, certainly not, and moreover that the Ministry was displeased with the 'elaborate arrangements' already made and communicated to the marchers beforehand. There was, however, a danger that official pressure might go too far. When Leicester seemed likely to impose the rule of detention for two nights and putting to work, the Ministry hastened to say that although it would be prepared to use the threat of the rule in order to get the marchers to find other accommodation, once they were in the casual wards it should not be enforced because of the likelihood of damage to property. The Ministry wanted to ensure that local authorities could not say, when there was disorder, that it was due to its insistence on all the rules. In Horsham, when the police stated that the intention to stick to the detention rule would lead to trouble, the Ministry was quite ready to tell the inspector not to insist.[15]

The Home Office, expecting trouble, required daily reports from chief constables of the progress and behaviour of each contingent. The reports showed each contingent's strength, progress (whether according to timetable), state of discipline, collections it made, the number of men who had convictions and for what offences. The Lancashire contingent was recorded as having seven men with convictions, including three of the leaders, for assault, incitement and breach of the peace. Each day the possibility of weapons being carried was examined, but it always faded away. One contingent was 'a very ugly crowd and armed with sticks adorned at the head with nail or safety razor blades', but later on while 'some had nasty looking sticks as they use both ends of the sticks it could be assumed that there were no razor blades or nails' and later still they were found to be carrying ordinary walking-sticks. On another route, although the Coventry police confirmed that the Scots were not carrying revolvers or other lethal weapons, the Bedford force reported that they had 'heavy cudgels, very formidable weapons', but these by the time they got to Luton had become walking-sticks. The Welshmen's pickshafts at Bath became walking-sticks later at Newbury, but it was suspected there were heavier sticks concealed in a van. Even the women's contingent did not escape scrutiny, 'most had light walking-sticks'. The persistent belief in the existence of weapons rested eventually on one actual piece of hard evidence. After six Scots had been to the cinema at Rugby an object was found near their seats, to wit: 'A root end of blackthorn; 8½" long, 1½" diameter at the business end, ¾" at the handle end, with a hole through to go round the wrist, six boot studs driven into the head. This weapon could easily be concealed on the person.' After such a discovery surveillance continued:

> The men in the Scottish contingent march well, appear to be well disciplined and are all determined and bitter in their attitude to the Government. Each one is equipped with a very heavy stick. A special look-out was kept for any indication of the marchers being in the possession of firearms or their sticks being studded with nails or razor blades.[16]

Shortly after the Scots entered England, the Home Secretary stated:

> The right to hold peaceful meetings and processions is one of our most cherished rights, but if this right is to be abused in such a way as to lead inevitably to grave disorder or public disturbance, the Government will have to ask Parliament to grant such powers as experience might show to be necessary to deal with such demonstrations.

Two days later the Attorney-General hinted at the possibility of bloodshed arising from the march and the measures the Government might have to take. The Movement replied:

> THIS IS A THREAT AGAINST THE MARCHERS. Gilmour and the Government for which he speaks know perfectly well that neither the Marchers nor the March and Congress Council have any intention or interest in bringing about 'disorder' or 'riots'. Therefore Gilmour is advertising in advance that any police chief or any Fascist body which provokes a conflict, will be rendering a service to the 'National' Government by giving them an excuse for using their police against the Marchers.
> We challenge the Home Secretary to find a single instance in any

Hunger March where disorder was begun by the workers. But we can give him plenty of cases where his police chiefs were responsible for a conflict. Thousands of workers can bear witness to the fact that again and again brutal police violence has been used against demonstrators who were 'exercising the right of the people of this country to march in procession along the streets' particularly the London workers can speak of how Lord Trenchard has enforced his illegal ban on meetings at Labour Exchanges by breaking workers' heads with batons.

The Council warns the working class; the Government is looking for trouble in order to break up the March, and when this Government goes looking for trouble, you may be sure they have plenty of agents whose job it is to help them to find it.

Therefore EVERYWHERE FIRM WORKING CLASS DISCI-PLINE! ON GUARD AGAINST PLAIN CLOTHES SPIES AND PROVOCATEURS! EVERY DEMONSTRATION AND MEETING STEWARDED AND MARSHALLED BY THE WORKERS' ORGAN-ISATIONS! OBEY ONLY THE DECISIONS OF YOUR OWN ELEC-TED LEADERSHIP!

Working-class discipline could not be taken for granted. The bulletin of the South Wales contingent made this clear:

Obviously, with 300 men and women brought together for the first time, it is not an easy matter to develop the iron discipline necessary to carry the march through to London. But these initial difficulties have now been overcome, and the experiences on the road have built up that mutual confidence which has resulted in a self-imposed discipline that could never be obtained in any capitalist army.

Arising from this is the matter of education. This has been accomplished by the organising of regular discussions in each Section under the guidance of the Section Leaders and also by allowing marchers who are inexperienced in mass work to domi-nate the platform of the marchers (Hannington Collection, Marx Memorial Library).

The Chief Constable of Cardiff considered this contingent to be an 'ill-conditioned crowd, they were peaceful and had given no trouble in Cardiff but there was no knowing what this type would do when they mixed with a mob'. He doubted 'if many possessed the stamina to walk very far. If they reached London he hoped the Authorities would not assist them to return to Wales.'[17]

There was also still an army flavour to discipline. The methods of the Lancashire contingent are described by its quartermaster, Robert Davies:

There was very little trouble on the march or in London. This was due mainly to the way in which it was organised both before and during the march. Instructions were given as to how the marchers should be equipped, strong boots, overcoat, a valise to hold one blanket, razor, soap, pint-cup, knife, fork, spoon, and a spare shirt and underwear. The valise was to be carried on the shoulders like a soldier's pack.

The march leader was Philip Harker, with George Staunton as assistant, Paul Farrel was sergeant major, for the first few days he marched at the side keeping men in step and in rank. Later he marched in front with the leader, assistant leader and Bob Edwards who was then fairly prominent in the ILP. On the march we marched army style 50 minutes' marching, 10 minutes' rest. We stopped on the road for our mid-day meal, a packet of sandwiches carried from our last night stop. In addition we had a 15 cwt motor lorry, very old and bad. Our lorry driver had an economics degree but he must have been a good motor mechanic to have got that lorry all the way to London, it needed constant mechanical attention. On the motor lorry we carried three boilers heated by wood or coal. This lorry went on ahead of the contingent and at a suitable road side space the three men in charge would unload the boilers, fill them with water and bring it to the boil to make tea ready for the mid-day meal. The mid-day break was usually only long enough to eat the sandwiches and drink the tea, it was too cold to stay longer.

I marched with the Ambulance Section, as my job was a sort of Welfare Quartermaster, I had charge of the boots and clothing that was given to us. We found fourteen or fifteen men with first aid qualifications. They marched at the rear of the contingent and soon improvised Red Cross armlets and got haversacks to wear across the shoulder. On the road they would run out of the march to visit every chemist's shop and beg bandages, cotton wool, lint, tins of ointment, etc., they soon could attend to any casualties, and they did very successfully as I could personally witness. I never knew methylated spirits was good for the feet, it is. I was hobbling some miles from Oxford, in between my toes had become raw and when we stopped for a rest an Ambulance man asked what was wrong with my feet. I didn't think anything short of rest could do any good. He insisted on looking at my feet. He took little pieces of cotton wool dipped in methylated spirits pushed them between my toes and told me to pull my socks on, they would keep the wool in position. When we restarted to march I felt in heaven.

It was these conditions and the organisation that made for the best discipline.

The police reports on Lancashire discipline were 'good' throughout.

Once established, discipline had to be maintained. Anyone acting against the interests of the march could be, and sometimes was, expelled. One example is given by Robert Davies:

Two men were expelled from the March by a roadside meeting of the marchers. These men had begun to work a racket. At our resting places or mid-day, men would ramble about going behind trees or bushes to answer the calls of nature and it was easy for these two men to slip away down the road. On arriving in the town, either on foot or by getting a ride, they would make a collection pretending it was for the March but they kept the money for themselves and quietly joined the contingent when it arrived. They were first warned about this and given another chance but when they did it again action had to be taken. Some of the marchers wanted to chase them off there and then in the middle of the country but the leaders argued to allow them to continue to Oxford, the next town. In Oxford these two men were taken to the railway station and tickets purchased for them back to Manchester. Another man was expelled in London for stealing money from a fellow marcher. He just disappeared in London, we never saw him again.[18]

The Tyneside and Teesside contingent, which had in previous years been rebuked by the Movement for its indiscipline, also expelled three men for disruption and pilfering the collecting boxes.[19]

The main test of discipline was the ability to avoid any conflict which might impede progress. When Wal Hannington spoke to three hundred and ninety-eight Scots assembled in a field near Bedford, he stressed the need to prevent disorder on the way to London. The Tyneside men narrowly averted a conflict with the police at Cambridge. The Public Assistance Committee had hired the Corn Exchange for the marchers with food not exceeding £5 in value and the loan of blankets. The Corn Exchange had been hired only until 8 a.m., and the marchers who had a day's rest scheduled at Cambridge, were still asleep at that hour. The police gave them half an hour to leave but at 8.40 they were still there showing considerable resentment. The police hustled them out before breakfast was finished; although there was some rough handling no blows were struck. As they formed up outside, Sam Langley their leader, veteran of 1932, addressed them. He commended their self-control; they had used no violence though they might easily have done so. In this heterogeneous crowd of forty-eight labourers, twenty-three miners, two pitmen, three drillers, two seamen, an apprentice, a fireman, a moulder, a hawker, an electrician, a compositor, an errand boy, a baker, a canteen hand, a machine feeder, a rivet-heater, a riveter, a salesman, a steel erecter, a stoker, a boilermaker and a turner, discipline prevailed.[20]

There were not many occasions when discipline was put to the test.

There were far fewer nights at the workhouse than before and the Ministry instructions became more irrelevant as they were made stricter. Solidarity committees or unity committees had multiplied, though the ban by the TUC and the Labour Party was still in force. They were based increasingly on an alliance of local labour organisations and middle-class sympathisers. The Cambridge solidarity committee was one amongst many such. At Wolverhampton the committee arranged accommodation for the Scots in the Temperance Hall. At Rugby it got the Brotherhood to take fifty of them, the Baptists fifty, the Wesleyans sixty, the Friends forty, the Spiritualists thirty, the Salvation Army fifty, the railwaymen's club fifty, and the engineering club forty. The ideal arrangement by which the committee found accommodation and food while the PAC supplied the basic casual rations and blankets, often succeeded. The marchers were frequently in a position to test out the attitude of the workhouse and if necessary could fall back on the solidarity committee and their own funds.[21]

The increase in working-class support took the form of cash as well as accommodation and food. The Tyneside men entered the march with money from the Durham miners: Follonsby Lodge £5, Harraton Lodge £5, Newbiggin Lodge £5, Marsden

Lodge £3, Heworth Lodge £3, New Hartley Lodge £2, Mainsforth Lodge 10s. In impoverished Wales £3. 10s was collected at Maerdy, £1. 5s at Caerau, 10s at Aberdare, £1. 5s at Bridgend, £6 in Cardiff, £25 in Monmouthshire. For the women's group £7. 5s came from the Association of Women Clerks and Secretaries. Sizeable sums were contributed over a range of industrial workers, Watford Typographical Association £25, Kings Cross Locomotive men £9, Rochdale textile unions £8.

The cash flowing into the collecting boxes indicated a marked response from middle-class pockets. The Scots collected £45 in Coventry and £20 at Birmingham; the Tynesiders £50 at Cambridge and £25 in Leeds, the Lancashire men £55 at Warrington and £120 in Oxford. Middle-class people, brought face to face with the unemployed, particularly in those prosperous places where they knew of them only by hearsay, contributed more freely than before. A Scot thanked the people of St Albans for their great kindness. 'But,' he said, 'you don't realise down here the vast amount of unemployment in the North or the misery resulting from it.' Many of these sympathisers could see no reason why the benefit cuts could not be restored. Some were brought to join the Labour Party, others, of whom a few later became eminent public figures, signed up with the Communist Party.[22]

The churches gave practical signs of such a change. Clergymen, Church of England as well as nonconformist, were often members of reception committees; parish rooms, church halls, churches themselves, were frequently used for shelter. Robert Davies recalled how 'in Manchester about half of us slept on the floor of the church because the school was not large enough. All Saints was a High Church but the vicar was very left wing. We rolled in our blankets on the floor, the pews were not broad enough, some that tried fell off during the night. In the morning we all gathered outside in the disused graveyard. . . .' At Saffron Walden the pastor lent the Congregational Church after the Tynesiders had refused to enter the workhouse and the next day at Bishop's Stortford they had St Michael's parish room; the Welsh in Bristol went to parish halls and the Society of Friends, and in Slough, to the Baptist and Methodist halls; the Yorkshiremen found that because of the churches' welcome in Dunstable it did not turn out to be the 'black spot' they expected from the experience of 1929. At the same time many of these same clergy disapproved strongly of the march as wholly mistaken. Some in fact feared its effect on the charitable work they were doing. The archdeacon of Newark wrote of the danger of such practical sympathy for the marchers affecting the efforts being made in the social service centres.[23]

For the first time a student contingent joined the march. Wal Hannington had addressed students earlier on at Oxford, Cambridge and Bristol; in London the London School of Economics had redressed the hooliganism he had met at King's College.

Robert Davies remembered the welcome at Oxford.

> On the outskirts we were met by a few hundred university students who fell in behind us and shouted slogans which caused some amusement among the marchers. The students along with TU members and branches gave us a good time in Oxford, providing food and sleeping accommodation in the Corn Exchange. They provided three doctors to give medical attention to anyone needing it. The distance from Oxford to our next overnight stop was about 28 miles, so the Oxford people provided us with bus rides for about ten miles.

An undergraduate of Queens' College lent them his own Morris Minor and as they departed they were preceded to the City boundary by eighty-three members of the University Labour Club and the October Club. The police had information that University College in London wanted the marchers to address them and that many students from the London School of Economics were expected to join the march.[24]

The surge of sympathy had its effect on local authorities. The poor law inspectors did not always succeed in keeping them in hand. Margarine was the bone of contention with the Scots at Birmingham. The issue for breakfast had not been used because the Co-op had supplied food. A revolutionary proposal by John McGovern, MP, that it should be given with the casuals' lunch of bread and cheese became the subject of grave dispute between the chairman of the PAC and the inspector, only to be eventually approved in spite of the latter's protest that such action was a direct encouragement to the marchers and their 'allied associations'. The local mayor often reflected the feelings of the townspeople. At Dunstable, Mayor

A. Cook mobilised the churches, tradesmen, the Women's Institute and the Independent Labour Party together, marched into the town with the Yorkshiremen, and lent a hand in cutting up loaves of bread. When the Scots arrived at Warrington it was due to the mayor's intervention that they found two night's rest in the Empire Hall instead of in the workhouse. The Welsh discovered that their hardship at Chippenham in 1932 was not to be repeated thanks to the mayor's efforts.[25]

Their leader Lewis Jones wrote in a letter intercepted by the police:

> Everyone is surprised at the courtesy of the authorities and the facilities provided for the mere asking, in some cases without asking ... We set off this morning for Swindon. The chief PAC officer of Swindon paid me a visit before we started. They have agreed to give us 400 lbs. of bread and we bring the 250 blankets we had from the PAC in Chippenham with us. In addition he offered us quarter cwt. of margarine. I am trying to negotiate for something more palatable in place of this but in any case it will come in handy to grease the wheels of the lorry we have bought outright ... We go into a town and then literally capture it ... doing everything we want to do ... going everywhere we want to go ... ignoring all bans and prohibitions. This has two good effects. It inspires the marchers with added strength and it encourages the workers in those towns where police chiefs have practically abolished working-class activity ... But we are keeping in mind the statement in the *Daily Herald* to the effect that 5,000 police are being mobilised in London to greet the Hunger Marchers and their friends.[26]

In London during February 1934 the question was what would happen when the marchers arrived. The Home Office intensified surveillance of reception plans. At a meeting of the national administrative council, when a large number of plain-clothes men were noticed outside, the council dispersed to meet elsewhere, fearing that the leadership was to be rounded up. The police tried, unsuccessfully, to follow Emrhys Llewellyn, Wal Hannington, Maud Brown, and Fred Copeman. Though they watched Friars Hall, the Builders Labourers' Hall, 16 King Street, 14 Doughty Street, 33 Ormond Yard and 269 Grays Inn Road, they could not find the new meeting place.

All open-air meetings were reported. Indoor meetings, except public ones, were not so easy, but when the detectives could not gain entry they could rely on informers, in spite of warnings by the Movement. A detective refused admittance to meetings of the West Ham reception committee in Canning Town and to a NUWM branch meeting in Cable Street, was able to give from 'a reliable source' the names of those present and the details of accommodation for the marchers. Reports indicated that there was 'much support for the Hunger Marchers'. At Bermondsey Town Hall there was a full house, 'great enthusiasm prevailed' and £18. 12s 8½d was collected; one thousand seven hundred showed 'ardent enthusiasm' in Shoreditch Town Hall and gave £35; Wal Hannington was 'much cheered' in Edmonton by a meeting of four hundred which contributed £6. 2s 0d including £1 from the Edmonton tramwaymen. A note of admiration occasionally crept into the police reports; at a Communist Party meeting in a Bromley public house a detective noted the 'high quality of reporting, persuasive, reducing ramblings to a splendid logic', and the trade-union support from the electricians, building workers, and railwaymen.

The detectives did not fail to note numerous references to recent events in France – the Stavisky scandal, the danger of the fascists taking over from a corrupt administration being defeated by the workers' action in the streets, and the example given to the working class in England. The sacking of Chiappe, the Paris police chief, was announced to a meeting of nine hundred in Battersea Town Hall; a crowd on Clapham Common was reminded that 'the French Government had been overthrown due to the mass opinion as expressed by the workers demonstrating in the streets; and what could be done in Paris could be done in London and there was nothing the authorities feared so much as organised street demonstrations'.[27]

In Parliament Conservative members were calling for a ban on the march. Lt.-Col. MacAndrew (Glasgow, Partick) asked for information about the use of funds collected and whether steps could be taken to prevent the march, as it was organised by the Communist Party, and got the reply that the Government had no power to prevent an orderly march. The Duchess

of Atholl tried to get the marchers banned from Trafalgar
Square, without success. They should be called 'Anger
Marchers' not Hunger Marchers declared Winston Churchill,
but he defended the liberty to march and present a petition. In
Scotland Yard the Commissioner had meetings with the Public
Assistance Officer of the London County Council and the Poor
Law Division of the Ministry of Health. They agreed that the
press would be persuaded to publish warnings to the public to
stay at home and that a draft of a BBC announcement should
be prepared. As regards the Special Constables, the experience
in 1932 had not been too happy, some people said that they
provoked trouble; they would therefore be kept in reserve.

The police would of course help the Ministry of Health, but
this year the intention was neither 'to enforce the law to the
utmost nor to encourage the marchers'. The question which
exercised the Home Secretary was how to handle the number
and size of deputations certain to go to Members at the House
of Commons. As he emphasised at a meeting with Lord
Trenchard, the Speaker's Secretary and the Deputy-Serjeant-
at-Arms, the position was different from last time, there were
now four Members in definite alliance with the Movement and
a good many more sympathetic. The Commissioner wanted to
limit deputations to six persons, but had to agree to ten when he
was told that that was well known to be the regulation number.
All agreed that 'tact and great discretion would be required to
control the numbers having access to the House'.[28]

The police plans when released to the press appeared to be
nothing if not thorough. Half of the twenty thousand Special
Constables available would take over the routine duties of the
regular police whose leave had been cancelled. The statement
that police duties would be similar to the last time sounded
ominous to the marchers, as did the warning to owners of shops
and premises near Hyde Park to take precautions against
damage. The popular press made the most of it; the *Sunday
Pictorial* announced:

BIG PLANS TO CURB 'HUNGER MARCHERS'
Foiling a New Red Plot.
Communists Bent On Stirring Up Trouble Next Weekend
POLICE READY
5,000 Flying Squad and Specials Called Up

Precautions on an unprecedented scale are being taken to prevent disturbances when the 'Hunger Marchers' reach London this week. It is known that sinister influences are at work to provoke trouble of a grave character and the authorities have not overlooked the possibility of repercussions in London following the desperate street fighting which recently took place in Paris and Vienna. Feverish attempts are being made by the Communists to whip up East End dwellers to participate in the demonstration. Occupiers of business houses have been warned to cover their windows with boarding. Efforts will be made to keep the marchers in the suburbs and prevent their meeting at Westminster. In 1932 the 'Hunger Marchers' cost the London ratepayers over £2,500 a week and could not pay their fares home.[29]

A different view of the marchers appeared in *The Times*. The vicar and rural dean of Bishop's Stortford was deeply impressed by his visitors:

A young Cambridge man arrived here on Sunday last, and secured the use of our parish hall for Tuesday night. We had no facilities for cooking food, but this difficulty was solved by the aid of a local tradesman. The men were to arrive at 6 p.m., 60 to come to us and 50 to the church hall of the next parish.

Unfortunately for them a public meeting was billed for one hall that night, so that when the first arrivals appeared there was no prospect of getting into the hall before 9.30 at the earliest. However, the men accepted the situation with the utmost good humour and appreciation of the circumstances, and sat down on the steps to await their comrades' arrival. The main body came in at 9 o'clock, with drums beating and singing songs. As soon as they realised that a meeting was in progress they desisted and stood quietly about the hall till they could be admitted. Though all must have been both hungry and tired, they were most orderly and quiet.

Although we did not attempt to hide our feeling that these marches are part of a mistaken policy, we clergy, the official purveyors of so called intellectual 'dope', were greeted with marked friendliness and respect. In the face of so much said to the contrary one would like it to be known that for real 'gentlemanly' feeling and courtesy one would have to look far and often to find anything superior to the conduct of the 110 marchers from Tyne and Wear side. This, I may add, is the testimony of our whole town.

Then their manners were so good. One could not help being struck with the curious neatness with which they took their food. Seated round the fire or leaning against the walls of the room, eating fish and chips, served in the usual newspaper, they picked up every crumb as it fell and put it in the fire, so that at the end of the meal the floor was as tidy as when it began. Also the food, the bread and the fish, was so used that when each had finished his supper what was over could be wrapped up in a neat parcel for future consumption.

When they left on Wednesday morning they expressed their thanks in the most generous and hearty manner. A squad of five or six 'daily workers' remained behind and swept up all dust and papers off the floors, cleaned up the hearth, tidied up the kitchen, and left everything in a most orderly condition. Indeed when one entered the hall after they had left it was difficult to believe that nearly 70 men had occupied the premises the night before and had had two meals there. I should like to say also that though I spent hours in their company I did not hear one single oath, let alone foul speech; not even the somewhat innocuous 'd--n'.

Without expressing any sympathy either with their politics or the manner in which they expressed them, one would like to say that it would be hard to imagine anything further removed from the truculent hectoring ruffians these marchers are often represented to be than the actual men one met. At least this is true of the column that visited Bishop's Stortford. For the most part they are men who for years have endured grinding want: a poverty extending even to a never appeased hunger and in winter time to unceasing cold. In spite of the inevitable bitterness engendered by such conditions of strain upon self-control and self-respect, there was not one of them of whom one could not have made a friend, or who failed to respond to a friendly gesture. If these men are samples of the body of the 'marchers', some of the above-stated facts are worth keeping in mind by the authorities responsible for law and order.[30]

At this point a new ally of the marchers appeared, a group of influential sympathisers, writers, academics, politicians, and lawyers. The origin of the Council for Civil Liberties was in the 1932 march. At that time Ronald Kidd reported that he saw police agent-provocateurs in working-men's clothes batoning and arresting orderly marchers after inciting violence among them outside Stanford's map shop at the top of Whitehall, and near Hyde Park. A. P. Herbert, soon to be independent Member of Parliament for Oxford University, asked Lord Trenchard for an inquiry. This found no truth in the allegation of provocation but admitted that plain-clothes men were working in the crowd and making arrests. Herbert accepted Trenchard's word but felt that it was necessary for the authorities to say where they stood on the use of agents-provocateurs. Kidd was less satisfied and called for a vigilance committee to watch for any police abuses. Such a body was formed and announced itself a few days before the marchers arrived on 25 February 1934.

The present hunger march has been preceded by public statements by the Home Secretary and the Attorney-General (who has already hinted at the possibility of bloodshed) which we feel justify apprehension. Furthermore, certain features of the police preparations for the present march – for example, instructions to shopkeepers to barricade their windows – cannot but create an atmosphere of misgiving, not only dangerous but unjustified by the facts.

All reports bear witness to the excellent discipline of the marchers. From their own leaders they have received repeated instructions of the strictest character, warning them against any breach of the peace, even under extreme provocation.

In view of the general and alarming tendency to encroachment on the liberty of the citizen, there has recently been formed a Council of Civil Liberties. One of the special duties of this Council will be to maintain a vigilant observation of the proceedings of the next few days. Relevant and well-authenticated reports by responsible persons will be welcomed and investigated by the Council.

(Signed)

Lascelles Abercrombie	C. R. Attlee
Ambrose Appelbee	V. R. Brittain
Dudley Collard	A. P. Herbert
Harold Laski	D. N. Pritt
G. H. Bing	Kingsley Martin

Evelyn Sharp Nevinson	H. G. Wells
Henry W. Nevinson	Ronald Kidd
Edith Summerskill	(*Secretary*)[31]

It became clear to the marchers as they entered Hyde Park on Sunday, 25 February, that the police had different instructions from those in 1932. The apparatus of control was more elaborate than before. The crowd was enormous – fifty thousand at the lowest estimate – but now there were no Special Constables in sight and no riding by mounted police into the crowds. Professor Harold Laski, watching events for the Council for Civil Liberties, reported: 'The police conduct was admirable and there was nothing to which one could take the slightest exception.'[32] The same restraint was apparent to the men and women who lobbied members of Parliament on the following days and by the ten thousand who gathered at Trafalgar Square the next Sunday. The authorities were well aware of the marchers' intention to avoid direct conflict whenever possible. The Movement intended to make all the constitutional moves available, whatever that meant.

The Cabinet had agreed on its position, in the light of a revolt of its own supporters who had voted with the Opposition in favour of an increase of child dependants' allowances. It had decided that Ministers should not receive any deputations and the Prime Minister should make a statement deploring 'the exploitation for political ends of the legitimate grievances of the unemployed'. Likewise, the Home Secretary was to reject the cooperation of the blackshirts and to discourage fascist bodies. The Cabinet agreed that the use of broadcasting to keep the public away might do more harm than good, showing some apprehension of popular interest, but authorised the Home Secretary to make use of it if he thought desirable.[33]

The United Front Congress, linked with the march, was attended by one thousand four hundred and ninety-four delegates who met for two days after an official welcome from the mayor of Bermondsey. Among the sponsors were the four ILP members of Parliament. The Congress resolved unanimously for the demands in the manifesto. Robert Davies was present:

Along with twenty men from our contingent I was a Marching Delegate representing my trade-union branch. The branch had donated £5 towards the marchers' expenses. When we got to our last night stop in Acton Elementary School, the Marching Delegates were notified to be ready the following morning to go to the Congress. I left the Lancs contingent there and only rejoined them in Hyde Park on the Sunday afternoon. Attending the Congress we had our food provided and slept on the floor on the Saturday night. On Sunday, just after mid-day, all the Congress Delegates formed up outside the hall with bands and banners to march to Hyde Park. We marchers were placed in the front ranks behind the band and the leaders. I remember James Maxton and Ellen Wilkinson among the fifty or so leaders. As we marched along, so many people joined in that by the time I got to Westminster Bridge I could not see the band, let alone hear it. The processions were the largest I have ever seen.[34]

The Congress had called on the Government to receive a marchers' deputation. This was the main issue in the following days. The demand that the marchers themselves should be heard in some way either at the Bar of the House or by the Prime Minister or by one of his Ministers was pressed home day by day in every constitutional way open to them. The petition was presented in Parliament by John McGovern, to be deposited in the bag provided for the purpose behind the Speaker's Chair, and heard of no more. Then on 7 February the adjournment was moved by George Buchanan (Gorbals) to call attention to 'the Prime Minister's refusal to grant any facilities for the unemployed marchers to voice their grievances either to himself, to the Government, or to the House'. As well as Buchanan, McGovern and Maxton, Attlee, acting leader of the Parliamentary Labour Party, spoke to explain why his party supported the motion; the charge of revolutionary leadership was irrelevant, a large body representing the unemployed ought to be heard. Sir Herbert Samuel put his weight, as a former Home Secretary, on the same side. He said:

No one can say that the grievances of these men, who have walked to this city from many parts of this island, are trivial or imaginary ... These men, who have been brought from all over the country, have been guilty of no disorder; those who have given them hospitality pay the highest tribute to their behaviour. What should they do, other than what they have done, if they want to draw the attention of the nation to their plight, to stir this nation out of what is really a shameful complacency, and to protest against the utterly inadequate measures that have so far been taken? Are we to say to them, 'If you are disorderly, we cannot listen to you; it would be to encourage disorder. If you are orderly, we need not listen to you?' . . .

It is said that they are Communists, and that therefore they ought to be ignored. Let us not attach so much importance to labels, but see the realities behind the name. There is not here, and everyone knows it, any deliberate plan or attempt to overturn society. This march is nothing more than a protest, a bitter cry. They say to us: 'Hear us; see us; help us.' It is that and nothing more. . . .

It is said that these men are not representative of the whole body of the unemployed. Perhaps not, but there is no one else to represent them; there is no other organisation that speaks urgently in their name. . . .

These men have come, many hundreds of them, tired, footsore, here to the capital of this country, to the seat of Government. Let them not go back feeling that every door is barred against them, every window shuttered, and, what is worse, every heart closed against them. Government and Parliament would be wise to wish them well and to show that we are anxious to help them' (Parliamentary Debates Commons, 1933–4, Vol. 286, pp. 1071–6).

Ramsay MacDonald fell back on the precedent of previous refusal to see the marchers, and the charge of subversive leadership. Conservative members rallied to him, and after an hour and half's debate the motion was lost: for – fifty-two, against – two hundred and seventy.

The next step was intensive lobbying. On the first of two days the marchers arrived in twos and threes outside the House. Eighty entered the lobby and met members, while the remainder, about six hundred, queued up. It was snowing hard. McGovern and Aneurin Bevan interrupted business to protest vigorously against marchers being kept waiting in the snow and alleged discrimination in admittance against people who were poorly dressed. 'Parliament is a farce,' McGovern shouted. Thereafter the queue lessened as entry became easier. Next day while two hundred men assembled in the central hall, others were let into the Strangers' Gallery where they repeatedly interrupted debate, shouting 'Hear the Hunger Marchers.

What about the marchers' deputations. Down with the starvation Government', only to be ejected each time. Those in the
central hall struck up 'The Internationale' and were hustled
out. No one was arrested. 'Some of our lads got rather badly
man-handled, bruised and their clothes were torn,' Robert
Davies remembered. It was his job to replace ruined clothing
from a secondhand stock.[35]

That was the only occasion that the marchers were heard by
the Government. The one further step possible was to approach
the throne. Before dark that day about a hundred marchers
with packs on backs began to parade in twos and threes in front
of Buckingham Palace where the King and Queen were in
residence. Mounted and foot police came up in haste and kept
them on the move until they scattered. Demonstration was not
quite over but law and order always prevailed. When on the
second Sunday, in Trafalgar Square, there was danger of
violence, the speakers appealed to the crowd to keep in good
order. One deputation did penetrate into 10 Downing Street.
Miss Ishbel MacDonald met a group of women led by Maud
Brown. They angrily rejected a suggestion from her that
unemployed women in the textile and clothing trades and in
office work should try domestic service. There was nothing
more to offer and nothing promised.[36]

The constitutional protest was finished for the time being.
The Times told its readers: 'Those who are seeking to make
political capital out of the lot of the unemployed may now be
supposed to have exhausted every artifice which might con-
ceivably represent them in the light of the rebuffed champions
of misery.' The Metropolitan Police congratulated themselves;
their extra work had cost only £2,000. The marchers had met
unprecedented generosity which helped to maintain them in
London and to raise the money to return home. The whole of
the £1,100 required for the reduced train fares negotiated with
the railway companies was raised by collections. Gifts in kind
were very various, according to Robert Davies:

> We stayed in the billet for most of a fortnight and were kept very
> busy. During the day we had groups going out foraging for food and
> they came back with some remarkable gifts. One lot brought a few
> hundred apple-pies or tarts, each in a little cardboard carton. They
> were castoffs from one of Lyons bakeries. They were piled in a

broad window ledge and a man took one when he felt like it. They were very good, some of them slightly burned on the crust. Another group brought a large leg of boiled ham with only about a quarter of it used. Of course most of the foragers brought in less fancy goods such as loaves of bread, etc.[37]

A month after the marchers returned home the Government raised benefits, whether because it felt obliged to give way to public opinion, or because the conditions under which they had been cut had disappeared some time earlier, the pound, no longer in danger, having left gold and the unemployment insurance fund having been made solvent. There was no apparent reason why the cuts should not have been restored earlier except for the fact that employers who paid low wages might have to raise them in relation to increased benefits. But this objection, a lively one among employers and in Whitehall, was overcome as the pressure increased from different sides. 'There is no doubt that the demonstration made an impression on public opinion', said *The Economist*. 'The hunger marchers themselves appeared anything but revolutionary. Their ranks were orderly; the slogans inscribed on their banners were cogent, but in the main, uninspiring; and the marchers probably secured most sympathy by their discipline, their confident humour, and their pinched and hungry faces.' *The Times* had explained to its readers what the marchers had been obliged to renounce when they started – any guarantee of food or shelter, of returning home, of dependants being maintained, of benefit or transitional payment while on the march, their freedom under the march discipline, and declared 'it was scarcely credible that this should be the only inducement to brave a month in the open in this inclement season of the year'. In the same columns praise came from Sir Cyril Cobb, chairman of the London County Council PAC for 'the high degree of discipline which contributed to a peaceful issue'. The Poor Law Inspector in London finally reported that he found the South Wales leader Lewis Jones 'particularly sensible and moderate like the rest of his Council'.[38]

The Chancellor of the Exchequer complained about the volume of letters urging restoration of the cuts. He particularly resented the advocacy of the Archbishop of York, and protested that the Government had its own humanitarian feelings.

Numerous influential bodies went on record for something to be done – increased child benefits, free school meals, public works schemes. The Movement itself organised a national demonstration for Budget Sunday. Finally, in introducing his budget on 17 April, the Chancellor announced that the :931 10 per cent cuts would go; this meant restoring the benefit for an adult male to 17s per week, for an adult female to 15s and for a dependant wife to 9s. The new rates would not be paid until July. The Movement felt it could claim another victory, though the battle against the Unemployment Bill was still to be fought.

REFERENCES

1. PRO Mepol 2/3071.
2. PRO Mepol 2/3071.
3. Miliband, *Parliamentary Socialism*, 1973, p. 212.
4. Hannington, *Unemployed Struggles*, 1936, p. 273.
5. McShane, *Three Days that Shook Edinburgh*, NUWM, 1933.
6. PRO MH 57/102; NUWM, NAC Report, 28.6.33.
7. PRO MH 57/102; NUWM, Notts & Derby District, *Why We Are Marching*, 1933; *The Spark*, No. 19, Staveley Tenants Defence Cttee, 1933.
8. PRO MH 57/102; *Western Mail*, 19.10.33; NUWM, NAC Report, 15.9.33.
9. *The Times*, 3.2.34.
10. PRO Mepol 2/3071; MH 57/103.
11. NUWM, NAC Report, 28.10.33.
12. National Congress & March Council, *Manifesto*, 1934; NUWM, Circular, 7.12.33; NAC Report, 13 & 14.1.34.
13. *Daily Telegraph*, 22.1.34; PRO Mepol 2/3071.
14. PRO MH 57/103.
15. PRO MH 57/103.
16. PRO Mepol 2/3071.
17. PRO MH 57/104A.
18. Private Communication.
19. NUWM, NAC Report, 7 & 8.4.34.
20. PRO Mepol 2/3071; Lincoln CRO PL 1934; PRO MH 57/104A; Cambridge CRO G/C/AM 44.
21. Warwick CRO 1238/9; *Birmingham Mail*, 15.2.34; PRO MH 57/104A; H. McShane and J. Smith, *No Mean Fighter*, 1980, p. 207 seq.
22. National Congress and March Council Bulletins, 3, 7 & 31.2.34; PRO MH 57/104A; *Hertfordshire Advertiser*, 23.2.34.

23. Private Communication; *Hertford Mercury*, 23.2.34; *The Times*, 24.2.34; PRO MH 57/104A; *Luton News*, 25.2.34.
24. Private Communication; PRO Mepol 2/3071.
25. PRO MH 57/104A; *Luton News*, 25.2.34; *Wiltshire Times*, 17.2.34.
26. PRO MH 57/103.
27. PRO Mepol 2/3071.
28. *The Times*, 16, 23, 24.2.34; PRO Mepol 2/3071.
29. The *Sunday Pictorial*, 22.2.34.
30. *The Times*, 26.3.34.
31. *Week End Review*, 4.11.33; National Council of Civil Liberties Archive, Feb. 1934.
32. *Daily Herald*, 26.2.34.
33. PRO CAB 23/78.
34. Private Communication.
35. *The Times*, 27 & 28.2.34; 1 & 2.3.34; PRO Mepol 2/3071.
36. PRO Mepol 2/3071.
37. PRO Mepol 2/3071; *The Times*, 2 & 3.3.34; 16.3.34; Private Communication.
38. *The Economist*, 15.3.34; *The Times*, 23.1.34; 9.3.34; PRO MH 57/104A.

8

The Last March on London, 1936

'What the eye does not see the heart does not grieve at' the *Hertfordshire Mercury* told its readers in the county town of Hertford in November 1936. The marchers from Yorkshire, Nottingham and Derby who had just passed through were, it continued, the kind of propaganda which was 'good for the souls' of that prosperous England unaffected by the suffering of the depressed areas. It was common knowledge that half the nation was not getting enough food and that the army could not get the physically fit men it wanted. The emaciated state of the marchers had been only too obvious evidence of this; several had been unable to enjoy the good meal set before them. Hearts had been moved by the appearance of these men who, however misguided, had chosen the rigours of a long march in order to raise their voices on behalf of the victims of a great social evil. Red-hot communists were certainly among them and 'The Red Flag' was not a welcome song in Hertford, but the town had been privileged to receive them and the Labour Party; the Co-op and the clergy had been true good Samaritans. Such sentiments were not expressed in the Conservative *Mercury* about any previous march, but much had happened since February 1934.[1]

Two years later the trends outlined in Chapter 7 provided the context for the 1936 march. The incessant campaign of the Communist Party for unity produced the same reaction as before. The Labour Party's condemnation of 'loose association' with Communists in 1934 and its rejection of yet another Communist application for affiliation in 1936 was followed by its expulsion of the Socialist League after the Unity Manifesto issued jointly by the Communist Party, the Independent Labour Party and the Socialist League. The Communist Party's gesture of withdrawing all but two of its candidates in the 1935 general election probably had little conciliatory effect on the Labour leadership. On the other hand, Communist support for Labour candidates on that occasion may well have promoted unity in the constituency parties. A similar effect on the trade unions may have occurred in 1935 during the widespread protest against the new regulations for relief issued by the Unemployment Assistance Board (UAB) in December 1934. The lead then given largely by the NUWM was followed by support from the National Council of Labour. According to Miliband:

> The leadership of the Labour Movement followed the agitation – it did not lead it; and it does not seem unreasonable to suggest that, had the unemployed solely relied on the efforts of that leadership, the Government would not have been quite so ready to withdraw the regulation which it did on the 5th of February.[2]

The NUWM gained much unofficial support thereby, including some from Labour leaders as well as rank and file. The effect of these developments on the 1936 march can only be estimated. Although Labour issued no ban, it advised against support of the march, in the same way as for the Jarrow march taking place at the same time. According to Ellen Wilkinson the intention of the TUC circular advising trades councils not to help was that they should judge each march on its merits and act accordingly.[3] They seem to have done just that.

The 1936 march took place in spite of the fact that unemployment had fallen considerably and the membership of the Movement with it. The Government's plan of reducing scales of relief had been defeated only a year before, but now five hundred marched from Wales alone. Other causes of protest had developed in the interval to draw in not only left-wing activists but also a multitude of sympathisers and fellow-travellers. Fascism in Britain had aroused strong opposition: the outbreak of civil war in Spain was already claiming the energies of anti-fascists; the invasion of Abyssinia by Italy, the 'peace ballot' in Britain, and warlike preparations, had all absorbed the attention of liberals, pacifists, and progressives. There was that much less left for the unemployed. On the other hand, the Movement gained rather than lost from the new movements of protest. If the general motive was to stop fascism, it was the Movement which was preventing British fascists from getting a hold among the unemployed. Protest against unemployment probably benefited from the growth of anti-fascist feeling. In the event the march was the biggest of all and scored notably.

The nature of unemployment was now seen more clearly. Although the total on the unemployed register had fallen during the two years from 1934, from about 2,200,000 to about 1,600,000 – that is from 17 per cent to 13 per cent of the insured workers – and the general recovery was obvious enough, there was no sign of this decrease in the worst areas – Scotland, South Wales, West Cumberland and Tyneside. These distressed areas, first called officially the Depressed Areas, were re-named Special Areas. It was already apparent in 1934 that unemployment was becoming mainly a matter of the distressed areas, and at the time the marchers were in London the Government appointed four investigators of conditions, one for each area. Their reports, made in the late summer of that year, but not published by the Government until November, were revealing. Pressure for special legislation resulted in the appointment of two commissioners to revive the areas, and an Act which defined the limits of their function. These were so restricted that Labour voted against the Bill, Dr Christopher Addison describing it as a 'pretentious imposture'. It seemed clear that the Government had no serious intentions for the distressed areas.

The concentration of unemployment in those areas had a particular bearing on the Government reform of unemployment relief. Most of the men out of work there were long-term unemployed; they had not had work for over a year and were therefore dependent on transitional payments made by the local PACs. Many of these paid right up to the legal limit, 26s for a man and wife. Part II of the Unemployment Bill, against which the 1934 marchers had demonstrated, transferred these men from the responsibility of the PACs, which in the distressed areas were mostly controlled by Labour, to a new central body – the Unemployment Assistance Board – remote from any direct political control. It was also known that the Board would issue its own scales of assistance which were to be on a national standard instead of being influenced by different local sympathies. Labour strongly contested the Bill in Parliament, creating a record of twenty-seven days' discussion, on the grounds that it did not recognise social need but was based wholly on the Government's determination to remove the local political influence of its opponents and to restore control of expenditure to the Treasury, but it became law in June 1934. The struggle, together with the opposition to the Special Areas Act, had drawn the Labour Party closer to the cause of the unemployed.

A campaign to get Part II withdrawn continued outside Parliament. By the autumn an outline of the implied threat to living conditions had become widely known. Before November there were local marches in the most affected areas. Monmouthshire unemployed marched on Newport, Dundee men on Forfar, Maesteg and Ogmore on Bridgend, and there were also marches in the Rhondda and in Glasgow. Not the least hostility to the Act was aroused by the intention to make relief conditional on the recipient going to a residential instruction centre to work without wages. These 'agencies of physical and moral rehabilitation, giving men a twelve-week course of fairly hard work, good feeding and mild discipline'[4] were labelled 'slave camps' by the Movement which issued a pamphlet entitled, *Work for Wages – not Slave Camps: Our Plan for Action.*

The new regulations for administration of relief by the UAB were debated in Parliament on 17 December 1934. They could not be amended, only confirmed or rejected. Labour moved rejection of the new scales of relief on the grounds that they were lower than those paid by some PACs. The Minister of Labour, Oliver Stanley, insisted that the new scales would cost three million pounds more than the existing transitional payments, and they were approved. When they came into operation there was an uproar of protest. In the second week of 1935 the majority of the 800,000 clients of the UAB found that their allowances were less than before; many found that their money had been cut drastically. A man and wife received 2s per week less, in any case, but the worst hit were single men and women living with their families, whose money was reduced by amounts varying from 3s to 9s. Under a strict operation of the means test, some allowances were abolished altogether. The impact was heaviest in the Special Areas where the PACs had been making the maximum possible payments.

Protest grew rapidly from all sides. In Wales employed and unemployed together numbering scores of thousands marched down the Rhondda Valley. Miners' unions called for a strike and the South Wales Miners Federation set up a council of action. When Parliament re-assembled on 28 January 1935 the Government was attacked by members of all parties who gave instances of insupportably harsh treatment. The Opposition forced a debate but the Government refused to withdraw the regulations, merely issuing instructions designed to soften the blow. It was preoccupied with other matters – the return of the Saar to Nazi Germany. The protest became a storm. Ten thousand marched through North Shields calling on the dockers to strike. The National Council of Labour issued a manifesto: 'An Appeal to the Public Conscience.' In the background was Lloyd George's *New Deal for Britain* which, with its positive ideas for employment, contrasted strongly with the Government's inaction. There were demands for the resignation of the UAB and of Government ministers. On Sunday 3 February some three hundred thousand people demonstrated all over Britain. Women in Merthyr Valley smashed the windows of the UAB offices, and in Llanelly the unemployed occupied the town hall. Thousands marched on Tyneside, in Scotland and in Lancashire. On 5 February the Government retreated. A standstill order gave the unemployed the best of two bad worlds. Applicants for relief were to be paid either under the old assessments by the PACs or on the new scales of the UAB, whichever was the higher, and reductions which had been made were to be refunded. Under more than half the PACs the assessments had been higher than the new scales.

That was not the end, for when the Government announced that it would take two weeks for the standstill to operate, the Movement demanded that it should start immediately. In Sheffield forty thousand people marched to the city hall, and such heavy fighting broke out in the streets that the councillors travelled to London and sought and got the Minister's permission to repay the cuts immediately.[5]

The Movement organised widespread demonstrations to oblige other authorities to follow suit. Public opinion was apparent in a Labour gain at the Liverpool, Wavertree, by-election that month. The Movement persisted in continuing the campaign for another two months to demand repeal of Part

II, i.e. abolition of the UAB. The biggest of a series of new demonstrations all over the country was a march of three thousand to Glasgow, in which men from Fraserburgh, Peterhead and Aberdeen were on the road for nine days.[6]

The Government made no move to end the standstill. The UAB had such a complicated administrative tangle to sort out that no new regulations could be got ready for over a year, until July 1936. In the meantime the Board was obliged to continue what it considered to be an abuse of public money. In many areas, especially South Wales, where Labour PACs had applied the means test only half-heartedly or even not at all, the Board had to maintain payments already made but which it considered excessive as well as anomalous. During a lull which lasted well into 1936, other matters occupied public opinion: the King's Silver Jubilee (with a week's bonus for the unemployed), and the warlike stances and war preparations in Europe.

In October 1935, the insurance benefit for a child, which had been 2s since 1924, was raised to 3s a week following a recommendation three months earlier by the Unemployment Insurance Statutory Committee under the chairmanship of Sir William Beveridge. The cost, a million pounds a year, was a small fraction of the large reserve that the Insurance Fund was now accumulating. The UAB had already fixed 3s to 4s 6d as a child's allowance and it was not thought appropriate for a family on unemployment assistance to be better off than one on insurance benefit. Unemployed families had been deprived of the increase for some weeks in order that its announcement might be timed for the general election. In the same month Baldwin dissolved Parliament in preparation for the election on 14 November 1935.

The chief issues were unemployment, housing, and the Special Areas. The churches were not behind in the widespread concern about domestic problems. During the election campaign, Archbishop William Temple, who had earned a reproof from Neville Chamberlain in 1934, called on the public at a meeting in the Albert Hall to 'revolt against malnutrition, bad housing, and the economic system which tolerates the degradation of unemployment. Give no rest to your consciences or to the consciences of your neighbours. Constitute yourselves a public nuisance until these and other far greater nuisances are remedied.'[7] The Conservatives could point to economic recovery and make promises for the Special Areas, old age pensions and education, while Labour lacked fire. At a time of alarums of war in Europe most electors still sought safety in the existing government, and the Conservatives retained a large, though somewhat reduced, majority. The year closed with a concession to poor children. Circular 1437 of the Ministry of Education had laid it down that a child should not be given free meals unless a doctor's report stated that there was malnutrition. The attempt to enforce the circular was now abandoned.

As 1936 wore on, the Special Areas became increasingly the main issue of home policy. The Government's inaction was matched by more publicity of the conditions in the areas. Under the 'pretentious imposture' of the 1934 Act, the Commissioners were not allowed to promote work for the unemployed and were hamstrung by lack of funds. A scheme for a bridge over the Severn proposed by the Commissioner for England and Wales was rejected because of opposition from the railway companies. The Commissioners themselves expressed disappointment at their lack of success. The Government passed the Special Areas Reconstruction (Agreement) Bill to finance firms willing to settle in those areas, but a derisory sum was actually expended. Almost as soon as the Bill appeared it was criticised as inadequate. The Church Assembly called on the Government to revise it 'in the light of the experience of the Commissioners by giving them adequate power to secure concerted and effective action over as wide a field as possible. To make every effort to expand productive enterprise within the depressed areas. . . .'[8]

Publication of various surveys of the areas made the facts of life there better known. The Medical Officer of Health for Stockton-on-Tees, Dr G. C. M. McGonigle, author of the widely read *Poverty and Public Health*, showed that the death rate among unemployed households in the North East was much higher than in employed households. More influential and more startling, concerned as it was with the state of the whole nation, was Sir John Boyd Orr's *Food, Health and Income*. It revealed that 30 per cent of the population were living on a food diet seriously inadequate to maintain health, and as many as 50 per cent fell below the diet required for good health because of low incomes. Put in another way, 10 per cent of the population was very badly fed (the unemployment rate was 13 per cent), and half the nation was ill fed.

In July the Government published the new scales of relief which were to replace the standstill in November. They showed a marginal improvement over the scales rejected in the previous year, for instance for single adult persons living with their families and for young people; but compared with the transitional payments which were still being made, they would impose severe cuts particularly for such single persons. For a man and wife the revised amount was to be 24*s* per week, whereas the ceiling for transitional payment had been raised earlier to 26*s*. The losses would be felt most in the Special Areas. The means test, although it was to be made less stringent, was now to be permanent, an essential part of the new regulations. The new scales were accepted in Parliament and the press with little criticism, but in the Special Areas there was strong resentment, especially in South Wales. Very soon a thousand Welsh were eager to march.

The Movement had already discussed the possibility of a march before the new scales of relief were published. The majority view was in favour of action. The Movement knew that Jarrow Town Council intended to organise a march on London and offered its support. The Special Branch at Scotland Yard reported that the Movement and the Communist Party had decided 'to exploit the intense opposition to the new unemployment regulations'. Their aim, in its view, was 'to keep the Party character of the March in the background and make it an "all in" protest by soliciting Labour and Trade Union participation'.[9] This did not exaggerate the possibilities of the march becoming the nearest of all to a national demonstration, in spite of its being essentially a protest from the Special Areas.

The National Council of Labour called a special conference and, although refusing to lead a march, did not, for the first time, ban support of it. For the Movement it was a useful point that the scales of relief it demanded were the same as those proposed by the TUC, i.e. 20*s* per week for all unemployed over 18 years, 5*s* for each dependant child, 15*s* for all between 16 and

18 years, 10s for those between 14 and 16 years. As the demand within the Movement for a march grew, and there were signs of greater official Labour support than before, it was decided that the march should take place to arrive on 8 November so as to give the Government a week in which to change its mind before the start of the new regulations on 16 November.

The signs were favourable. The Movement had already organised a Petition of Public Representatives against the means test, signed by teachers, local councillors and aldermen, doctors, magistrates, clergy, members of Parliament, including C. R. Attlee – altogether over a thousand people – which the Parliamentary Committee of the Labour Party had presented to the Minister of Labour. The idea of marching on London could no longer be regarded entirely as a nuisance committed only by the Movement. Not only Jarrow but the National League of the Blind and ex-service-men were now following suit. The general climate of political feeling had grown more disturbed and more favourable to protest. Many who had been politically inactive were drawn by their sympathy for the Spanish Government into demonstration against fascism. The Left Book Club with its fifty thousand members and a thousand discussion groups appeared. In such a changed atmosphere, the march and the Movement, obviously anti-fascist, could hardly fail.

The motives for marching were as strong as ever – the means test and the new regulations. The Special Branch report that the Movement was 'not missing the opportunity this year of again creating sufficient enthusiasm among their supporters in various parts of the country to stage another so-called "Hunger March"', was misleading though it was true enough that 'little trouble was experienced in finding leaders for this venture, they, as previously, were the old and trusted stalwarts who are very well known to the police'.[10]

Police and poor law authorities made their preparations as before. At first their instructions harked back to 1932 and what they called the unfortunate results of leniency by the poor law authorities and lack of coordination. Once again the Home Office circulated chief constables to ensure adequate protection against disorder arising from the treatment of the marchers in the casual wards where all 'depended on the grit of the Master who should get full support from the police'.[11]

All this was beside the point since the marchers had little need to use the casual wards. 1936 was to be as different from its forerunners as 1934 had been. The different complexion of affairs was soon realised by the Metropolitan Police from its reports of meetings in London. The influential London Trades Council was now a sponsor. It was reported that a meeting of the reception committee, held this year – it was noted – at the National Trade Union Club, included as well as the 'trusted stalwarts' and Aneurin Bevan, both the Council secretary, A. M. Wall, and Dr Edith Summerskill, and that the appeal for funds was signed by Ellen Wilkinson, herself about to lead the Jarrow March, by members of Parliament G. R. Strauss, S. O. Davies and John Jagger, and by well-known clergy in addition to trade-union figures like J. R. Scott and Ted Hill.[12] The appeal, headed 'People of London', was addressed to a wider audience, 'Friends and Comrades'.

Scotland Yard, assessing reports and issuing instructions, shifted its stance somewhat. Councillor Lewis Jones, again leader of the South Wales contingent, might well say: 'We are going to London to meet the Government and the House of Commons and if they refuse to see us we will force ourselves in upon the Cabinet and if necessary upon the King, and we will force this pack of gangsters to abolish for ever the means test. They are ruining our country'; but it should be seen in the context of five hundred angry men about to march. The danger of weapons being carried was not so great as before. This year it was to be dealt with tactfully, recognising the discipline of the march. If a marcher was known to have a weapon, he himself would not be asked to give it up but the request would be made to the man's contingent leader in the first place. As for other precautions, there was no change, it was all routine: collections to be allowed if there was no obstruction, road materials to be removed, no sticks to be carried, and film companies to be requested not to take pictures of demonstrations for newsreels.[13]

The march programme, while sticking close to the bread and margarine issue, had broadened out to appeal to all citizens to withstand fascism and war as well as the National Government. This was the new style and the new situation. The march itself was now called the National Protest March.

There were other indications that the march might become a national Labour protest. At Cardiff on 29 August five hundred and ninety-five delegates from trades councils and local Labour parties took a unanimous decision to sponsor it. The South Wales Miners' Federation was in support. In Nottinghamshire so was the Broxtowe divisional Labour Party, on Tyneside the Durham miners' lodges, in Dundee the Bakers' Union, in Edinburgh and Aberdeen the trades councils. Consequently the Movement emphasised the need for improved organisation and discipline. There would be competition for publicity and sympathy from the Jarrow march. The marching instructions were therefore fuller and more precise:

> From the moment when the full contingent sets out from the starting centre, the local units of marchers (groups from a locality) cease to exist as separate units.
>
> The full contingent should be divided into companies, consisting of twenty men in each company plus one company leader who should march at the head of his company, or at the side.
>
> The companies should be known by numbers – Company No. 1, Company No. 2, etc. There should be a space of six yards between each company.
>
> The company leader must see that his men march in step. This is very essential. It has a much more striking effect upon the public, and demonstrates efficiency and control, and further, it is possible to cover much more ground with a minimum of fatigue. A steady swinging step will be found much better than a quick step.

Each contingent's control council of six or eight 'of the most capable comrades' was of prime importance. 'Any complaint or request from any man in the ranks must first be raised with his company leader.... The control council must fix a definite time each night for lights out.... Any serious case of misconduct must be strongly dealt with by the control council.' It was essential that the position of Road Treasurer was held by a trustworthy comrade....

> Further there will be no objection to a payout to the men of one shilling each twice a week if the funds will allow. But in order to ensure that all contingents are treated alike in this respect, we lay it down definitely that the shilling pay out to the men must not exceed two payments in one week.

Daily reports to headquarters and to the men were equally important:

> Each morning when the men are assembled following breakfast the chief leader or deputy should give a report to the men on the matters that have been before the Control Council.
>
> After the decisions of the Control Council have been announced, any news from the Press concerning the March should be read to the men. It will therefore be necessary to purchase each morning copies of various newspapers. Even when the newspaper report is an unfavourable one, it should be read just the same and the necessary comments made to the men concerning any lying statements that may have been published. The men will then see for themselves the character of the capitalist press, including the *Daily Herald*.[14]

Proper health arrangements were essential; as well as orders for the Red Cross personnel, detailed first aid notes were drawn up by a group of doctors.

It was mainly from the Special Areas that the six contingents set out: Scottish West via Lancashire and Staffordshire; Scottish East from Edinburgh via Yorkshire and Derby; Northumberland and Durham; Lancashire plus Merseyside and North Staffs; Yorkshire, Notts and Derby; South Wales; with a women's group from Coventry. On arrival in London their numbers were 276, 185, 130, 225, 115, 500 and 32 respectively, a total of 1,463. Banners and slogans stuck close to the basic issues – 'Against the UAB, Down with the Means Test'. International problems rarely came into it; Merseyside, exceptionally had a banner reading 'We Want Bread Not Gun and Lead'.[15]

There was little doubt this year of the strength of Labour support, official as well as unofficial. The West Scots leader Peter Kerrigan told the press: 'One thing we have noticed is that we have increased support this time from Co-op Society members and trade unionists.' In the Potteries, the Scots found, as well as a welcome from the trades council, the local members of Parliament speaking for them – Alderman Hollis and Ellis Smith – saying that the marchers had given 'a magnificent display of discipline', and in Stockport the trades council rooms were available. The Manchester alderman who was treasurer of the reception committee said: 'In their hearts and bones and homes they were having a rotten time.' At St Albans they were again looked after by the trades and labour council. The Lancashire men were received at West Bromwich by the trades and labour council which collected £10 for them. The Yorkshire men, on arriving at Nottingham, were so much helped by Labour organisations and promised every possible help from the PAC that the Conservatives charged Labour with bringing the marchers into the city for its own political advantage in the municipal elections.[16]

The Welsh found the full parliamentary strength of Labour deployed at Cardiff. After being met by officers of the South Wales Miners' Federation, they were addressed by five members of Parliament – James Griffiths, Ted Williams, S. O. Davies, George Hall and W. H. Mainwaring.

James Griffiths declared that the march was no party manœuvre but 'the march of a nation – the protest of the soul of a nation against ten years of degradation, poverty and destitution'.[17]

An unprecedented degree of sympathy and material help came from beyond the labour movement. 'This hunger march has taught us that there are more decent people in the world – of all classes – than some of us believed existed,' the Lancashire leader told the *Birmingham Mail*:

> We have been welcomed by Unionist and Liberal mayors and ministers of religion and all kinds and creeds have helped. We have slept on the floors of workhouses, schoolrooms and public baths, wrapped in blankets provided by the Public Assistance Committees. We have marched on an average 18 miles a day. We have been extremely well fed by sympathisers, and our only hardship has been one stormy day.

At West Bromwich a dinner of roast beef, potatoes, cabbage and bread pudding had been served by the mayoress and councillors, with a thousand cigarettes, a pound of tobacco, cigarette papers and matches from the mayor. 'Oxford's friendly reception was eloquent of the deep sympathy that is felt for these courageous pilgrims of poverty,' the *Oxford Mail* reported. The women students of Lady Margaret Hall peeled the marchers' potatoes; the male undergraduates (except for the Ruskin men) were forbidden to march through the city. Cambridge was more forward. After the Girton students had given the Tynesiders coffee and snacks on their approach to the town, the male undergraduates marched in the ranks and fed the marchers in the colleges.[18] 'The marchers would never forget the warmth of welcome in Leeds,' Harry McShane, leading the East Scots, told the *Yorkshire Evening Post*. 'We have had a rough time so far but Leeds people have shown us great kindness and we feel much better for the substantial Yorkshire meals they have served us.' Sheffield was an exception, being one of only two places after Edinburgh where there had been no official reception. Even so, the marchers were well looked after by the Methodist Church and an anonymous donor of break-fast. The first stop, after coming over the border, at the small town of Brampton in Cumberland had set the standard. The local NUWM secretary sent the marchers' thanks to the *Cumberland News*: 'The men were heartily grateful for the support and the solidarity shown in their gifts of food, clothes, money and the warm interest shown in their cause. Thanks were due to Lady Cecilia and Mr Charles Roberts for the use of the Temperance Hall and to Toc H, the British Women's Total Abstinence Union, and the Badminton Club for foregoing their use of the hall.' To 'these and many others the men extend their greatest thanks'.[19]

Some of the earlier hostile attitudes persisted in officialdom. In Scotland many public assistance committees were generous compared with the English, some treating the wives of marchers as householders and paying them on that scale instead of the married woman's allocation. Only the Jarrow wives were treated so generously, because the Jarrow marchers could be shown to be looking for work while the hunger marchers were, in official eyes, only looking for trouble. It so happened that the few difficulties with the poor law were experienced by the Scots contingents. The PAC at Ripon insisted at first that the marchers, as vagrants, would have to stay two nights in the casual wards. When the marchers rejected this ruling and additional police were sent in, conflict seemed imminent until the PAC gave way.[20]

In Warwickshire, which was to receive four contingents at different points, memories of 1932 were still vivid. The inspector wrote to put the county public assistance officer on his mettle. 'I trust,' he wrote, 'you are ready to meet the contingents from Glasgow, Edinburgh, Lancashire and the women. All the reports seem to show that the various groups of marchers are well behaved and obedient to their leaders. I am sure that you are anxious to avoid a repetition of anything like the difficulty at Stratford-on-Avon on the last occasion. I think it is to everyone's interest to endeavour to avoid any "incidents" which only result in a cheap martyrdom.'

The difficulty came at Warwick workhouse where the public assistance officer had arranged for a force of seventy police to be installed in the building. The marchers demanded the removal of the police and permission to stay out until 11.30 p.m. The master agreed to 10 p.m. but negotiations with the police ended with their refusal to withdraw. Discipline among the marchers prevailed, violence was avoided but the threat of it was strongly resented. Under a headline in the local press, 'What They Could Not Understand', Peter Kerrigan asked why was it necessary to have such a large force; they would not have objected to five or six police. The cost appeared later. The casual diet of bread, margarine, tea and sugar supplied to the three hundred marchers cost £1. 18s. Seventy police had those basics (butter instead of margarine), plus beef, bacon, sausage, jam and cake for £5. 3s 6d. Three halfpence was spent on each marcher, 1s 7d on each policeman. Where, however, the poor law was required to do no more than cooperate with a reception committee, the result was entirely satisfactory, as indicated by a letter to the public assistance officer at Warwick:

> I am instructed by the Rugby Reception Committee of the Recent Marchers to express thanks for your very generous and practical help rendered in the shape of three blankets per man and woman. This was a very Christian act, quite spontaneous on your part, and for that reason we look upon your contribution as fine work. We have covered expenses for food by subscription, collections, etc., they pass this way but once, and having passed move on, we collectively in Rugby – Police, Public Authority and all, have no regrets, we did our job to souls not so fortunate as ourselves; again gentlemen, a sincere thank you. Best wishes in your labours.
>
> Very sincerely,
>
> G. T. Grant, Secretary.[21]

When the Cabinet discussed the march, the Home Secretary, Sir John Simon, reminded the meeting that the statute under which persons could be required to enter into recognisances and find sureties to keep the peace had been successfully operated in 1932 but had not been found necessary in 1934 because of the marchers' disciplined behaviour. Legislation on the subject had since been in abeyance. At present it was impossible to stop the march. Something could be done, however, to discourage interest and support, and the best course would be for selected journalists to be given material for 'exposing the origin, motive and uselessness of the march'. The Government's press statement, after expressing customary concern about unnecessary hardship for the marchers and the virtues of the parliamentary system, emphasised again – 'Ministers cannot consent to receive any deputation of marchers, although, of course, they are always prepared to meet Members of Parliament.'[22] This was widely published, headlined 'Warning to Marchers', and on the radio the Prime Minister advised the marchers to return home.

How far the march could claim to be a national protest was indicated when all fifteen hundred men and women marched into Hyde Park at 2.30 p.m. on Sunday 8 November, exactly as programmed. Headlines in the *Daily Herald*, a consistent enemy in the past, read '250,000 Greet the Marchers – Means Test Must Go'. The police, putting the figure much lower, reported 'the great "welcome" was robbed of much of its warmth by the elements'. On six platforms, speakers from the Labour Party and the London Trades Council and ten Members of Parliament were alongside the Movement and the Communist Party. Aneurin Bevan proclaimed the cause of unity: 'This demonstration proves to the country that Labour needs a united leadership'. Clem Attlee put the march on a national footing; 'The marchers are rousing the people against the lingering poverty caused by long unemployment.... Let us take our enthusiasm from the marchers. Let us sweep away this Government.' When hot heads shouted 'Let's go to Downing Street', Will Thorne, veteran stalwart of the Social Democratic Federation and the Gas Workers' Union, calmed them down. Finally, according to the *Daily Herald*:

> For a moment there was silence as the resolution was read, then a quarter of a million voices suddenly lifted in one great flaming challenge: 'Down with the Means Test – Work for the Unemployed!' It was the dramatic climax – the fitting climax to one of the mightiest demonstrations London has ever seen.[23]

The new understanding with the Parliamentary Labour Party, the London Labour Party, and the London Trades Council was evident during the following days. On Monday the rank and file held local rallies, while the Tynesiders took tea at the London School of Economics. The leaders spoke to a meeting of two hundred Members of Parliament convened by Labour in the House of Commons. When the House met that day Aneurin Bevan spoke:

> I beg to present a humble Petition from unemployed marchers showing the grievous hardship which is being endured by great numbers of unemployed men and women by reason of their loss of physical well-being, the breaking up of many of their homes, the wretched condition of the villages and towns, and the harsh incidence of the family means test. Wherefore, your Petitioners pray that they, or some of their number, be heard at the Bar of the House as the representatives of the unemployed, to set forth their grievances and to urge, on behalf of the unemployed men and women, the provision of decent maintenance or employment at trade union rates of wages.

On Tuesday, the day for mass lobbying, all was peaceful until one group found its Member so objectionable that they raised a shout, 'The means test must go', and were promptly expelled. On Wednesday the 11th, Remembrance Day, the contingents assembled in Horse Guards Avenue to march past the Cenotaph after the service. Two marchers laid a wreath inscribed, 'We do not and will not forget, from the Hunger Marchers, 1936'; the women's wreath read: 'They gave their lives, we dedicate ours to the future of youth.' There was grumbling in the ranks, and there were some who asked: 'Why should we take part in this hypocrisy?' The Independent Labour Party paper, the *New Leader*, came out with an attack, on behalf of its marcher members, on the ceremony as a militarist and imperialist one. The *Daily Worker* replied that the act of mourning was rather for all those who had been killed in the interests of capitalism.

The same day Attlee moved in the Commons that the marchers should be allowed to appear at the Bar and explain their grievances. He argued for the distressed areas. The march was no communist demonstration but was simply an organised body of unemployed passing peaceably through the country in an endeavour to bring home their position to a House which needed to be reminded of it. The recent report by the Commissioner for England and Wales had not and could not deal with the basic problems of the distressed areas and the marchers ought therefore to be heard. Baldwin's reply only restated the view that representative government should not be weakened by any unconstitutional body of people having the right to appear at the Bar, or to see the Prime Minister or the Cabinet. After three hours' debate the Opposition motion was duly defeated by 237 to 119. It may well have been that it was this stand by the Opposition, together with the massive popular support that did induce the Cabinet Minister responsible, against all expectation, to see a deputation.

The Cabinet had changed its mind, or had it quite done that? Despite the ban on deputations, a powerful one of all the leaders was about to call at 10 Downing Street when it was informed by William Gallacher and Aneurin Bevan that the Minister of Labour would in fact receive a deputation of Members of Parliament and their constituents. Thus the marchers would be received, but only as constituents from the Special Areas and with their Members of Parliament. In the event the formula was stretched so that the deputation just assembled was seen by the Minister, though Gallacher and Bevan could not have been the Members for more than two of them. Whichever side won, something definite was achieved.[24]

After listening for two hours to an indictment of the neglect of the Special Areas and the inhumanity of the means test and of the new scales of relief, the Minister made a concession. The scales which were due to start in four days' time would be postponed for two months. Moreover, those who were due for an increase under the regulations would get it at once, but the cuts would be introduced only gradually and spread over a period of eighteen months. The deputation realised that this would mean much to hundreds of thousands and their dependants. About 230,000 persons who were clients of the UAB would get increases, however small, immediately. The remainder, about 370,000, would not suffer the full reductions until the summer of 1938. By that time they might be fewer.

The rest of the week was spent quietly in local fund-raising marches and attending football matches on Saturday. At the farewell rally in Trafalgar Square on Sunday, 15 November, Ben Tillett and Tom Mann represented past struggles, G. R. Strauss and Aneurin Bevan stood for the Labour Party, Harry Pollitt for the Communist Party, and the journalist Hannen Swaffer for the broader reading public. Wal Hannington could tell the marchers that they had scored two victories. They had gained access to the Minister; the cuts in public assistance had been postponed. Nothing more had ever been on the cards.[25]

The marchers left London on Monday 16 November; 586 from St Pancras and Euston, 343 from King's Cross and 500 from Paddington. The Welshmen had their return tickets; the rest were paid for with cheques for £411. 18s all from collections.[26]

They felt well satisfied with the result. The wretchedness of the distresssed areas had been brought before everyone. Almost the whole weight of the Labour movement had been brought behind them.

In the meantime the Special Areas remained depressed. In the Tyneside Area there was the special case of Jarrow.

The march from that town started on the day before the West Scots set out from Glasgow, and was due to arrive in London a week before them. In spite of the differences between the two marches there was no competition or feelings of rivalry. They had the same motives for action. Unemployed men, whether in Jarrow or Scotland or, from closer to hand, among the North-East contingent of the NUWM, all wished for the same thing – the restoration of work. In Jarrow 73 per cent of the insured workers were unemployed. Heavy unemployment was no new thing in the town; it had been at a similar level since 1931. The main industry, shipbuilding, came to an end when Palmers' shipyards were closed down in 1933 during rationalisation carried out by National Shipbuilders' Security. The town would have been relieved of destitution if a proposal to build a steelworks had not been smothered by the Iron and Steel Federation which was engaged in re-organising that industry in the same way. This last blow led, in July 1936, David Riley, a town councillor, to suggest a march to publicise the treatment which the town had received. The march was different from any other. There was to be no political party flavour, still less any association with the Movement or the Communists. The town council, with a Labour majority, sanctioned the march and it was organised from the town hall by the town clerk. Accordingly the town did not respond to the Movement's offer of co-operation, though Ellen Wilkinson, MP for Jarrow, who was to lead the march with David Riley, asked Wal Hannington for his advice and received it freely. The Home Secretary reported to the Cabinet that the march 'was not a Communist movement and it is represented as non-political'.[27]

Other differences were apparent. With the council and the town in support, money came in freely from a poor community to an initial sum of £800, or £4 per head, more than any NUWM contingent had accumulated. As though to emphasise the non-party character, the divisional agents for both Conservative and Labour Parties were sent ahead to prepare the way, and support came from the political right as well as the left. At Harrogate the Territorial Army took care of the Jarrow crusaders; at Leeds a newspaper owner gave food and drink; at Sheffield the Conservative Party were the hosts, and at Chesterfield it gave meals and accommodation, and again at Nottingham. At Bedford the Rotary Club gave tobacco, the butchers sausages, the cinemas free seats, Toc H a concert. At Edgware the mayor and the Rotarians gave a three-course meal. Mayoral welcomes were forthcoming at Bedford, Luton, St Albans. Ellen Wilkinson described such occasions:

> Sometimes we came in from the dark road to beautifully set tables, napery and crockery and bright lights. Immediately the men smartened up. Where it was not possible for them to wash before tea, they surreptitiously combed tousled hair and rubbed soiled fingers on their handkerchiefs.[28]

The symbolic figure was Councillor David Riley wearing his bowler hat at the head of the crusaders all the way.

There were also some similarities with the NUWM marches. When Ellen Wilkinson asked the annual conference of the Labour Party for its backing, she met with official disapproval, in line with discouragement from the TUC. This had a similar effect: the cold shoulder from Labour officials at a few places such as Chesterfield, but at most, a warm welcome. The Inter-Hospital Socialist Society gave a free medical service throughout. Boots were looked after at Leicester where the Co-op gave leather and the cobblers worked all night without pay. The Ministry of Health followed the same policy for all marches whatever their composition – application of the regulations for casual wards and workhouses, though this rarely arose.

Ellen Wilkinson wrote:

> But in those towns . . . mercifully few . . . where the tables were bare boards, and tea was poured from buckets into our own tin mugs, the men who had appeared so smart and alert at the well-set tables, suddenly looked 'poor law' and just as grubby as their angry MP who still had to smile and return thanks for the bread and marge as politely as she had done for the hot pies.[29]

In the Church of England there was a similar ambiguity of attitude. The crusaders themselves, however, were attentive to the established church. On their departure prayers were said for them in every church and chapel in Jarrow, and in Christ Church the Bishop of Jarrow bade them 'godspeed'. They attended service in Ripon cathedral; at Sheffield the bishop gave his blessing and £5; at Bedford the vicar of St Paul's church blessed their cause; in London Canon H. R. L. Sheppard supported their meeting at the Memorial Hall, Farringdon Street; and when they returned to Jarrow the Mayor asked them to accompany him to church on mayor's Sunday.

But from on high there was condemnation. The Bishop of Jarrow, in a long letter to *The Times*, denied his earlier support for the crusaders, and was followed, a week later, by outright rejection from his superior, the Bishop of Durham, of 'revolutionary mob pressure' on a matter which should be left to Parliament. Rebuttals of this criticism came from the chairman of the Tyneside Council of Social Service, himself an archdeacon, and from the Mayor of Jarrow, claiming that the crusaders were merely exercising their constitutional right to present a petition and to lobby Members of Parliament, a point which was emphasised by Councillor Riley, and taken up by *The Times*.[30]

In London the crusaders trudged through the rain to the London County Council Institution in the Mile End Road and supper given by the National Union of Distributive and Allied Workers. On the following day, 1 November, in Hyde Park, the Communist Party offered them the use of its meeting, organised in preparation for the arrival of the hunger marchers, and according to Ellen Wilkinson, 'generously gave way for an hour and asked their great audience to swell our Crusade which grew to enormous size when it was known that Jarrow Crusaders were there'.[31]

Parliament duly received two petitions on 4 November: one from Jarrow, bearing nearly 12,000 signatures, which had been carried all the way; the other, with 68,500 signatures, from Tyneside, presented by the Conservative Member, Sir Nicholas Gratton Doyle. The crusaders in the gallery were disappointed with the brief episode. They were entertained to tea in the House. Later they heard of the crowded meeting in a committee room where their case had been put. They had a steamer trip on the Thames (paid for by Sir John Jervis) and received a cheque for £100 from Sir Albert Levy to replace their clothes. One crusader got work as a baker's assistant in London. There was no other effect before they returned home.[32]

There were some results later. Sir John Jervis, High Sheriff of Surrey where large sums of money had been collected for welfare work in Jarrow, established several firms there: a furniture factory, a tube works, a metal-casting factory, a ship-breaking yard. Finally the construction of a steel works, promised in 1937, got under way in 1939. The result of five years' campaigning was work for about eight hundred men and boys. Thousands had found work in Tyneside shipyards when naval orders arrived. The crusade, itself only too real, gave rise to the myth that it was representative of British protest against unemployment. The newspapers gave it great prominence and much favourable comment: *The Times* devoted twice as much space to it as it had to the hunger marchers. In the public memory of the 1930s, the crusade earned for Jarrow the image and name of hunger marching which belonged properly to the NUWM.

REFERENCES

1. *Hertfordshire Mercury*, 13.11.36.
2. Miliband, R. *Parliamentary Socialism*, 1973, p. 215.
3. Wilkinson, E., *The Town That Was Murdered*, 1939, p. 206.
4. Davison, R. C., *British Unemployment Policy*, 1937, p. 117.
5. Cohen, M., *I Was One Of The Unemployed*, 1945, pp. 20–7.
6. NUWM Circular, 12.3.25; Hannington, *Never On Our Knees*, pp. 305–12.
7. *The Times*, 6.11.36.
8. Hannington, *Ten Lean Years*, 1940, p. 156.
9. NUWM, NAC Report, 6.7.36; PRO Mepol 2/3091.
10. PRO Mepol 2/3091.
11. PRO Mepol 2/3091.
12. PRO Mepol 2/3091.
13. PRO Mepol 2/3091.
14. NUWM, Hunger Marchers' Bulletin, September 1936, Circular nd (1936).
15. *Bolton Evening News*, 21.10.36.
16. *Cumberland News*, 17.10.36; *Manchester Guardian*, 22 & 23.10.36; *Birmingham Mail*, 30.10.36; *Nottingham Journal*, 29.10.36; *Worksop Guardian*, 30.10.36.
17. Branson, N. and Heinemann, M., *Britain in the 1930s*, p. 35; *Western Mail*, 26.10.36.
18. *Birmingham Mail*, 30 & 31.10.36; *Oxford Mail*, 4 & 5.11.36; *Daily Worker*, 2.11.36.
19. *Yorkshire Evening Post*, 17, 19 & 22.10.36; McShane, H. and Smith, J., *No Mean Fighter*, 1980, p. 217; *Sheffield Telegraph*, 24.10.36; *Cumberland News*, 17.10.36.
20. *Manchester Guardian*, 22.10.36; *Yorkshire Post*, 17.10.36; *Bradford Telegraph*, 19.10.36.
21. Warwick CRO 1238/9.
22. PRO CAB 24/264; Hannington, *Ten Lean Years*, p. 144.
23. PRO Mepol 2/3091; *Daily Herald*, 9.11.36.
24. PRO Mepol 2/3091; *The Times*, 10, 11 & 12.11.36.
25. *Daily Herald*, 16.11.36; Hannington, *Never On Our Knees*, pp. 318–19.
26. PRO Mepol 2/3091.
27. NUWM, NAC Report, 6.7.36; McShane and Smith, op. cit., p. 217; PRO CAB 24/264.
28. *The Times*, 27, 29, 30 & 31.10.36; *Yorkshire Evening Post*, 17 & 22.10.36; Wilkinson, *The Town That was Murdered*, 1939, pp. 202–3.
29. Wilkinson, op. cit., pp. 202, 207.
30. *The Times*, 15, 17, 20, 24 & 28.10.36, 5.11.36.
31. Wilkinson, op. cit., p. 209.
32. *The Times*, 3, 5 & 6.11.36; Wilkinson, op. cit., p. 209.

9

Instead of Marching, 1937–40

The mind of many people is naturally centred upon the grave international situation but let us not forget that there are still two million unemployed in Britain who have a just claim to the right to work or the right to live (Wal Hannington, NUWM Circular, 2 May 1939).

There were to be no more marches on London, not even from Wales. Only in Scotland did the unemployed continue to protest in the old way. Why did the marchers not take to the road in 1937, or 1938 or even 1939? Was it wholly because of public preoccupation with the advance of fascism in Europe and the growing danger of a Second World War? That general situation dwarfed other issues but there were other factors, some of which were part of the situation, others not so, and these may go to explain the significant exception of Scotland.

Economic fluctuations produced changes in unemployment which in turn affected the size and influence of the Movement. There was also the question, after the conflict over the setting of national scales of relief by the Unemployment Assistance Board appeared to have been ended, whether there was an issue large enough to promote a national march. The demand for winter relief might have been such an issue in different circumstances. There was little improvement in the distressed areas, the growth of trade and of general prosperity hardly affected them, and the deadening effect of years of unemployment on the minds of their people was not diminished. Within the Movement, however, there was considerable change. The Spanish war engaged the energies of thousands of its members, while hundreds of its activists went to Spain, many to their deaths. Weakened, in one sense, in this way, neither the Movement nor the Communist Party succeeded in achieving any greater unity with the Labour Party or the TUC than had been reached on the platform in Hyde Park in 1936.

From the beginning of 1937 unemployment fell continuously

until September, from 1,677,000 or 12½ per cent to 1,334,000 or 9½ per cent. This was to be the lowest point until the outbreak of war. It seemed possible for a time, with the revival of international trade and the first stirrings of rearmament, that Britain had climbed out of depression. The UAB, with fewer clients, proceeded gradually to liquidate the standstill and bring all relief down to its standard. The Movement shrank and, as Hannington put it, 'mass activity declined during this period'. The Movement organised a national petition with half a million signatures, calling again for abolition of the means test and for a national plan of public works, and presented it at Westminster on 5 May, without effect. Its demands at the UAB head office for increased scales of relief, based on the rise of eight points in the official cost of living index during the previous twelve months, was rejected. This was not unexpected, but the Board's rejection of the demand for special allowances during the coming winter as well, came as a surprise. Winter relief, granted by the boards of guardians and subsequently by the Public Assistance Committees, had been an accepted practice for some twenty-five years but now it appeared that the regulations made no such provision. The unemployed would have to do without the extra money for fuel and warm clothing. Winter relief became the main issue during the next year or two. At the time, there was something to celebrate. During the week of festivities to mark the coronation of George VI, the Government gave a special bonus of 2s 6d to each applicant for assistance, a useful sum for a family receiving 30s a week.

The attempt continued to carry the cause of unity of Labour, with which the marchers had been identified, and with it the basic demands of the Movement into the Labour Party. In January 1937 the Communist Party, the Independent Labour Party, and the Socialist League, representing the left wing of the Labour Party, issued a joint manifesto. The first purpose was 'the struggle against fascism, reaction and war', but an essential part of the same struggle was the marchers' demands for abolition of the means test, trade union scales of unemployment benefit, and development of the distressed areas. The Labour Party rejected the manifesto and the unity it called for as spurious, and expelled the Socialist League.

In Parliament the Members for the distressed areas continued to press for concessions to the unemployed. As the cost of living continued to rise throughout the year, James Griffiths, William Mainwaring, Aneurin Bevan, and others who had signed the unity manifesto, continued their efforts until the Minister gave way. He announced that the UAB would meet cases of hardship arising from increased prices and winter conditions, although there would not be an increase in the scales of relief for all. These adjustments in relief for those families who were considered to need them turned out to be for amounts ranging between 1*s* and 3*s* per week. Nothing was done to raise insurance benefits to meet the cost of living.

During 1937 the Spanish war began to have a direct effect on the Movement. The British Battalion, some six hundred strong, of the International Brigade, was formed in January. Many leading members of the Movement found their way over the Pyrenees, among them Fred Copeman who had led the Eastern Counties contingent in 1932, Peter Kerrigan who led the West Scots in 1936 and William Paynter, prominent with the Welsh. By April, over a dozen NUWM activists had been killed. They had come from London, Liverpool, Scotland, Sheffield, Sunderland, Birkenhead, Portsmouth, and West Hartlepool. By October 1937 three members of the National Administrative Council of the Movement had died fighting with the battalion. They were Bob Elliott who, as Councillor R. S. Elliott, had led the marchers from Co. Durham in 1936, Wilf Jobling of Tyneside and Eric Whalley of Notts and Derby. In November 1937 the battalion was named the Major Attlee Company in Attlee's presence. At home the Government, in the light of evidence of civilian slaughter from the air in Spain, passed the Air Raid Precautions Bill, thereby starting a sharp controversy as to how far local authorities should go in discharging their duty of protection against bombers. The Movement, seizing on the issue, demanded deep shelters for all and the great amount of employment on construction which they would give.

Early in 1938 it was clear that the revival of trade was only temporary. In January the unemployed numbered 1,818,000 or 13 per cent, an increase of half a million in six months, and that level was to remain until early in 1939. The Movement, however, had lagged behind and was weaker than for some years. So critical were its finances that it became necessary to economise in headquarters' staff, three of whom, the national organiser, the national propagandist and the women's organiser, were taken off the payroll. By the autumn strenuous efforts and the influx of unemployed produced some improvement, permitting the re-engagement of the national organiser. In London the number of branches which had fallen to only six recovered to twenty-seven; the money raised had come mainly from trade-union branches, Co-op Guilds and Left Book Club groups on whom there were also heavy demands for Spanish Aid.[1]

At the same time, the Movement had been campaigning on another front, against what it saw as the danger of 'slave camps' in Britain. The authorities had had power since 1934 to send claimants for relief to the Ministry of Labour Instructional Centres. In thirty-five residential camps the unemployed worked for three months, usually at heavy manual labour, without wages, receiving only food and 4s per week pocket money, together with allowances for their families. Under increased pressure to attend, the number of admissions rose from 18,474 in 1935 to 23,772 in 1938, but the proportion of those who found work afterwards was never more than 15 per cent. It was this fact as well as the Movement's campaign which produced passive resistance among the unemployed. The possibility of fascist methods of labour control in Britain existed, in left-wing opinion, since there was no lack in governing circles and in the press of advocates of labour camps for unemployed youth on similar lines to those in Nazi Germany. The Movement saw its efforts to persuade the unemployed to refuse to go to the camps as a part of the struggle against fascism, of which the sacrifices in Spain were another aspect.

While the political left attempted to form a Popular Front movement, the bread and butter issue of winter relief arose. This became the basis of a lively campaign in London and of the only major march of those years, the march of the Scots on their capital city. In April the unemployed were told that what they had understood to be extra allowances to meet the increased cost of living was, in fact, winter relief and would be withdrawn, and that, in any case, the cost of living had fallen a few points. Astonishment and dismay gave way to anger. Attlee told the Minister responsible, Ernest Brown, of the likely effect on thousands of homes. In July the Government authorised the Unemployment Winter Adjustment Regulation 1938. Extra relief might now be given 'in a case where special needs due to winter conditions exist'. The claimant was still, for this small extra, subject to the means test and the discretion of the UAB officer. It was clear that winter relief would be difficult to get when it was due to start on 14 November. In the event few claimants got the extra allowance; most were adjudged not to have 'special needs' either by the local official or the Appeals Tribunal. The Movement's demand was for 2s 6d per adult and 1s per child for all; the allowances granted never exceeded 3s per family and were often less.

The Movement had realised earlier that a strong protest would have to be made and now saw that it would have to be soon if the unemployed were not to suffer in the coming winter. But as Wal Hannington wrote:

> The international situation seemed to be dominating the mind of the nation and the widespread unemployment and distress at home were being lost sight of by those in more comfortable circumstances. The Press was silent.... Starvation it seemed, was not news in Fleet Street.[2]

The unemployed were not news.

During the lull after the Munich Crisis, the Movement began to assert itself by indicting the capitalism which refused humane treatment to its surplus labour while it appeased fascism. Action in London began in October with sixty members occupying the UAB head office, but without effect. In Scotland it was different. In that distressed and far-away country, the political crisis in London had not pushed all other matters into the background, nor did its capital city see itself as the target of Goering's bombers as London did. The Scots had always been the most eager and steadfast marchers, and their organisation was still strong. Local marches in Dundee and Glasgow prepared the way for the march on Edinburgh in November.

Over five hundred men came from all parts. On the outskirts

of Edinburgh the Highland contingent, which had marched for a fortnight, met the others from Glasgow, Ayrshire, Lanarkshire, Aberdeen, Dundee, Alloa, and Fife. Harry McShane and Wal Hannington were again in command. Along Princes Street the bands struck up, 'The Internationale' rose in the air and clenched fists saluted. In the ranks were veterans of the International Brigade, wearing the blue berets of Spain. Others had been in the 1936 march. The Trades Council and Borough Labour Party had looked after them in Waverley Market and they held meetings at the Mound.

In the morning the long column, a thousand strong, marched to the Ministry of Labour. McShane, leading the deputation, developed the main theme of their memorandum. There must be work schemes, he said, the Forth and Tay road bridges, a ship canal across the country, development of the Highlands. All these schemes were well known and widely advocated. Why would the Government not provide the finance? The Government stood condemned for its 'mean and contemptible policy towards the unemployed'. Its training schemes were exploiting the workers. In the training-centres men were being designated fully-fledged tradesmen after six months, something which it took an apprentice five years to achieve; in the instructional centres, the 'slave camps', the demand was that men should be paid at trade-union rates.

Unless these wrongs were righted Scotland would remain what it was – the most distressed country in the British Empire, with Lanark its most distressed county. If the demands were met it would be a happier place for all. The officials complimented the marchers on their presentation: their representations would be noted and sent to the proper quarters. Outside, the marchers had begun to feel restive in the bitter cold, but at a whistle blast they fell in and marched back to Waverley. At a mass meeting in the Synod Hall there was little Wal Hannington could say, except that in all his experience of deputations that day's had been the most purposeful. There was no way of measuring the success of the marches but there was no doubt that they impressed those in authority.

The marchers went home quietly that evening. There had been a sharp debate on winter relief in the city's Public Assistance Committee. While it was clear that only those families who were 'in need' would receive relief, it was argued that the least the committee could do would be to receive a deputation, especially as it had done so the year before. The committee rejected this by seven votes to six. Such was the result of the last march.[3]

In London the Movement, recognising that a national march was not feasible, was determined at least to bring the unemployed into the news and to shock the public conscience. Surprise was the vital element in a series of unorthodox, carefully-planned demonstrations. Five days before Christmas, when the West End of London was crowded with shoppers, two hundred men lay down in Oxford Street, carrying posters 'Work or Bread', while they chanted 'We Want Extra Winter Relief'. Two days later a hundred unemployed sat down in the Ritz Grill and demanded tea for twopence. On Christmas Day a hundred and fifty unemployed carol singers appeared outside the home of the chairman of the Unemployment Assistance Board. As City workers were leaving for lunch on 30 December they saw a banner on the top of the Monument, proclaiming 'For a Happy New Year the Unemployed Must Not Starve in 1939'. The New Year was celebrated with a mock funeral procession, which followed a black coffin bearing the words, 'He Did Not Get Winter Relief'. Some onlookers respectfully bared their heads, but the police diverted the procession from St Pauls, afraid that it might desecrate the cathedral. The black coffin continually reappeared, rebuilt when necessary after rough treatment, at 10 Downing Street, at Bow Street Police Court, and at Victoria Station, with the slogan, 'Appease The Unemployed Not Mussolini', as Chamberlain left to meet the Duce.

The unemployed became news. Invasion of expensive restaurants in Piccadilly and Regent Street continued through January and February. At a world conference on recreation and leisure in the Savoy Hotel, fifty unemployed displayed 'Hungry Leisure is no Pleasure' on their recumbent bodies, and on the same evening the Lord Privy Seal, as guest of the Allied Brewers, was confronted by men lying on the floor of the Grosvenor House Hotel, chanting 'Work for the Unemployed on ARP'. Crufts Dog Show was not spared.

The aim of the next tactic – of the chain-gangs – was different: to make an impact on the unemployed as well as gain publicity.

Locked to the railings of the house of the Minister of Labour, a chain-gang demanded with placards 'Release us from Hunger' and delivered a letter to the Minister which said:

> You are the Minister of Labour. You have refused to meet our national deputation. You are the Minister chiefly responsible in the field of unemployment for the starvation and suffering of our families. We are compelled to resort to this method of protest in order to get you to see the justice of our demand for work or bread.[4]

The press was informed that the chain-gangs would operate at five Labour exchanges simultaneously. As the long queues formed outside Camden Town Exchange, two labourers, a cabinet maker, a fitter's mate and a shop assistant, having chained themselves to the railings, displayed posters – 'We Demand Winter Relief' – while the police got busy with hacksaws. They were bound over in the sum of £2 for twelve months. At Stepney Exchange ten others fastened themselves in position. They did not get off so easily; some were fined. The magistrate made some uncomplimentary remarks, saying of one man, 'I suppose he has been got hold of by this movement and incited to make a guy of himself.' Three men at Holloway Exchange were discharged under the Probation of Offenders Act. A fourth, french polisher by trade, previously convicted of chalking in the streets and illegal bill-posting, was fined £1 (with time to pay) for obstructing the police in the execution of their duty. He was alleged to have offended the police while they were sawing through his chains with the words, 'These interfering sods'.[5] There were also lie-downs in Liverpool and Edinburgh, a chain-gang in Alloa, and banners flew from steeples in Dundee and Kirkintilloch. In London much publicity had been gained in the press. In spite of the overriding international problems the unemployed had forced themselves into the news. The UAB felt obliged to state publicly its policy on winter relief. In the upshot many who had been denied relief received it.

When the winter was over, unemployment fell rapidly, from two million in January 1939 to one and a quarter million when war was declared in September. Expansion of the armed forces and the first stage of conscription gave employment where industry had failed. It became clear that the Movement had served its purpose and would soon have to close down. Wal Hannington started looking for a job, but although there were vacancies enough, particularly for skilled men, his reputation was well known by the engineering employers. Eventually, in 1940, he was taken on as a centre-lathe turner, again became a prominent shop steward, and, soon after, national organiser of the Amalgamated Engineering Union.

The National Unemployed Workers' Movement lingered on until unemployment had virtually disappeared. One of its last circulars, signed by Hannington, showed how marginal it had become. The main item concerned an appeal, one of thousands over the years, on behalf of a member. He had been disallowed benefit because, by working on a lifeboat while it was rescuing a British air-crew who had been brought down in the sea, he had been deemed to be in gainful employment and therefore not genuinely unemployed. The result of the successful appeal was an amendment to the regulations that 'for the purposes of Section 35 of the 1935 Act the manning or launching of a lifeboat shall not be deemed to be an occupation from which an insured contributor derives any remuneration or profit'.[6]

Nothing could illustrate better the care with which the Movement had protected the rights of the unemployed, the administrative detail with which it had had to contend, and the times which had made hunger marches a thing of the past.

REFERENCES

1. NUWM, NAC Reports, April & September 1938, January 1939.
2. Hannington, *Ten Lean Years*, 1940, p. 221.
3. *Edinburgh Evening Despatch*, 24, 28 & 29.11.38; NUWM, NAC Report, November 1938.
4. NUWM, Report of 11th National Conference, 28–29.1.39; Hannington, op. cit., p. 235; *Never On Our Knees*, pp. 324–8.
5. NCCL, File Freedom of Speech & Assembly NUWM, 4, 11 & 18.1.39.
6. Hannington, *Never On Our Knees*, pp. 333–5; NUWM, Circular No. 8, 2.7.40.

10

Acceptance or Protest

Looking back from the eighties, the question may be asked: what did the marches amount to? The effort, the hardship, the broken heads and sore feet, the determination, and the comradeship – were these all futile?

Survivors of the marches look back on them with pride. They see them as a great achievement, for the effect on themselves and on Government policies. 'The spirit of these men. What comrades!,' recalls J. Fisher who, at the age of eighteen, was leader of a youth contingent in the 1932 march. He was struck by a mounted policeman in Hyde Park as he went to defend a woman with a baby in her arms who was being roughly treated by a special constable. Herb Morgan of Abertillery, a survivor of the 1934 march, sees it as one which prepared the ground for the outburst of anger in the following year against the reductions in relief, and the consequent standstill order. The sense of achievement is also based on the mere act of protest, the release of deep tides of resentment. 'I sometimes wondered how low you would get if nobody raised their voices about it,' said Maggie Nelson, a marcher of 1932 and 1934, on the BBC in 1973. The community from which each contingent came shared the same feelings and hopes during the lengthy preparations for marching, and felt the disappointment of volunteers who were rejected as medically unfit or, as Mrs Robinson of Pontypridd recalls, 'because the only pair of shoes he had were nearly off his feet'.[1]

After an incident at a labour exchange in which the unemployed accepted that a shortage of pennies was an adequate excuse why they could not be paid, Hugh Dalton remarked, 'Such meekness is a mouldy miracle.'[2]

Of the alternatives open to the unemployed – acceptance of their lot, revolt, or the exercise of organised pressure in order to extract concessions – the last mentioned offered the best prospect. It could not have been adopted without the National Unemployed Workers' Movement. Revolt, though sometimes not far away, was hardly on the agenda for the Communist leaders of the Movement, even in the phase of the 'new line' in 1930.

If there had been no Movement, it is likely that there would have been sporadic protests, more or less violent. The cuts in 1932 and those which accompanied the coming of the Un-employment Assistance Board in 1935 must have provoked spontaneous protest. That the unemployed should accept their lot was the devout wish of all governments. It is arguable that to a large extent, and for long periods of time, that wish was fulfilled. But the question of how much deprivation the unemployed would accept was a nicely balanced one. Every influence seems to have been in favour of unemployment being accepted as a fact of life, and also whatever treatment was thought appropriate for the unemployed. The persistence of large-scale protest seems all the more remarkable. After the slump of 1921 and the following recovery, the general view was that the only answer to trade depression and unemployment was to wait for the upturn of the trade cycle. When the international depression stimulated criticism of the economy it was not thought any other solution was available. Keynesian ideas on the imbalance between saving and investment had little influence until the end of the 1930s. The distressed areas were not, apparently, capable of improvement. Successive governments were unable or unwilling to deal with unemploy-ment in spite of their pledges. There was, it appeared, nothing to be done. If you were unemployed you would have to live with it. If you lived in the prosperous regions you could forget about the problem.

If the unemployed were to accept this apparent inevitability, something else was required – a dole. In the early 1920s when there were fears of a revolt by demobilised and unemployed soldiers, the major consideration appears to have been how much money would prevent trouble, following the donation to ex-soldiers and war workers. Thereafter, as heavy unemploy-ment became an accepted feature of society, this motive gave way to the necessity of preventing starvation. There was the additional requirement: that the money given to the un-employed man should be less than the lowest wage of an employed man, or else either he would not work or wages would be forced up. These two motives combined governed the amount of the dole, and largely explain, in the light of changes in the profitability of business, the successive variations in the standards of living of the unemployed. During the second crisis of unemployment in 1931–2, fear of disorder, if not of revolt, revived, as evidenced in the press campaign against subversion, the police violence, and the imprisonment of the marchers' leaders. The Movement was the only force to be reckoned with that might push the dole above the current level and thereby affect the level of wages.

If the dole was the chief emollient of mass unemployment, there were subsidiary ones. Charity, in the shape of the Lord Mayor's million pound fund, was seen as the conscience money of the well-to-do. The marchers did not regard proceeds of their collecting-boxes as charity, nor themselves as beggars. This money was a comradely gift, a token of support from employed to unemployed, or from the prosperous to the poor, when 'a toff in a motor car saw us at a distance and his hand went out of the side window and to our surprise a pound note was pushed out. We don't know who he was as the car never stopped.'[3] Social service had perhaps a more reconciliatory effect. The clubs under its aegis had some appeal for men and women who could learn something useful there or find distraction from the daily struggle to make ends meet. The effect was limited; by 1938 when the clubs had been in existence for six years, only about one in fourteen unemployed belonged to them. According to Ellen Wilkinson, it became fashionable to do something for the unemployed, but such efforts had only modest success. A Jarrow man provides a typical comment: 'As for being grateful for what is done for us – why should we be? We are willing to work for what we get.' Perhaps the attitudes of social workers did not help. The Pilgrim Trust's survey entitled *Men Without Work*, categorised men in language of a different class from that of the marchers: 'Very good type, happy-go-lucky type, rather inferior type, fine normal type.'[4]

Resignation to unemployment meant numerous mental and emotional constraints as well as the knowledge of physical deterioration. To the inquisition of the means test man was added the realisation that officials and courts were not interested in helping, but only in preventing fraud. Confusion arose from an administrative jungle which frequently changed shape. 'I can remember the days when it was thought shameful to accept poor relief', said one man: 'Now there's so many doing it that there's nothing to it, and as far as I can hear, it all comes from the same places as the dole anyhow.'[5]

For a large number of the unemployed, politics and politicians offered no solution. Those who were members of a political party learnt how little their party had been able to help them. The trade unionists among them had no greater hope of a better future from their organisations. Many unemployed drifted out of their unions. Those that remained members could not see their unions actively pressing for a better deal for them. They could read how the TUC in London had condemned Government policies but there was little evidence of their trades councils effectively caring for them as instructed by the TUC. The prevailing attitude Labour took was a defensive one during the decade after the General Strike. There was little point, it seemed, in men protesting instead of accepting their lot. One of them told the Bishop of Guildford: 'I feel like an animal in a cage. I can't get out of it.'[6] Apathy, increasing with the length of unemployment, was only to be expected. At its highest point, the membership of the Movement amounted to only one in eighty of the unemployed army.

The fact of repeated protest on a large scale is not easy to explain fully. It is clear that the leadership which the Movement provided, with men like Wal Hannington and Harry McShane and the contingent leaders, men of great ability who inspired unbounded confidence among the marchers as well as the intense dislike of authorities, was vital. Their well-known communist faith made little difference to the marchers. The motives of the led, the rank and file are less clear. No definition will apply equally to different persons marching from various places on contrasting occasions, to a boilermaker from South Shields in 1922, a hotel worker from Plymouth in 1930, and a miner from South Wales in 1936, each in his personal situation and with his own expectations.

Hope and despair were perhaps the general motives. For some their decision was a despairing if temporary escape from their homes. Anything was better than vainly waiting about for work. They went because there was nothing else to do. For others it was a rough holiday. For the many who had never been near London, an adventure for the lads, a jaunt. On one level there was the chance of better feeding on the way, as a Scot recorded in 1929:

> The men were getting out of hand at meal times today. This being due to some elements in our ranks who are here for a gutsful of food and because it is not plentiful just now some of them are getting out of hand. Wal H. gave them a hell of a dressing down tonight. It will do a lot of good.[7]

Many more set out with hopes of some improvement. On another level there was the hope of wresting from the authorities a reward for their endurance, any gain which could be called a victory. D. O. Williams of Nantymoel felt that possibly (though he doubted it greatly) 'something good might come of it.'[8] Few could have believed that the demand for work or full maintenance at trade-union rates would be fully met, but anything less was possible. Concessions by the authorities could serve to create the belief on a subsequent march that its demands too would be met in some degree. There were such concessions whether or not attributable to the marches: the suspension of the thirty stamps qualification for benefit in 1929, the removal of the 'not genuinely seeking work' rule in 1930, the Transitional Payments (Determination of Needs) Act of 1932, and the modification of the UAB regulations in 1936.

Mixed with hope and despair may also be seen anger against 'the men who are ruining our nation', as one contingent leader put it; and resentment of the neglect of distress by prosperous Britain and by the authorities.[9] These were perhaps the driving force of the determination to demonstrate at the centre of power and to be seen and heard there. There was also the satisfaction to be gained from the mere fact of arrival and presence in London. The harder the struggle to overcome opposition, the greater the achievement felt, even if arrival in London was the main noticeable success of the march.

If preservation of self-respect and independence, of not only the ten thousand or so who marched at one time or another, but also of the hundreds of thousands in towns and villages who saved and organised in support, were the only result of the marches, they may be thought to have been worth while. In the longer term there was probably a wider effect.

It is impossible to estimate the number of people of all classes on whom the marchers made an impact, or to weigh with any accuracy the critical thoughts which arose from it. There was nothing like a repeated invasion by large bodies of hungry men to spread awareness of them from the distressed to the prosperous areas. In hundreds of towns people saw for the first time the victims of unemployment. At the time some were impelled to join the labour movement, and to become its post-war leaders. Prosperous places comforted their shocked conscience by giving food and shelter. The marches may be seen, in A. J. P. Taylor's words, as 'a propaganda stroke of great effect. The hunger marchers displayed the failure of capitalism in a way that mere figures or literary description could not'.[10] A large shift of public opinion towards 'never again' was indicated in the subsequent defeat in 1945 of the politicians held responsible for the 1930s. In wartime the Army Bureau of Current Affairs found that full employment and social security were matters of prime interest. The marches had made a deep mark on the Britain of the inter-war years, and on a society which sought to maintain its unemployed at the lowest possible level of existence. Effective resistance to that ruling intention had been left to the marchers. They had shown that enforced idleness, human dereliction, neglect and misery, 'the expense of spirit in a waste of shame', were not to be taken lying down. Those upright men, and the women who accompanied or supported them, had had, as their guide, clear, simple and reasonable aims, comradeship, discipline and a trusted leadership which knew its purpose. We may still have reason to be thankful for their use of those essentials and for their example of fortitude and endeavour.

REFERENCES

1. Private Communication; BBC Radio programme, 17.1.73.
2. H. Dalton, *Call Back Yesterday*, 1953, p. 296.
3. Private Communication.
4. Wilkinson, *The Town That Was Murdered*, 1939, p. 231; Pilgrim Trust, *Men Without Work*, 1938, p. 418.

5. M. Bruce, *Coming Of The Welfare State*, 1967, p. 223.
6. *The Times*, 26.6.34.
7. Private Communication.
8. Private Communication.
9. Private Communication.
10. A. J. P. Taylor, *English History, 1914–1945*, 1965, p. 349.

Index

Aberdeen, 36, 171, 210

Abertillery, 47

Amalgamated Engineering Union, 18, 28, 231

Ambulance Section, 182

arrests, 20, 24, 26, 29, 31, 68, 78, 126, 139, 152, 155, 167, 159, 161

Attlee, C. R., 14, 153, 194, 208, 215, 216, 225, 227

Bagshot, 44

Baldwin, Stanley, 74, 107, 205, 217

Banbury, 69

Barnet, 44–6, 64

Barrow-in-Furness, 33, 37, 42, 54, 56, 60, 61, 136

Basingstoke, 29

bathing of marchers, 64, 68, 100, 102

Battersea, 14, 46, 48, 151, 188

Bevan, Aneurin, 195, 209, 215, 216, 217, 218, 225

Bevin, Ernest, 76

Bicester, 70

Birkenhead, 60, 139

Birmingham, 25, 31, 69, 101, 134, 147, 166, 178, 185

Bishops Stortford, 102, 105, 185, 190–1

Blanesburgh Committee, 80

Bolton, 37–8, 48, 97, 144

Bonar Law, Arthur, 33–4, 47, 54, 59

Bondfield, Margaret, 114–15

Bradford, 61, 88

Bridgend, 172, 185, 203

Brighton, 68

Bristol, 23, 41, 120, 185

British Broadcasting Corporation, 156, 215

Bromsgrove, 147–8

British Socialist Party, 17, 18

Brown, Maud, 142, 146, 187, 196

Buchanan, George, 152, 194

Burton-on-Trent, 147

Cabinet, 66, 132, 158, 162, 193, 214, 217; Cabinet Committees, 66, 132, 162

Cambridge, 98, 167, 183–4, 185, 212

Canterbury, 43, 68

Cardiff, 24, 40, 181, 210, 212

Carlisle, 122, 145, 179

Casuals' diet, 40, 42, 57, 64–5, 68, 70, 100–5, 123, 145, 147, 214; Casual Poor (Relief) Order 1925, 100; Casual Wards, 57, 64, 121, 213

chain gangs, 229–30

Chamberlain, Neville, 80, 103, 171, 229

Chippenham, 122, 187

churches, 68, 184, 185, 187, 206, 213, 220

Churchill, Winston, 107, 189

Citrine, Walter, 82

clergy, 36, 123, 185–6, 190–1, 209, 220

coffin, black, 229

Commissioner of Metropolitan Police, 13, 25, 36, 137, 138, 189

Communist International, 90–1, 161

Communist Party of Great Britain, 18, 19, 21, 59, 73, 74, 83, 90–1, 113, 150, 152, 164–5, 167–8, 174, 175, 177, 185, 188, 200, 207, 215, 221, 223, 224

Conservative Party, 219

Cook. A. J., 82, 90, 91, 107

Cooperative Societies, 95, 121, 122, 142–3, 186, 211

Copeman, Fred, 187, 225

Coventry, 42, 46, 120, 140, 179, 185

Crediton, 123–4

Cripps, Sir Stafford, 153

Currie, Gordon, 46, 49, 53, 64

Daily Herald, 25, 32, 46, 48, 52, 92, 107, 211, 215
Daily Mail, 85
Daily Worker, 154, 216
Davies, Robert, 182, 186, 193, 196
Davies, S. O., 82, 209, 212
Depressed (Special) Areas, 202, 203, 206, 207, 211, 217
Deptford, 13, 46, 151
Derby, 39, 60, 61, 88, 172, 200
detention, workhouse, 43, 64
Devon marchers, 37, 43, 44, 47, 93, 97, 105, 123, 146, 149
Dingley, Tom, 18, 19, 46, 50, 53, 54, 64, 66, 68
discipline, 35, 40, 50, 62, 79, 84, 171, 176–7, 181–2, 192, 209, 210, 214, 215
domestic service, 54, 196
Doncaster, 43
Dundee, 56, 60, 87, 171, 203
Dunstable, 185, 187
Durham, 121, 184; Bishop of, 164, 220

Edinburgh, 60, 69, 87, 171, 210, 227, 236
Edmonton, 20, 58, 59, 64, 98, 151
Elias, Sid, 41, 92, 118, 135, 138, 159, 160, 161
eviction, 31, 77
ex-servicemen, 31, 33, 38, 45, 50, 84, 208

factory raids, 27
fascism, 130, 167, 174, 201, 208, 224
France, 188
Fulham, 13

Gallacher, William, 175, 217
Garrett, George, 43, 49
General elections, 1922, 33, 41, 42, 48; 1923, 75; 1924, 76; 1929, 91, 111; 1931, 135; 1935, 205–6
General Strike, 80
Gilmour, Sir John, 158, 180

Glasgow, 25, 31, 36, 60, 134, 171, 176, 203, 205, 228
Gosling, Harry, 15
Greenwood, Arthur, 114
Griffiths, James, 212, 225
Guardians, poor law, 19–20, 23, 24, 28, 30, 34, 35, 37, 40, 42, 43, 44, 56, 57, 58, 61, 62, 66, 67, 68, 69, 70, 80, 88, 100, 115
Guildford, 120, 124

Hackney, 14, 64, 151
Hammersmith, 14
Hannington, Wal, 18, 19, 22, 25, 47, 48, 53, 55, 60, 64, 66, 67, 70, 74, 76, 78, 79, 82, 86, 90, 113, 116, 122, 126, 131, 133, 135, 138, 149, 156, 158, 160, 161, 164, 175, 183, 186, 187, 188, 218, 219, 223, 224, 227, 228, 231
Haye, Percy, 19, 22, 33, 51, 54, 59
Health, Ministry of, 29, 42, 56, 58, 66, 80, 120, 125–6, 139, 174, 178, 179, 189, 220
Hertford, 200
Hicks, George, 153
Holt, Jack, 19, 22, 33, 76
Home Office, 40, 53, 56, 66, 120, 178, 179, 187, 208
Home Secretary, 66, 180, 189, 192, 193, 214
Honiton, 93–4
Horner, Arthur, 82, 91
Hughes, J., 82

Independent Labour Party, 17, 119, 130, 147, 167–8, 174, 175, 187, 193, 200, 216, 224
Instructional Centres, 203, 226
International Brigade, 225
Islington, 20, 27, 64

Jarrow March, 201, 207, 210, 213, 218–21
Jennett, Dennis, 20, 24
Jones, Lewis, 187, 197, 209

Kent marchers, 43, 47, 48, 124

Kerrigan, Peter, 211, 214, 225
Kettering, 42
Kidd, Ronald, 192
Kilmarnock, 36

Labour Government, 1924, 75–6;
    1929, 112–19, 130, 132
Labour, Ministry of, 54, 56, 87, 126
Labour Party, 21, 22, 43, 76, 77, 78,
    90, 110–11, 118, 130, 146, 165,
    168, 185, 200, 210, 215, 216, 219,
    224
Lambeth, 20
Lancashire marchers, 33, 37–9, 42,
    48, 53, 103, 147, 172, 179, 182–3,
    185, 194, 212
Lancaster, 37
Langley, Sam, 62, 65, 138, 184
Lansbury, George, 56, 59, 65, 113,
    118, 152, 163, 164
Laski, Harold, 192–3
Leeds, 61, 97, 185, 213
Leek, 38
Leicester, 24, 42, 62, 99, 150, 179
Ley, Donald, 98, 99
lie-downs, 229, 230
Lincolnshire marchers, 43, 60
Liverpool, 24, 33, 60, 230
Llewellyn, Emryhs, 107, 138, 141,
    159, 161, 162, 164, 187
Lloyd George, David, 13, 26, 33, 111,
    204
Local Government Act 1929, 80
London County Council, 13, 15, 127,
    151, 154, 160, 189, 197
London School of Economics, 186,
    216
London Trades Council, 63, 83, 106,
    209, 215, 216
Loughborough, 40, 99, 101, 121, 145
Lowestoft, 21
Luton, 63, 67, 180

MacDonald, Ishbel, 196
MacDonald, J. Ramsay, 75, 118,
    132, 133, 153, 195
McGonigle, Dr G. C. M., 206

McGovern, John, 156, 158, 174, 186,
    194, 195
McKay, Tom, 38, 39, 45, 49, 53
McShane, Harry, 25, 31, 135, 138,
    149, 158, 175, 213, 228
Maidenhead, 70, 106
Mainwaring, W. H., 40, 212, 225
malnutrition, 174, 206
Manchester, 37, 38, 134, 136, 185,
    211
Mann, Tom, 78, 91, 118, 161–3, 164,
    218
Marches, 1st national (1922), 33–71;
    2nd national (1929), 89–108; 3rd
    national (1930), 109, 118–27; 4th
    national (1932), 129, 139–65; 5th
    national (1934); 166, 175; 6th
    national (1936), 200–1, 208–18;
    South Wales Miners, 82–6;
    Scottish miners, 87
marshalls, 36, 38, 39, 42, 46, 50, 54,
    57, 59, 64
Maxton, James, 154, 156, 159, 194
May Committee, 131–2
Means Test, 131, 134, 135–6, 143,
    153, 169, 203, 207, 216, 217, 224
Middleton, George, 92, 93, 95
Midlands marchers, 33, 48
Miliband, Ralph, 21
Miners, Durham, 184, 210; South
    Wales, 33, 82–6, 185; Scottish, 87
Mond, Sir Alfred, 26, 130
Monmouthshire, 41, 136, 185, 203
Moscow, 150, 151, 152, 160, 161, 163
Mosley, Sir Oswald, 113, 118, 127,
    130, 131

National Council for Civil Liberties,
    161, 192–3
National Government, 129, 132, 135,
    144
National Minority Movement, 74,
    78, 83, 113, 141, 165
National Shop Stewards & Workers
    Committee Movement, 17
National Unemployed Workers
    Committee Movement; origin, 22;

National Unemployed Workers
  Committee Movement—*cont.*
  Conferences, 1921, 26; 1924, 73,
  76; 1926, 78; 1929, 116
National Unemployed Workers
  Movement: conferences, 1929,
  116; 1931, 131; membership, 130,
  235
Newark, 186
Newcastle, 33, 61, 62
Newport, 41, 203
Newton Abbott, 44
Northallerton, 33, 104, 121
Norwich, 21
'not genuinely seeking work', 81,
  88–9, 114, 119, 236
Nottingham, 24, 43, 129, 172, 200,
  212

Oldham, 136, 178
Openshaw, 38
Orr, Sir John Boyd, 206
Out of Work, 22, 25, 32, 77
Oxford, 27, 148, 185, 186, 212

Pall Mall Gazette, 52
Parliamentary Labour Party, 107,
  152, 208, 216
Paynter, William, 225
Peterborough, 43
Pickering, Rev. Thomas, 46, 49, 56,
  67, 99
Pilgrim Trust, 234
Plymouth, 37, 56
police, 24, 44, 66, 68, 69, 70, 101, 102,
  124, 139, 140, 146, 148, 150–1,
  161, 174, 178, 179, 184, 214;
  Metropolitan, 13–15, 20, 26, 67,
  126, 140, 149, 151–3, mounted, 14,
  26, 152–3, 154–5, 159
Poor law, 19, 26, 80, 139, 168
Poor law inspectors, 57, 61, 70, 104,
  105, 109, 122, 126, 129, 140, 145,
  146, 147–9, 172, 178, 186, 197, 213
Poor relief, 26, 34, 80
Poplar, 20, 23, 31, 48, 65
Preston, 96, 172

Public Assistance Committees, 80,
  124, 134, 135, 136–7, 139, 144,
  172, 183, 186. 187, 197, 202, 204,
  205, 212, 213, 228

Reading, 42, 68
Reception Committees, 141–5, 150,
  151, 185, 209, 214
Recruiting marches (1923), 66–70
Rees, Noah, 82
reinforcements (1922), 56, 59, 60–4,
  65
relief work, 29, 79
Rhondda, 40, 82, 84, 203, 204
Ripon, 103, 133, 145, 121, 213
Rochdale, 29
Rotherham, 146, 147
Royal Commission on
  Unemployment Insurance 1932,
  130, 131, 169–70
Rugby, 43, 67, 184, 214
Russia, 18, 19, 21, 55, 143

Saffron Walden, 185
St Albans, 64, 120, 125, 142–4, 185,
  211
St Pancras, 14, 19, 20, 64
Saklatvala, Shapurji, 49, 91
Salford, 38, 60
Salvation Army, 48, 62, 146, 184
Samuel, Sir Herbert, 132, 158, 168,
  194
Scotland Yard, 24, 53, 149, 151, 154,
  155, 159, 175, 189, 207, 209
Scottish marchers, 33, 36, 39, 42, 46,
  47, 59, 61, 62, 63–4, 89, 92–3,
  95–7, 102, 122, 141, 144, 145, 171,
  177, 179, 180, 183, 185, 186–7,
  205, 211, 213, 223, 227–9, 236
searching of marchers, 64, 68, 100,
  127, 102, 121
Seditious Meetings Act 1817, 162,
  164
Sheffield, 22, 31, 56, 60, 121, 124,
  204, 213
Shop Stewards, 15–19, 27
Shoreditch, 13, 23, 65, 66, 188
Sittingbourne, 68

Slough, 185
Smethwick, 29, 31, 42
Social Service, 170, 234
Socialist Labour Party, 17
Socialist League, 200, 224
Solidarity committees, 184
Southampton, 68, 136
South Shields, 33
South Wales Miners' Federation, 204, 210, 212
Spanish Civil War, 223, 225
Special Areas, 203, 206, 207, 211, 217, 225
Special Branch, 24, 53, 78, 138, 140–1, 175, 207, 208
Special constables, 154, 159, 189
Steel-Maitland, Sir Arthur, 85
Stepney, 13, 20, 230
Stoke-on-Trent, 136, 179
Stratford-on-Avon, 148, 178, 214
students, 186, 212
Sumner, Charles, 31
Sunderland, 25
Swindon, 41, 187

Task work, 115
Taylor, A. J. P., 237
Thirsk, 102–3, 121
thirty-stamps qualification, 89, 108, 236
Thomas, J. H., 39, 112, 115, 117, 127
Tottenham, 20
trades councils, 21, 37, 38, 40, 41, 42, 43, 83, 95, 96, 97, 98, 99, 119, 120, 145, 210, 211, 212
Trades Union Congress, 21, 63, 73, 76, 77, 80, 83, 86, 90, 92, 107, 133, 138, 168, 170, 207, 235
Training centres, 228
Transitional payments, 134, 169, 202, 203
Transitional Payments (Determination of Need) Act 1932, 163, 169, 236
Transport & General Workers Union, 68
Tremaine, George, 93, 105, 106, 123

Tyneside marchers, 33, 43, 62, 93, 97, 102, 103–5, 121, 145, 149, 183, 184, 185, 190–1, 216

Unemployed Insurance Act 1927, 88
Unemployed Workers' charter, 73
Unemployment Act 1934, 203
Unemployment Assistance, 203, 205, 207, 217, 227;
    Unemployment Assistance Board, 201, 202, 203, 204, 205, 217, 222, 224, 225, 227, 229, 230, 233, 236
Unemployment benefit, 15, 21, 22, 26, 30, 34, 35, 42, 75, 81, 119, 131–2, 134, 169, 197, 198, 205, 225, The Gap, 30–1, 75
Unemployment rate, 15, 19, 75, 130, 202, 207, 224
United front, 175, 176, 193, 200

violence, 15, 20, 24, 26, 31, 101, 129, 133, 134, 139, 147–9, 154–6, 159, 166, 181, 192, 196

wages, 29, 37, 79
Wakefield, 124, 172
walking sticks, 149, 156, 179, 180, 209
Walsall, 42, 53
Wandsworth, 23, 46
Warrington, 185, 187
Warwick, 140, 145, 214
weapons, 149, 155, 179–80, 209
Welsh marchers, 33, 40–2, 47, 58, 122, 133, 149–50, 172, 180, 181, 185, 201, 203, 204, 209, 212, 218
West Bromwich, 29, 212
Wigan, 60, 178
Wilkinson, Ellen, 194, 201, 209, 219, 220, 221, 234
Willesden, 14, 20, 58, 151
winter relief, 130, 160, 222, 224, 226, 229, 230
Wolverhampton, 25, 136, 184

women marchers, 109, 124, 126, 129, 142–4, 146–7, 185, 216
Workers' committees, 17
workhouses, 23, 33, 37, 38, 44, 48, 61, 65, 67, 68, 69, 94, 99, 101, 102, 103, 104, 105, 121, 122, 124, 125, 126–7, 145, 146–8, 160, 212; workhouse masters, 48, 94, 103, 104, 105, 121, 123, 124, 145, 149, 150; workhouse regulations, 100–6

Yeovil, 37, 105
Yorkshire marchers, 43, 121, 145, 149, 172, 185, 200, 212